CSI:
CRIME SCENE INVESTIGATION™

DOMINOS

WRITTEN BY **KRIS OPRISKO**

ART BY **GABRIEL RODRIGUEZ**

AND **STEVEN PERKINS**

IDW Publishing

Operations:
Ted Adams, President
Clifford Meth, EVP of Strategies
Matthew Ruzicka, CPA, Controller
Alan Payne, VP of Sales
Lorelei Bunjes, Dir. of Digital Services
Marci Kahn, Executive Assistant
Alonzo Simon, Shipping Manager

Editorial:
Chris Ryall, Publisher/Editor-in-Chief
Justin Eisinger, Editor
Andrew Steven Harris, Editor
Kris Oprisko, Editor/Foreign Lic.
Denton Tipton, Editor
Tom Waltz, Editor

Design:
Robbie Robbins, EVP/Sr. Graphic Artist
Neil Uyetake, Art Director
Chris Mowry, Graphic Artist
Amauri Osorio, Graphic Artist

www.idwpublishing.com

ISBN: 978-1-60010-171-7
11 10 09 08   1 2 3 4 5

CSI: CRIME SCENE INVESTIGATION: DOMINOS TPB-DIGEST. MAY 2008. FIRST PRINTING. CSI: CRIME SCENE INVESTIGATION
™ CBS © 2000-2008 CBS Broadcasting Inc. and Entertainment AB Funding LLC. All Rights Reserved. © 2008 Idea and Design Works,
LLC. The IDW logo is registered in the U.S. Patent and Trademark Office. All Rights Reserved. IDW Publishing, a division of Idea and
Design Works, LLC. Editorial offices: 5080 Santa Fe St., San Diego, CA 92109. Any similarities to persons living or dead are purely
coincidental. With the exception of artwork used for review purposes, none of the contents of this publication may be reprinted without the
permission of Idea and Design Works, LLC. Printed in Korea.
IDW Publishing does not read or accept unsolicited submissions of ideas, stories, or artwork.

Originally published as CSI: CRIME SCENE INVESTIGATION: DOMINOS Issues #1 to 5.

CSI: Crime Scene Investigation

Created by **Anthony E. Zu**

Licensed to IDW by CBS Consumer Produ

"Dominos

Written
Kris Oprisk

Pencils and Inks
Gabriel Rodrigu
Sulaco Stud

Colors
Fran Gamb
Sulaco Stud

Painted Artwork
Steven Perki

Lettering
Robbie Robbins and **Tom B. Lo**

Design
Robbie Robbi

Original Series Edited
Jeff Mariotte and **Chris Ry**

Edited
Alex Garn

Cover and Chapter Photos
CBS Photo/Robert Voe

Book Design
Cindy Chapm

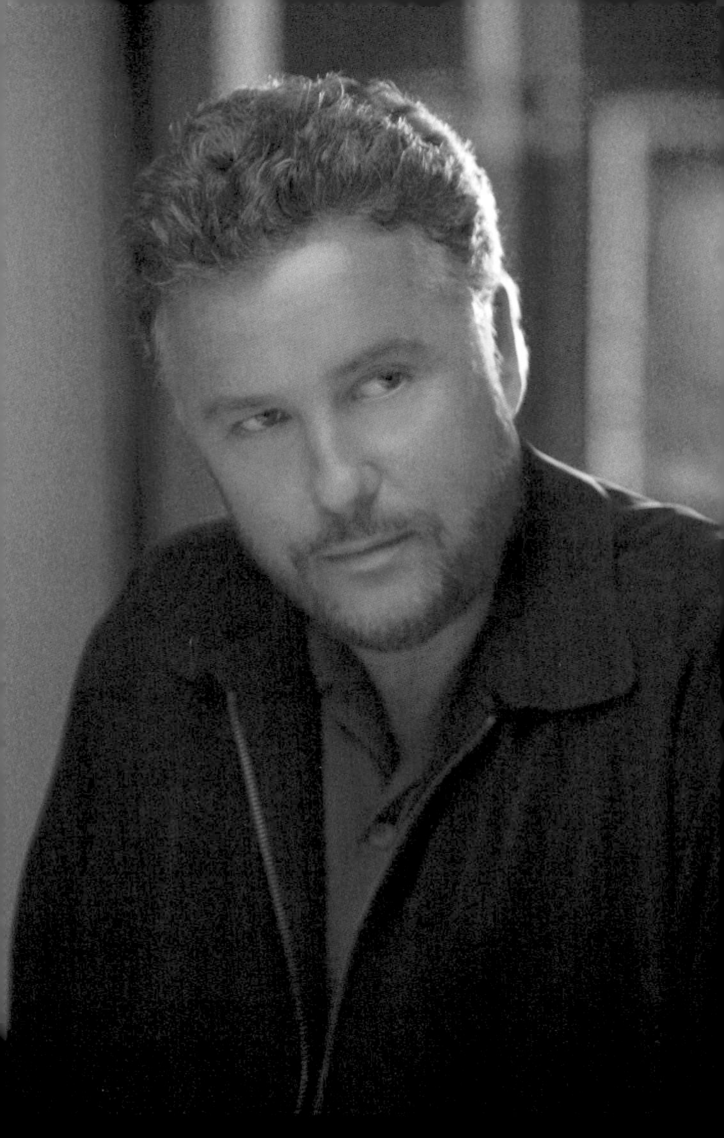

Chapter One

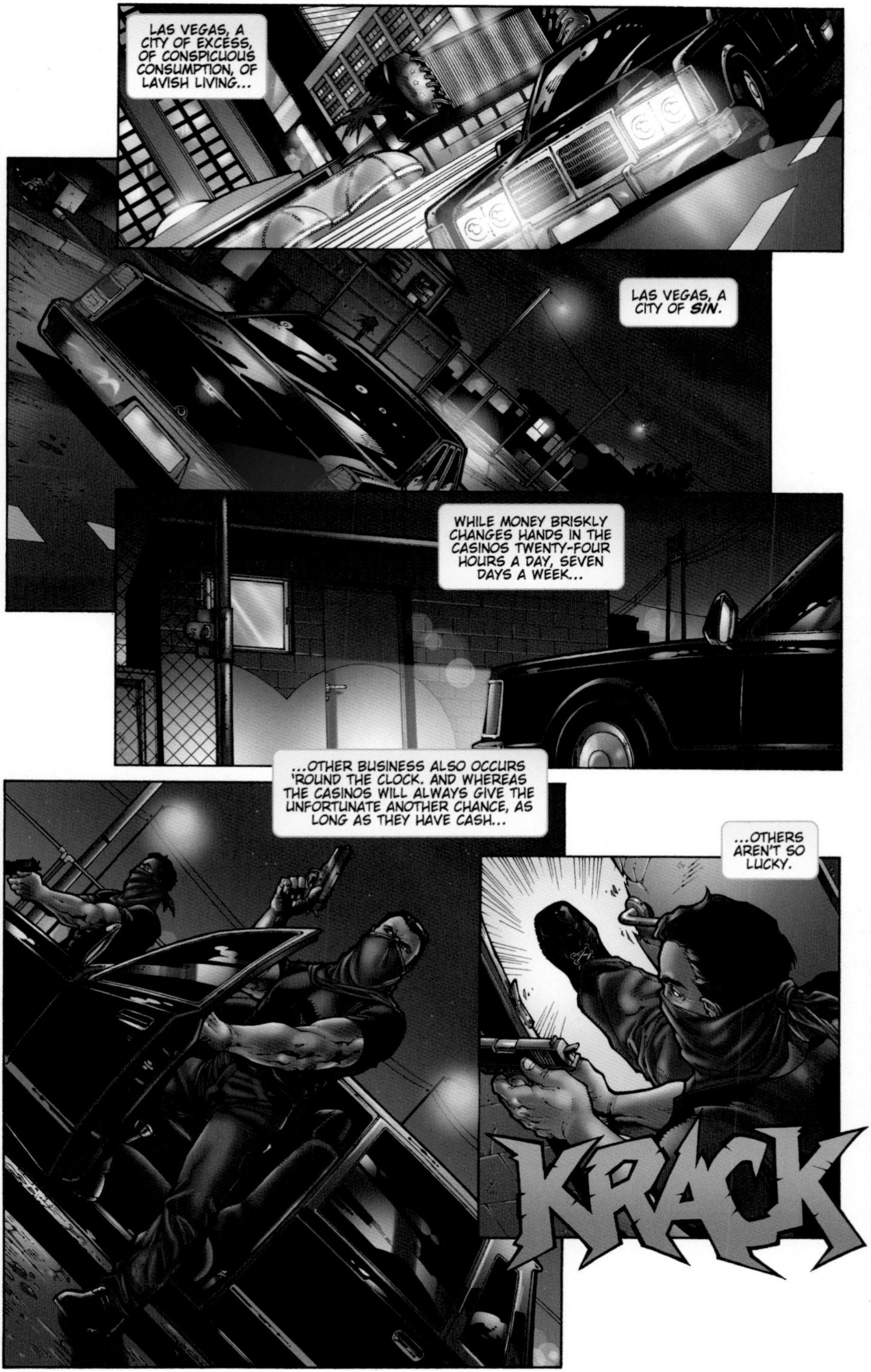
LAS VEGAS, A CITY OF EXCESS, OF CONSPICUOUS CONSUMPTION, OF LAVISH LIVING...
LAS VEGAS, A CITY OF SIN.
WHILE MONEY BRISKLY CHANGES HANDS IN THE CASINOS TWENTY-FOUR HOURS A DAY, SEVEN DAYS A WEEK...
...OTHER BUSINESS ALSO OCCURS 'ROUND THE CLOCK. AND WHEREAS THE CASINOS WILL ALWAYS GIVE THE UNFORTUNATE ANOTHER CHANCE, AS LONG AS THEY HAVE CASH...
...OTHERS AREN'T SO LUCKY.
KRACK

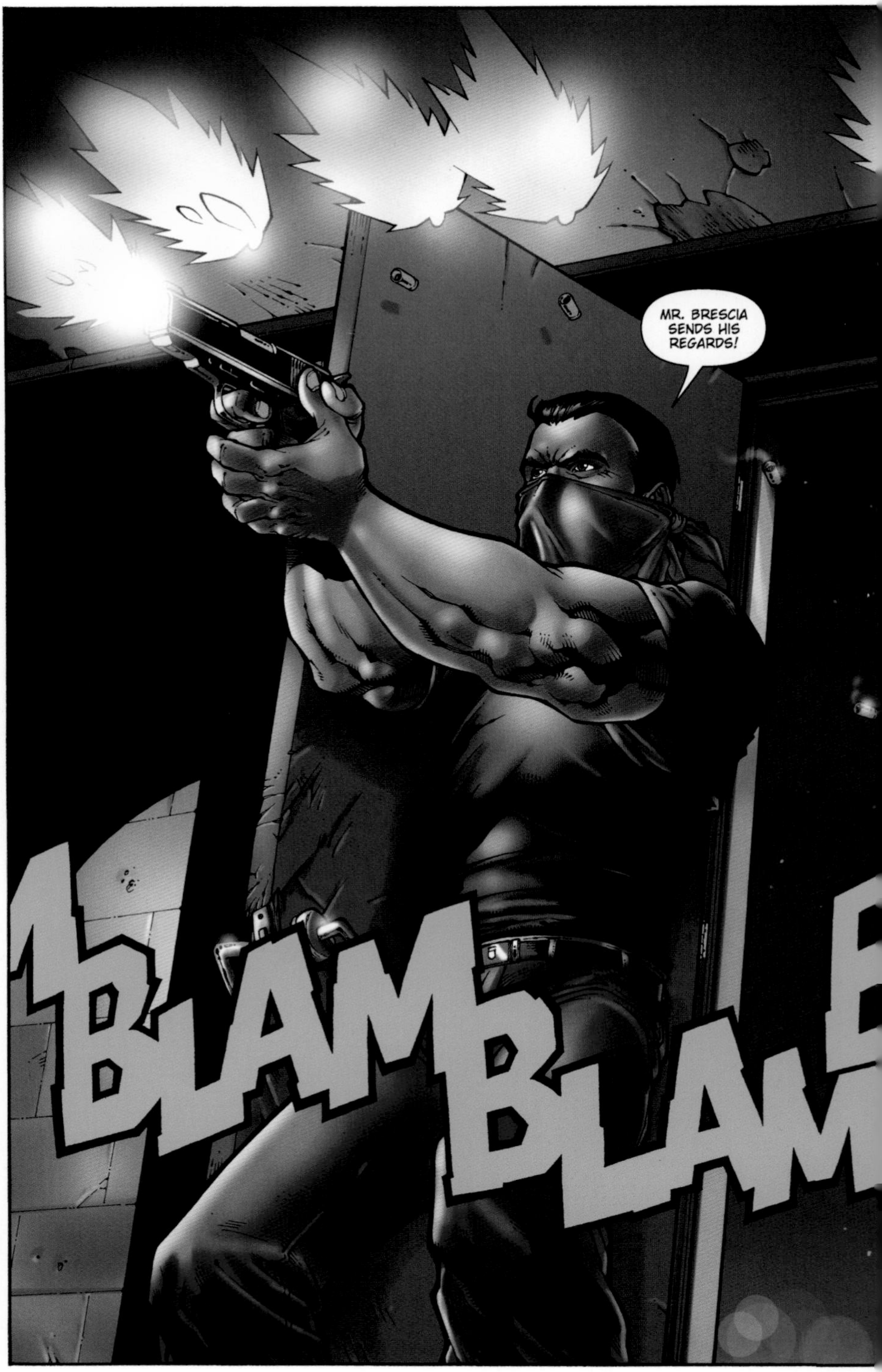
MR. BRESCIA SENDS HIS REGARDS!
BLAM
BLAM

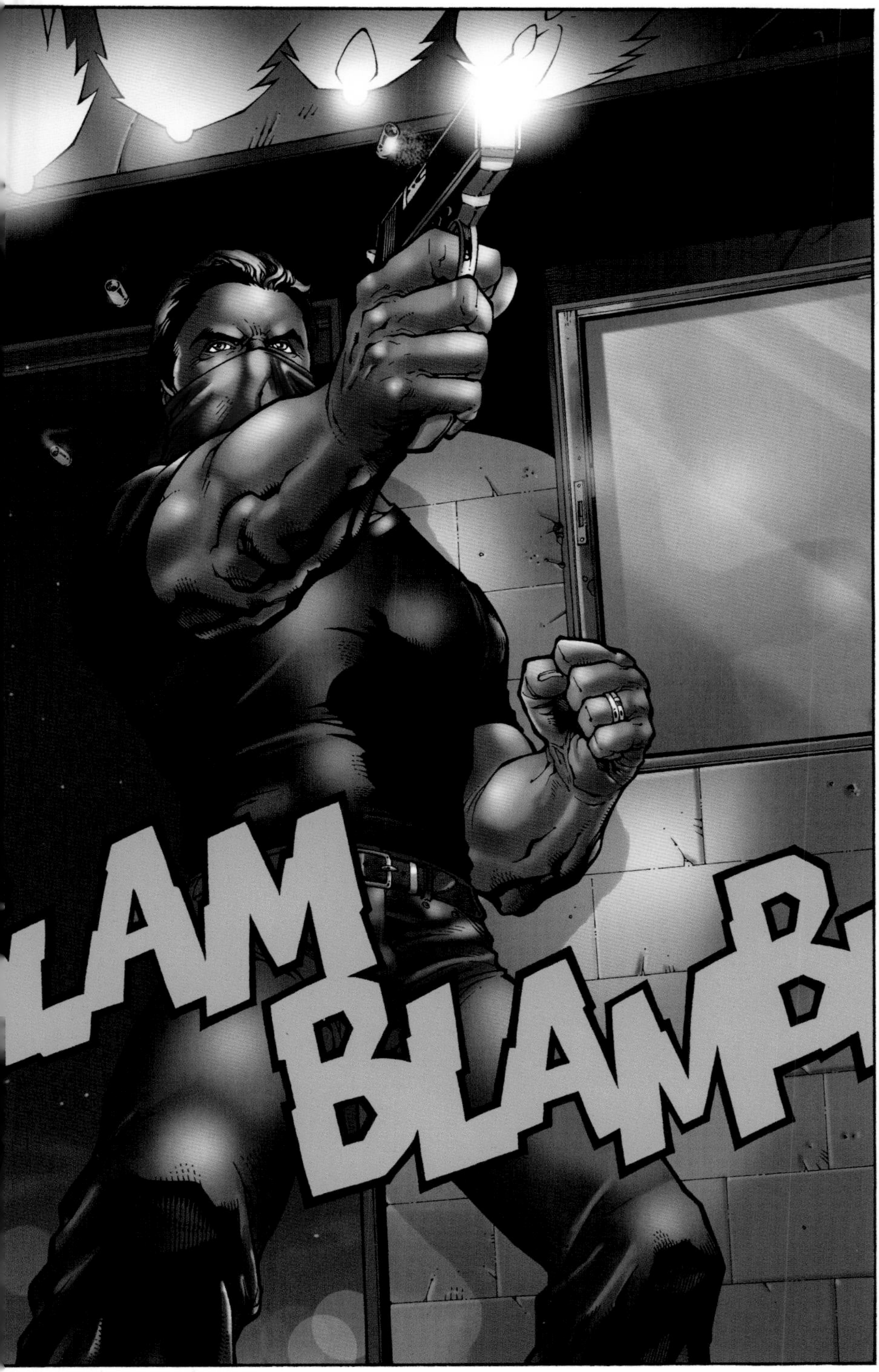
LAM
BLAM

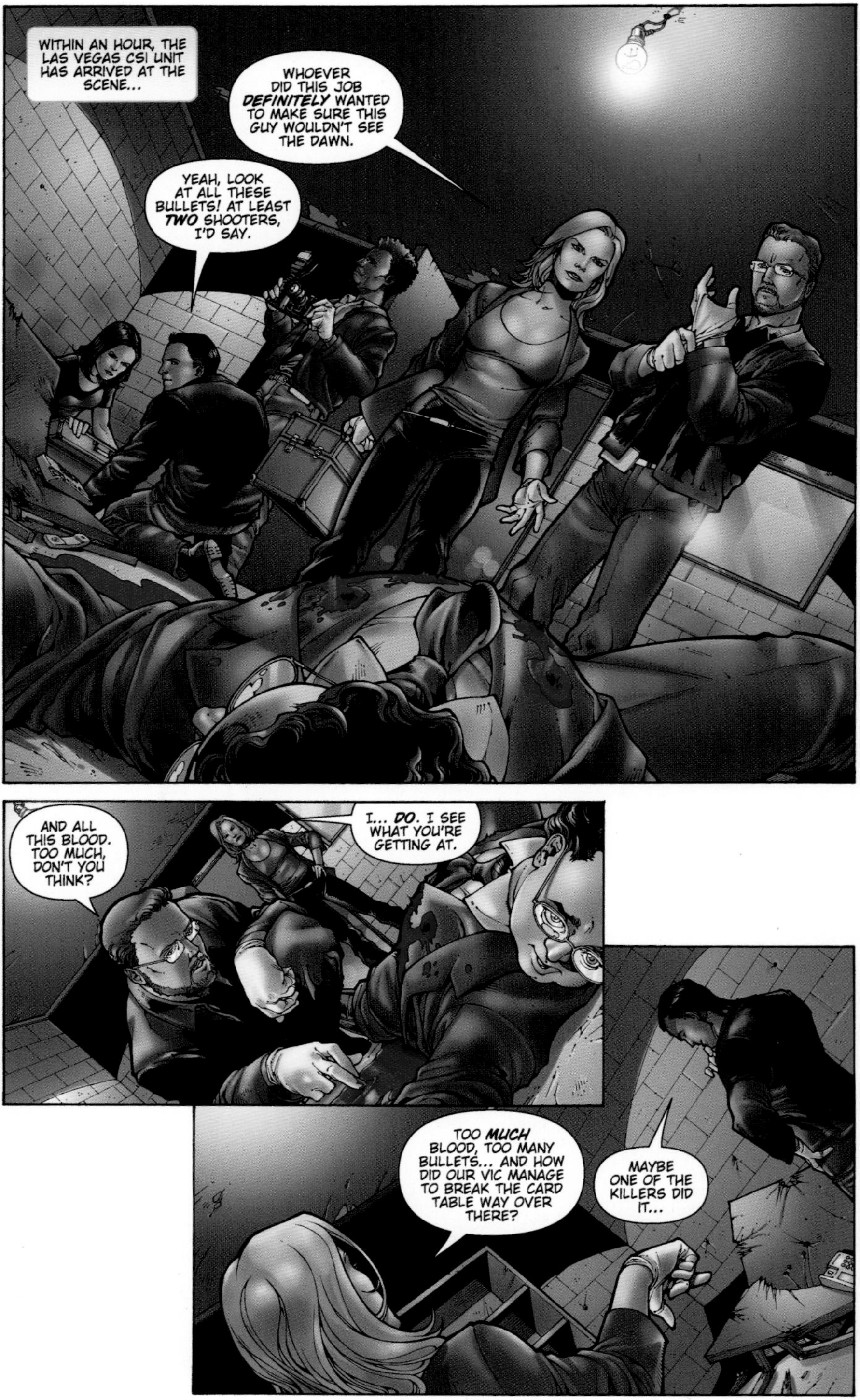

WITHIN AN HOUR, THE LAS VEGAS CSI UNIT HAS ARRIVED AT THE SCENE...
WHOEVER DID THIS JOB *DEFINITELY* WANTED TO MAKE SURE THIS GUY WOULDN'T SEE THE DAWN.
YEAH, LOOK AT ALL THESE BULLETS! AT LEAST *TWO* SHOOTERS, I'D SAY.
AND ALL THIS BLOOD. TOO MUCH, DON'T YOU THINK?
I... *DO*. I SEE WHAT YOU'RE GETTING AT.
TOO *MUCH* BLOOD, TOO MANY BULLETS... AND HOW DID OUR VIC MANAGE TO BREAK THE CARD TABLE WAY OVER THERE?
MAYBE ONE OF THE KILLERS DID IT...

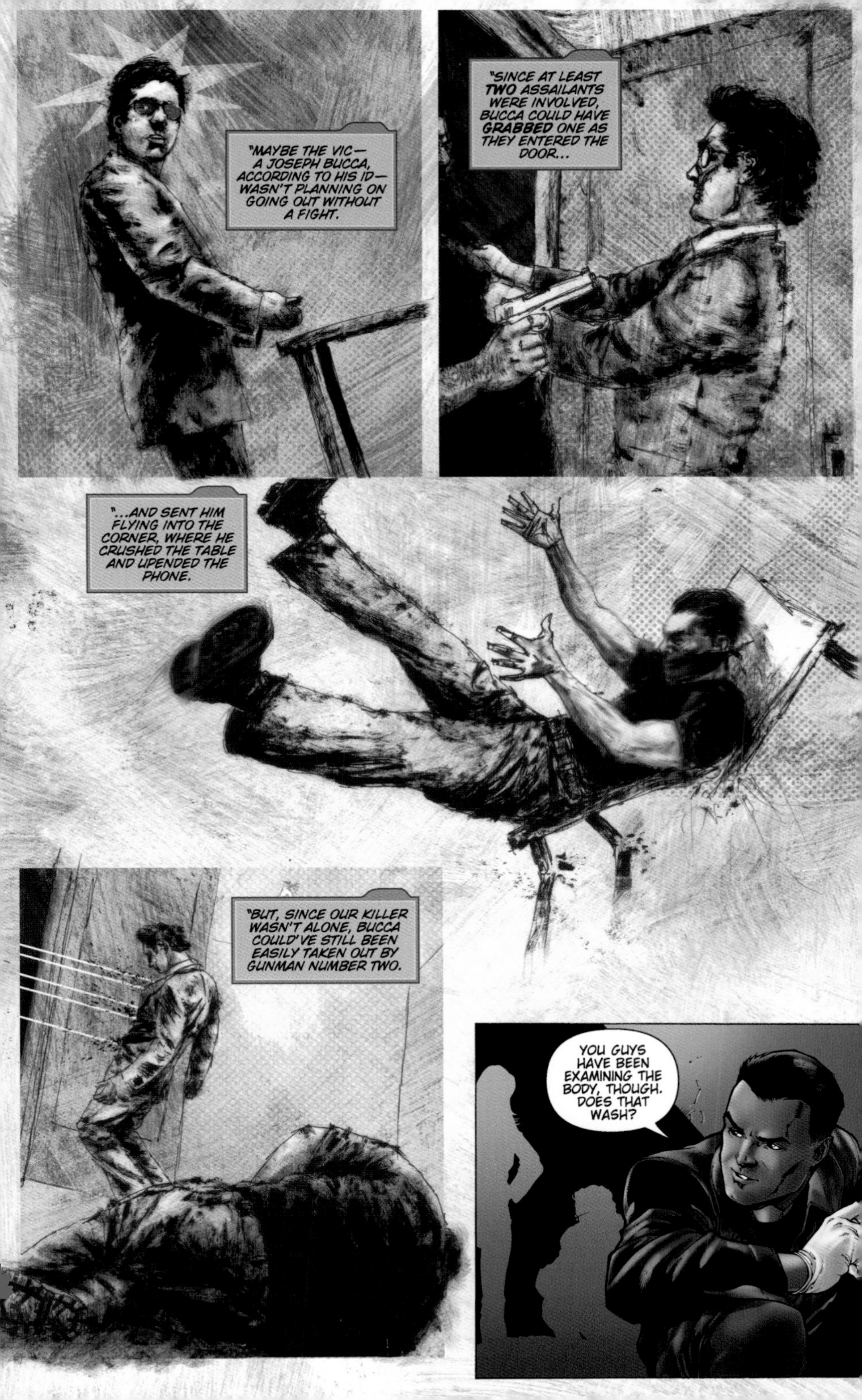
"MAYBE THE VIC—A JOSEPH BUCCA, ACCORDING TO HIS ID—WASN'T PLANNING ON GOING OUT WITHOUT A FIGHT.
"SINCE AT LEAST TWO ASSAILANTS WERE INVOLVED, BUCCA COULD HAVE GRABBED ONE AS THEY ENTERED THE DOOR...
"...AND SENT HIM FLYING INTO THE CORNER, WHERE HE CRUSHED THE TABLE AND UPENDED THE PHONE.
"BUT, SINCE OUR KILLER WASN'T ALONE, BUCCA COULD'VE STILL BEEN EASILY TAKEN OUT BY GUNMAN NUMBER TWO.
YOU GUYS HAVE BEEN EXAMINING THE BODY, THOUGH. DOES THAT WASH?

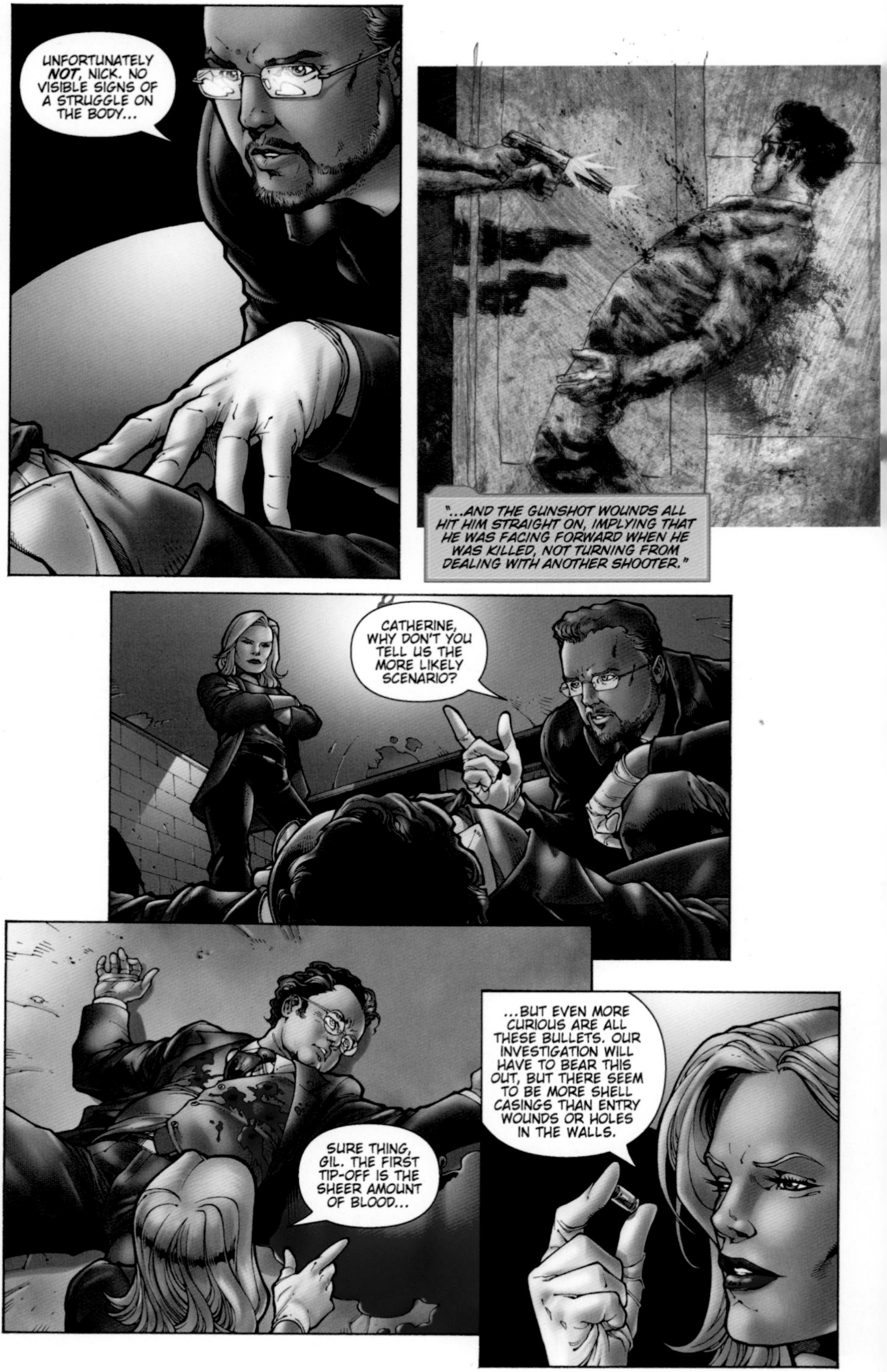
UNFORTUNATELY NOT, NICK. NO VISIBLE SIGNS OF A STRUGGLE ON THE BODY...
"...AND THE GUNSHOT WOUNDS ALL HIT HIM STRAIGHT ON, IMPLYING THAT HE WAS FACING FORWARD WHEN HE WAS KILLED, NOT TURNING FROM DEALING WITH ANOTHER SHOOTER."
CATHERINE, WHY DON'T YOU TELL US THE MORE LIKELY SCENARIO?
SURE THING, GIL. THE FIRST TIP-OFF IS THE SHEER AMOUNT OF BLOOD...
...BUT EVEN MORE CURIOUS ARE ALL THESE BULLETS. OUR INVESTIGATION WILL HAVE TO BEAR THIS OUT, BUT THERE SEEM TO BE MORE SHELL CASINGS THAN ENTRY WOUNDS OR HOLES IN THE WALLS.

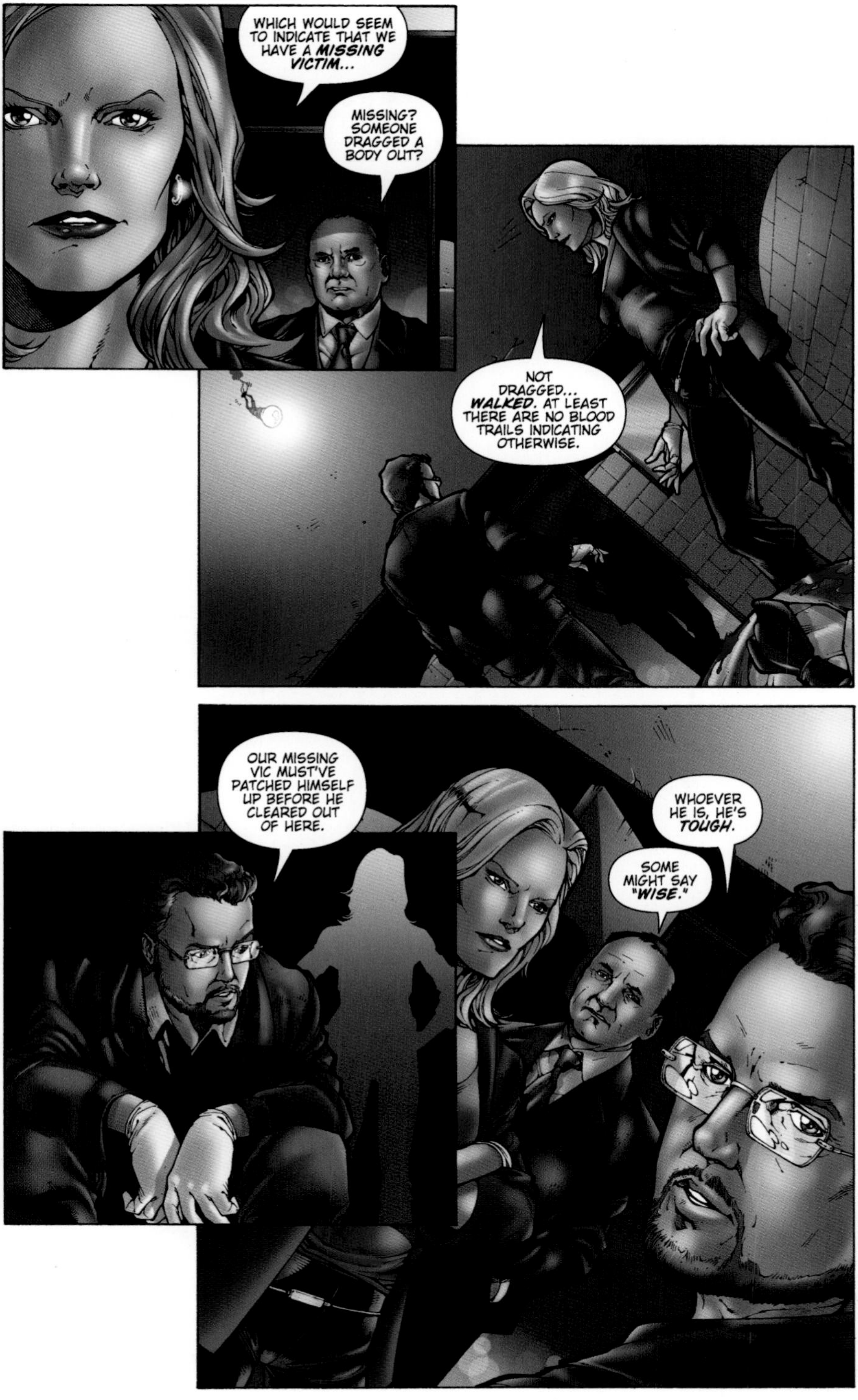
WHICH WOULD SEEM TO INDICATE THAT WE HAVE A MISSING VICTIM...
MISSING? SOMEONE DRAGGED A BODY OUT?
NOT DRAGGED... WALKED. AT LEAST THERE ARE NO BLOOD TRAILS INDICATING OTHERWISE.
OUR MISSING VIC MUST'VE PATCHED HIMSELF UP BEFORE HE CLEARED OUT OF HERE.
WHOEVER HE IS, HE'S TOUGH.
SOME MIGHT SAY "WISE."

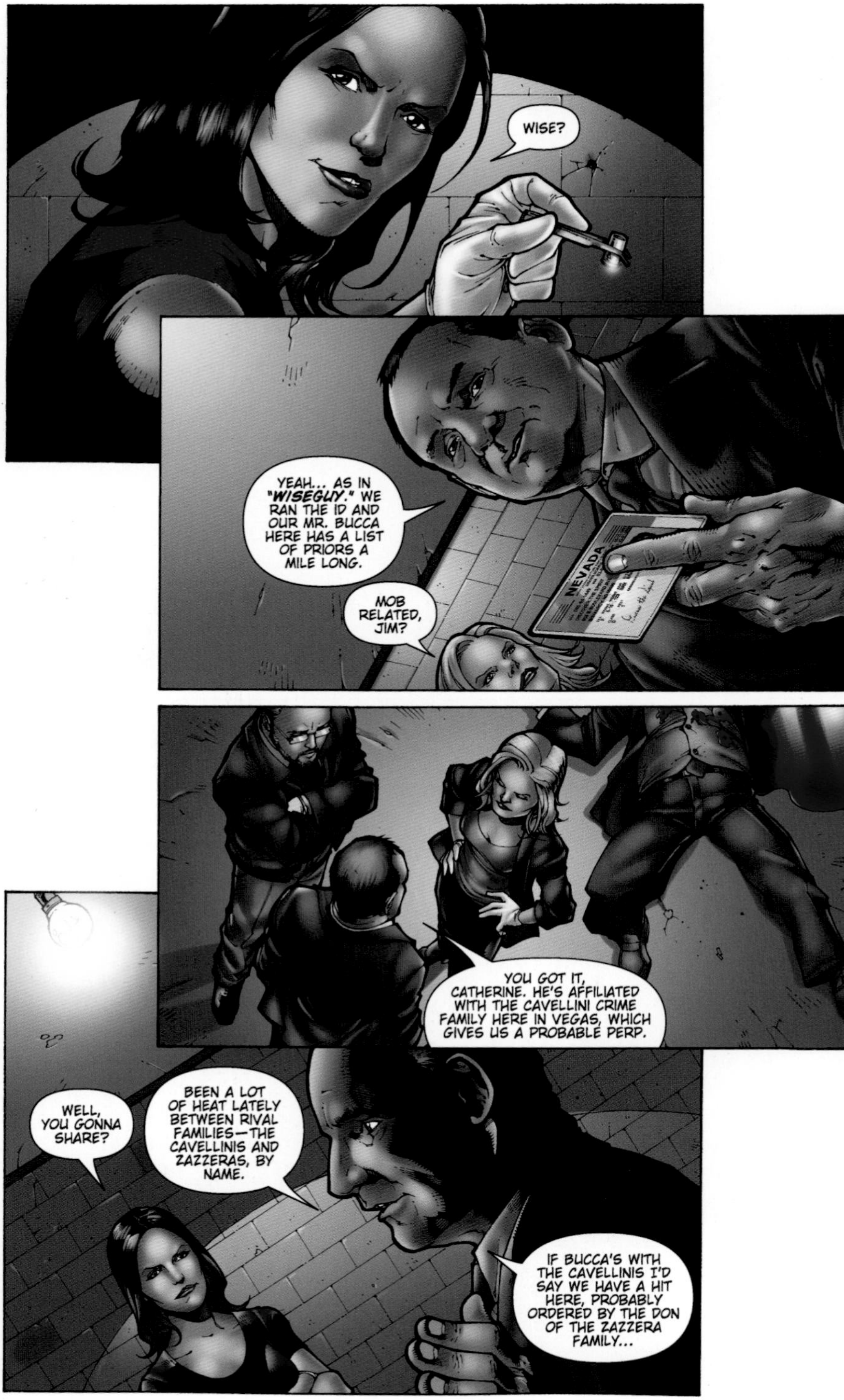
WISE?
YEAH... AS IN "*WISEGUY*." WE RAN THE ID AND OUR MR. BUCCA HERE HAS A LIST OF PRIORS A MILE LONG.
MOB RELATED, JIM?
YOU GOT IT, CATHERINE. HE'S AFFILIATED WITH THE CAVELLINI CRIME FAMILY HERE IN VEGAS, WHICH GIVES US A PROBABLE PERP.
WELL, YOU GONNA SHARE?
BEEN A LOT OF HEAT LATELY BETWEEN RIVAL FAMILIES—THE CAVELLINIS AND ZAZZERAS, BY NAME.
IF BUCCA'S WITH THE CAVELLINIS I'D SAY WE HAVE A HIT HERE, PROBABLY ORDERED BY THE DON OF THE ZAZZERA FAMILY...

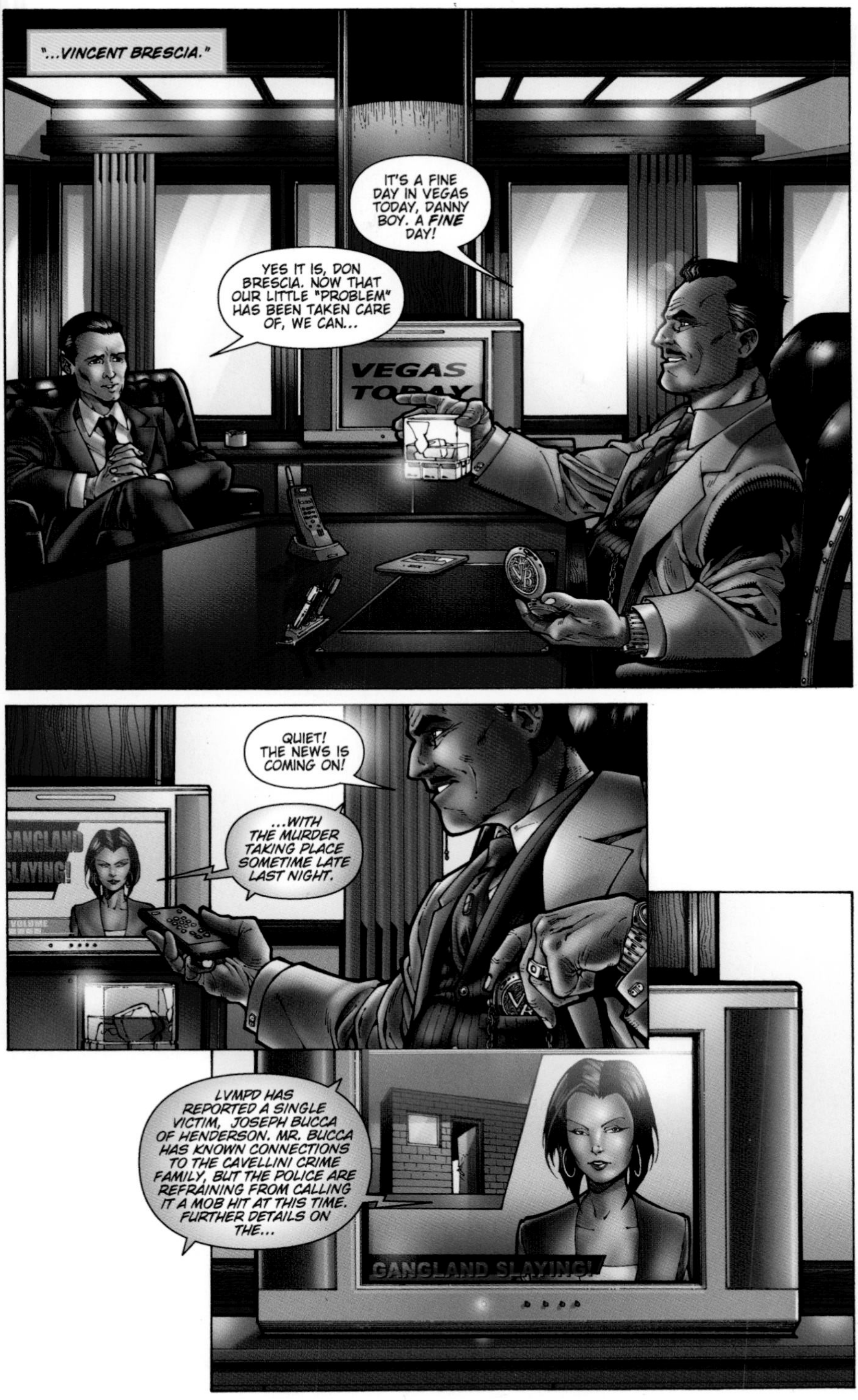
"...VINCENT BRESCIA."
IT'S A FINE DAY IN VEGAS TODAY, DANNY BOY. A FINE DAY!
YES IT IS, DON BRESCIA. NOW THAT OUR LITTLE "PROBLEM" HAS BEEN TAKEN CARE OF, WE CAN...
VEGAS TODAY
QUIET! THE NEWS IS COMING ON!
...WITH THE MURDER TAKING PLACE SOMETIME LATE LAST NIGHT.
GANGLAND SLAYING!
VOLUME
LVMPD HAS REPORTED A SINGLE VICTIM, JOSEPH BUCCA OF HENDERSON. MR. BUCCA HAS KNOWN CONNECTIONS TO THE CAVELLINI CRIME FAMILY, BUT THE POLICE ARE REFRAINING FROM CALLING IT A MOB HIT AT THIS TIME. FURTHER DETAILS ON THE...
GANGLAND SLAYING!

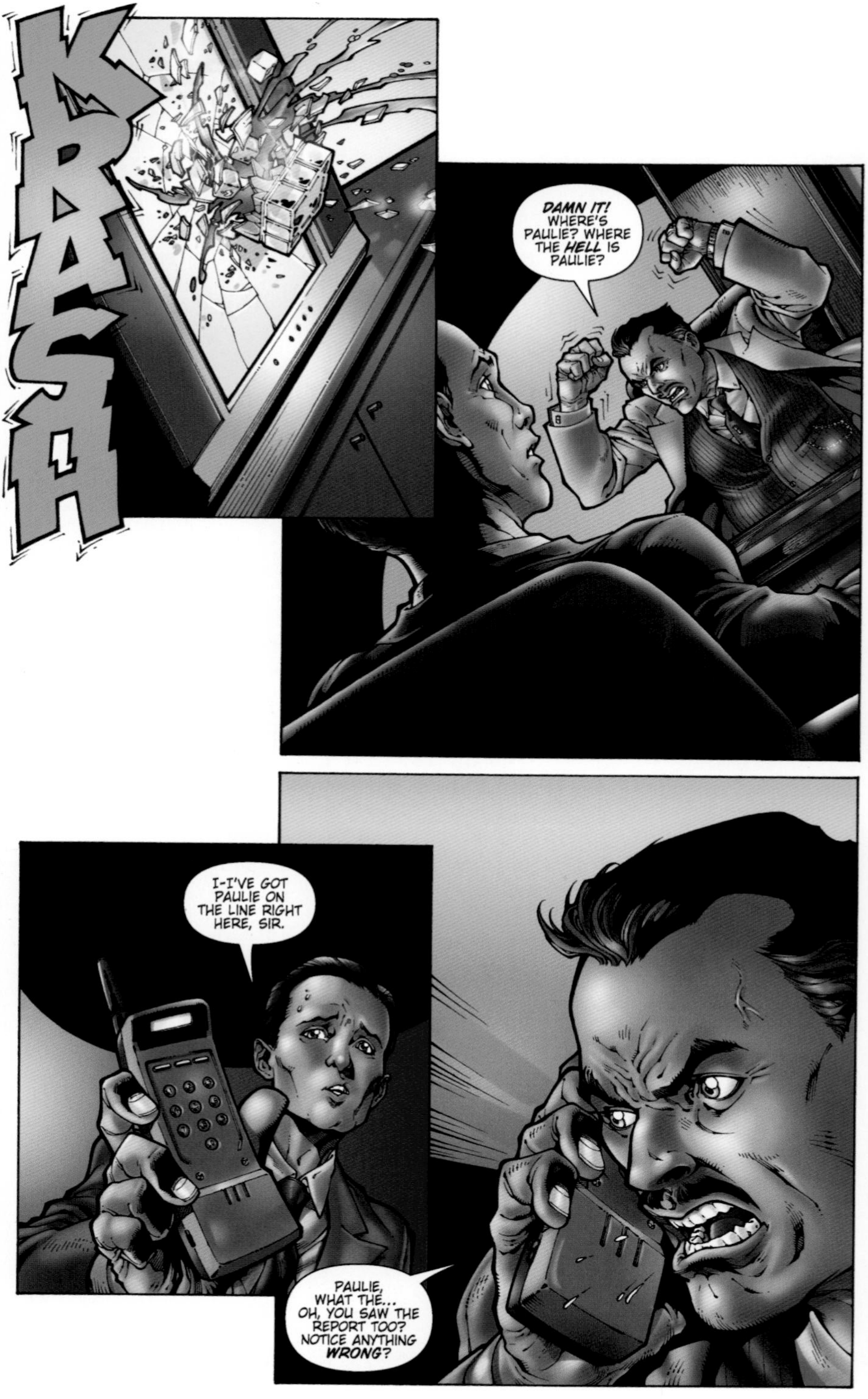
KRASH
DAMN IT! WHERE'S PAULIE? WHERE THE HELL IS PAULIE?
I-I'VE GOT PAULIE ON THE LINE RIGHT HERE, SIR.
PAULIE, WHAT THE... OH, YOU SAW THE REPORT TOO? NOTICE ANYTHING WRONG?

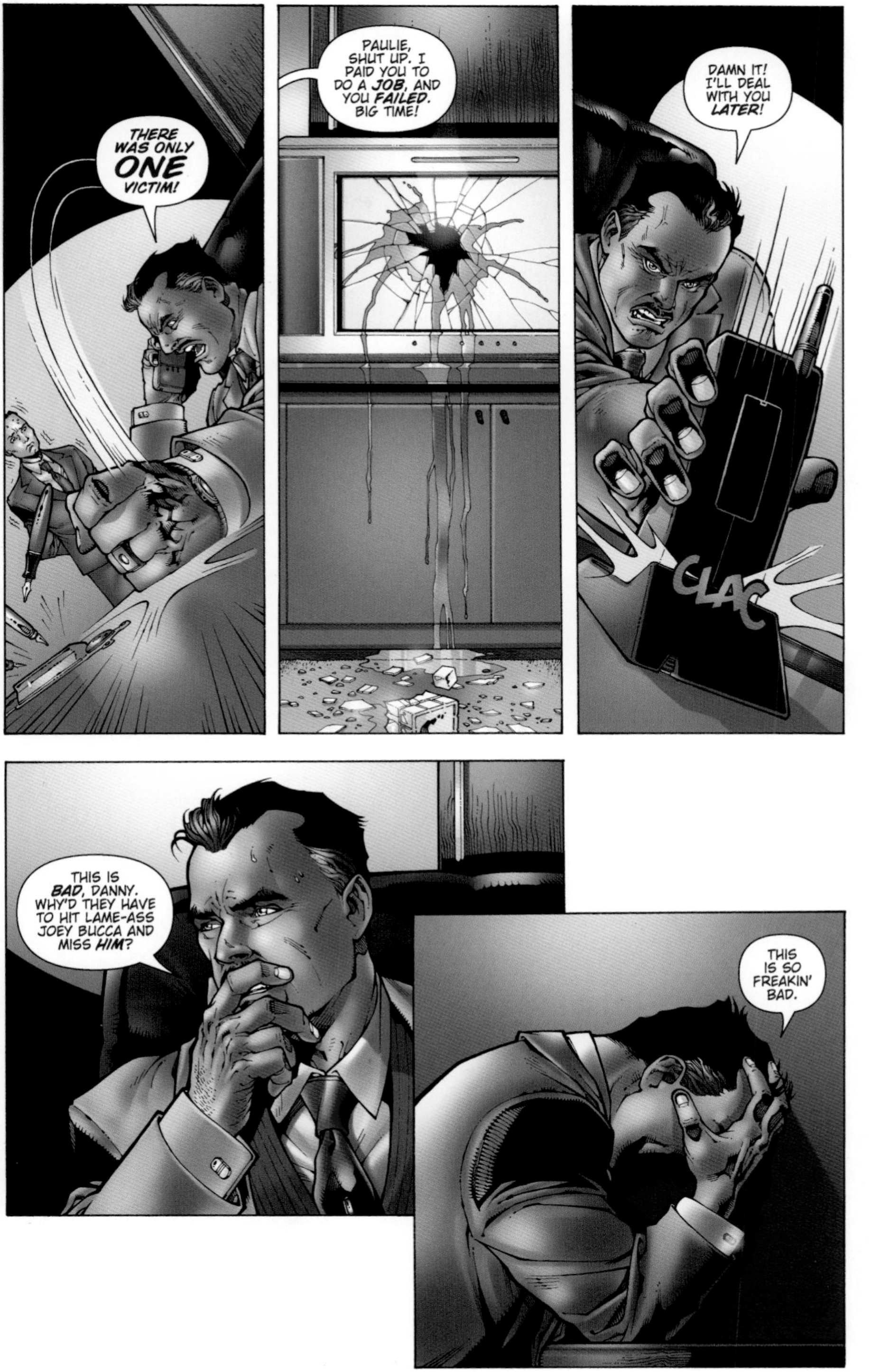
THERE WAS ONLY ONE VICTIM!
PAULIE, SHUT UP. I PAID YOU TO DO A JOB, AND YOU FAILED. BIG TIME!
DAMN IT! I'LL DEAL WITH YOU LATER!
CLAC
THIS IS BAD, DANNY. WHY'D THEY HAVE TO HIT LAME-ASS JOEY BUCCA AND MISS HIM?
THIS IS SO FREAKIN' BAD.

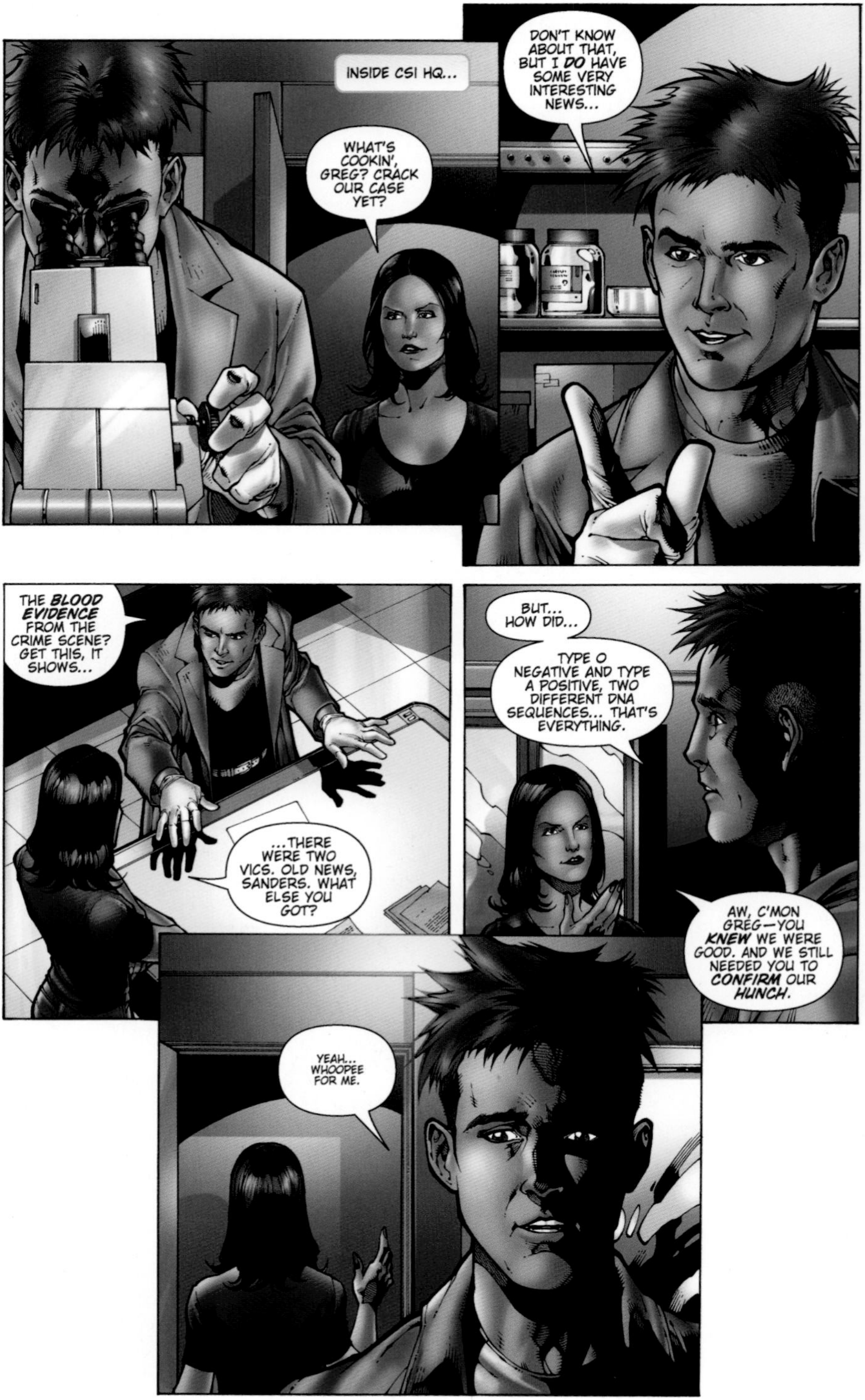
INSIDE CSI HQ...
WHAT'S COOKIN', GREG? CRACK OUR CASE YET?
DON'T KNOW ABOUT THAT, BUT I DO HAVE SOME VERY INTERESTING NEWS...
THE BLOOD EVIDENCE FROM THE CRIME SCENE? GET THIS, IT SHOWS...
...THERE WERE TWO VICS. OLD NEWS, SANDERS. WHAT ELSE YOU GOT?
BUT... HOW DID...
TYPE O NEGATIVE AND TYPE A POSITIVE, TWO DIFFERENT DNA SEQUENCES... THAT'S EVERYTHING.
AW, C'MON GREG—YOU KNEW WE WERE GOOD. AND WE STILL NEEDED YOU TO CONFIRM OUR HUNCH.
YEAH... WHOOPEE FOR ME.

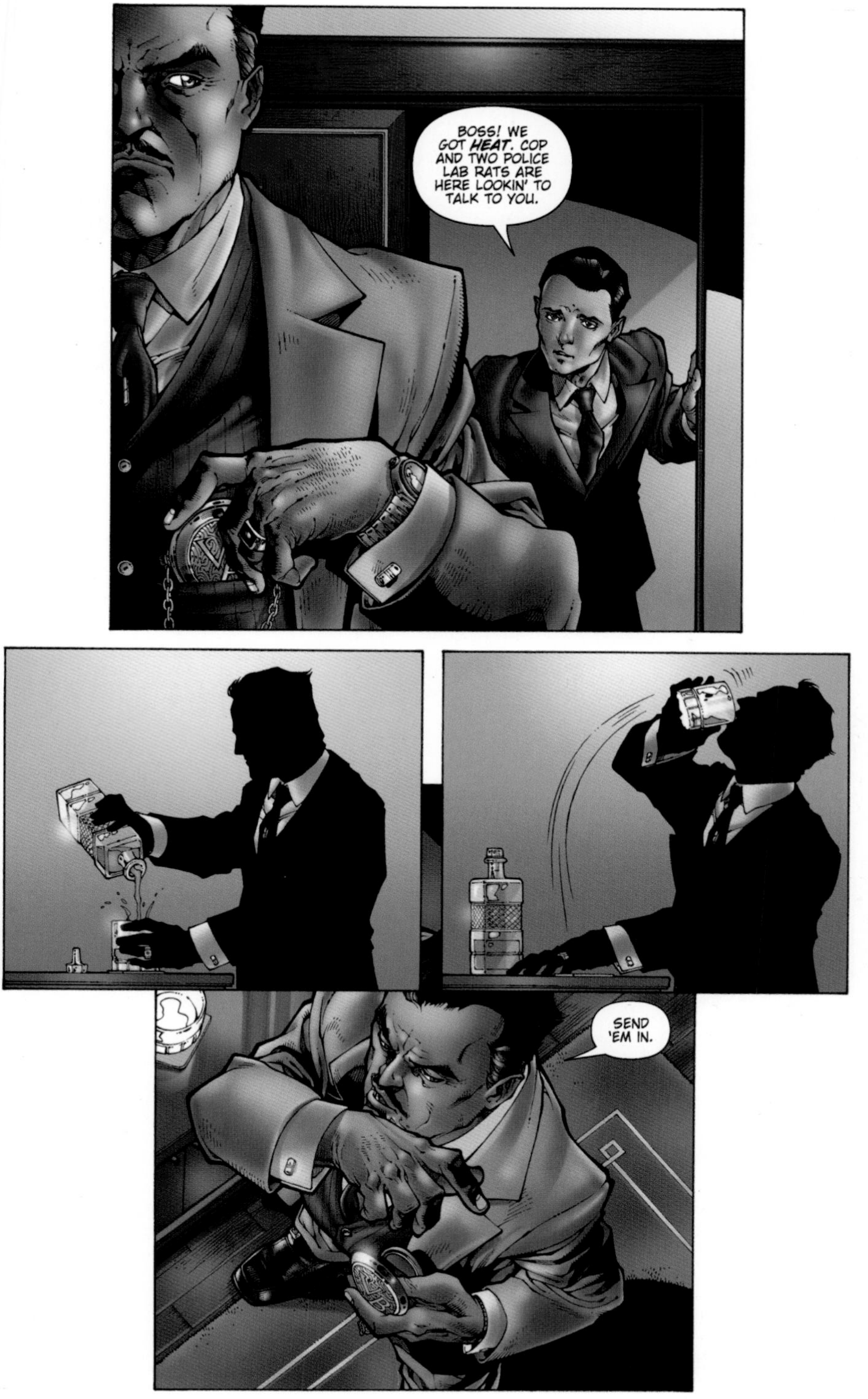
BOSS! WE GOT HEAT. COP AND TWO POLICE LAB RATS ARE HERE LOOKIN' TO TALK TO YOU.
SEND 'EM IN.

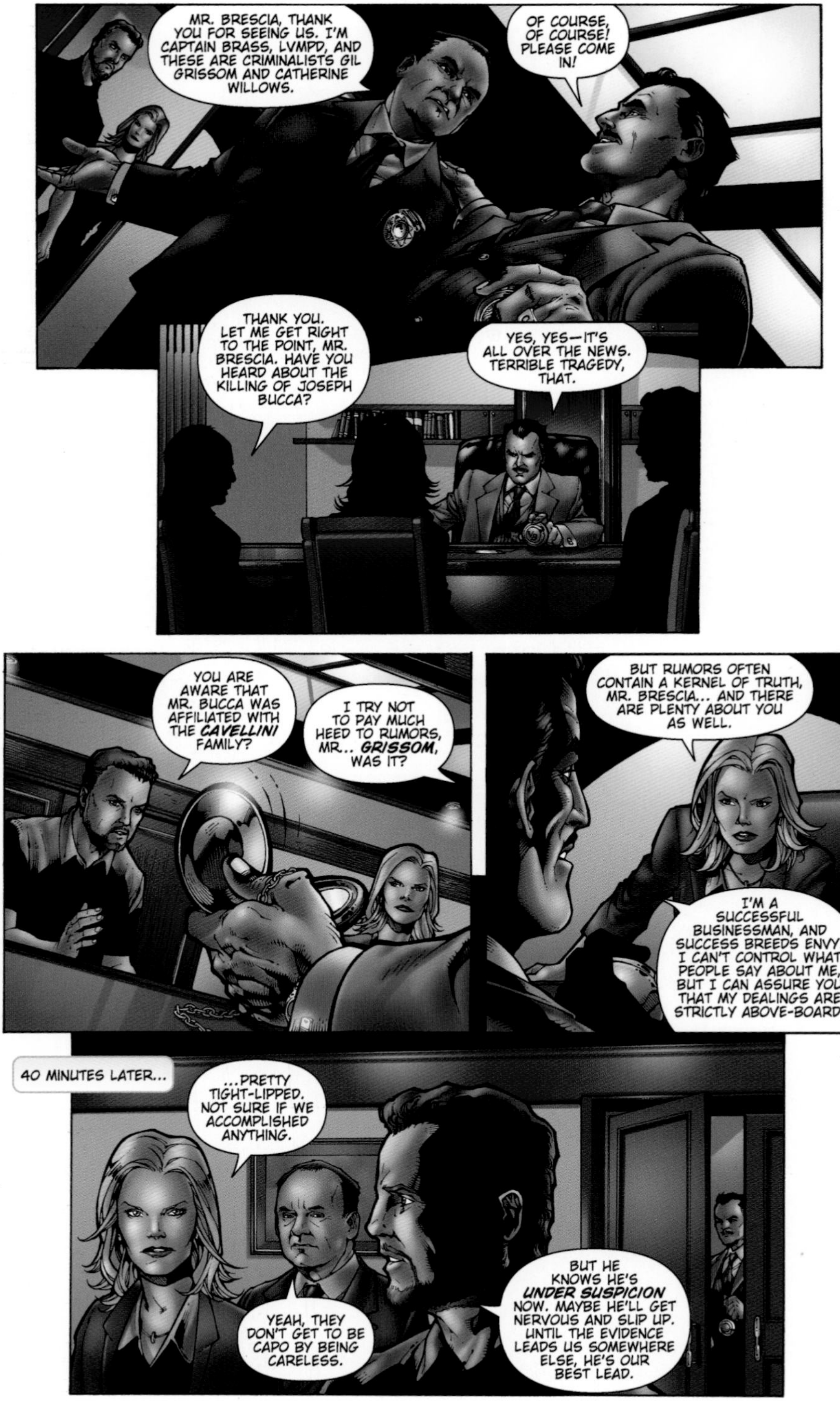
MR. BRESCIA, THANK YOU FOR SEEING US. I'M CAPTAIN BRASS, LVMPD, AND THESE ARE CRIMINALISTS GIL GRISSOM AND CATHERINE WILLOWS.
OF COURSE, OF COURSE! PLEASE COME IN!
THANK YOU. LET ME GET RIGHT TO THE POINT, MR. BRESCIA. HAVE YOU HEARD ABOUT THE KILLING OF JOSEPH BUCCA?
YES, YES—IT'S ALL OVER THE NEWS. TERRIBLE TRAGEDY, THAT.
YOU ARE AWARE THAT MR. BUCCA WAS AFFILIATED WITH THE *CAVELLINI* FAMILY?
I TRY NOT TO PAY MUCH HEED TO RUMORS, MR... *GRISSOM*, WAS IT?
BUT RUMORS OFTEN CONTAIN A KERNEL OF TRUTH, MR. BRESCIA... AND THERE ARE PLENTY ABOUT YOU AS WELL.
I'M A SUCCESSFUL BUSINESSMAN, AND SUCCESS BREEDS ENVY. I CAN'T CONTROL WHAT PEOPLE SAY ABOUT ME, BUT I CAN ASSURE YOU THAT MY DEALINGS ARE STRICTLY ABOVE-BOARD.
40 MINUTES LATER...
...PRETTY TIGHT-LIPPED. NOT SURE IF WE ACCOMPLISHED ANYTHING.
YEAH, THEY DON'T GET TO BE CAPO BY BEING CARELESS.
BUT HE KNOWS HE'S *UNDER SUSPICION* NOW. MAYBE HE'LL GET NERVOUS AND SLIP UP. UNTIL THE EVIDENCE LEADS US SOMEWHERE ELSE, HE'S OUR BEST LEAD.

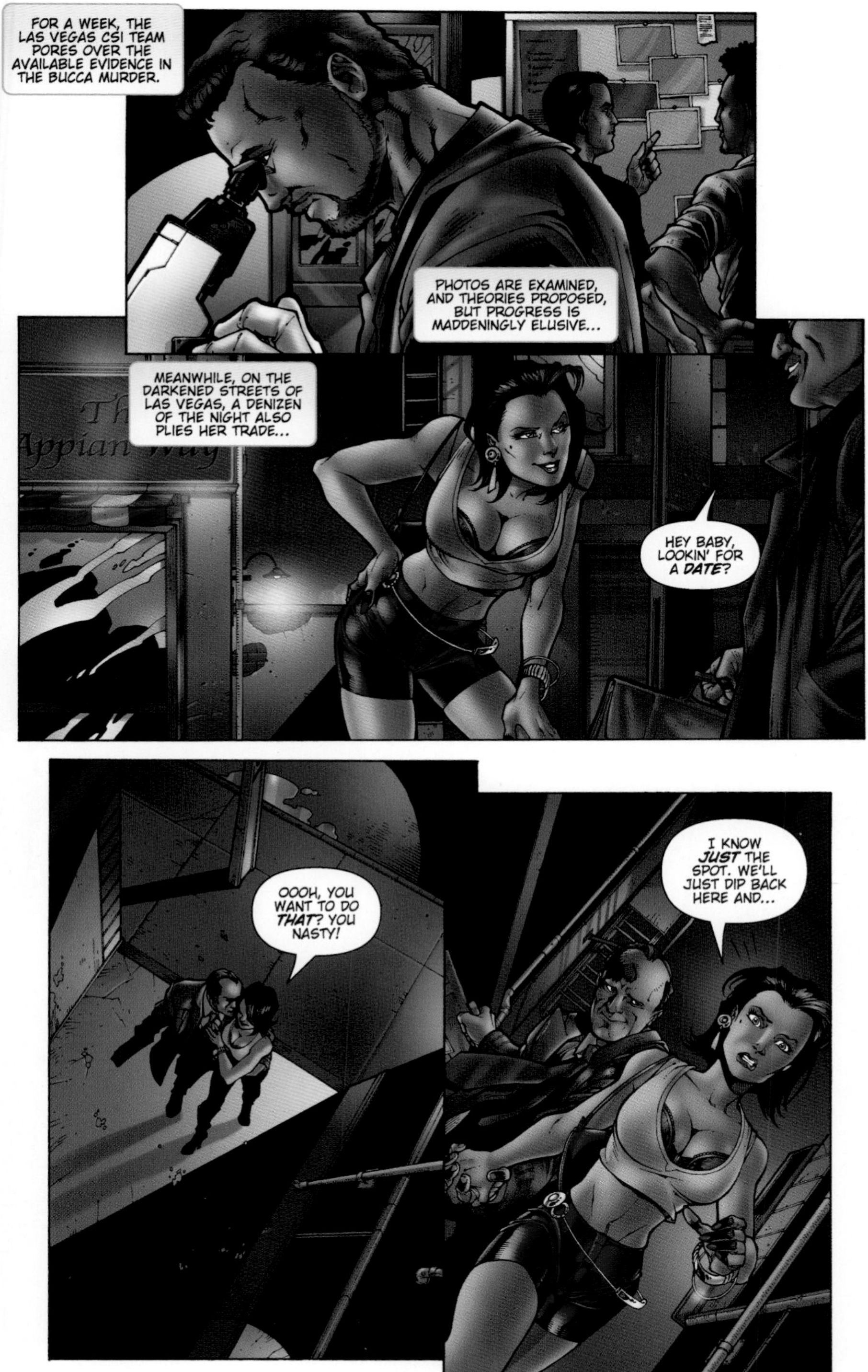
FOR A WEEK, THE LAS VEGAS CSI TEAM PORES OVER THE AVAILABLE EVIDENCE IN THE BUCCA MURDER.
PHOTOS ARE EXAMINED, AND THEORIES PROPOSED, BUT PROGRESS IS MADDENINGLY ELUSIVE...
MEANWHILE, ON THE DARKENED STREETS OF LAS VEGAS, A DENIZEN OF THE NIGHT ALSO PLIES HER TRADE...
The Appian Way
HEY BABY, LOOKIN' FOR A *DATE*?
OOOH, YOU WANT TO DO *THAT*? YOU NASTY!
I KNOW *JUST* THE SPOT. WE'LL JUST DIP BACK HERE AND...

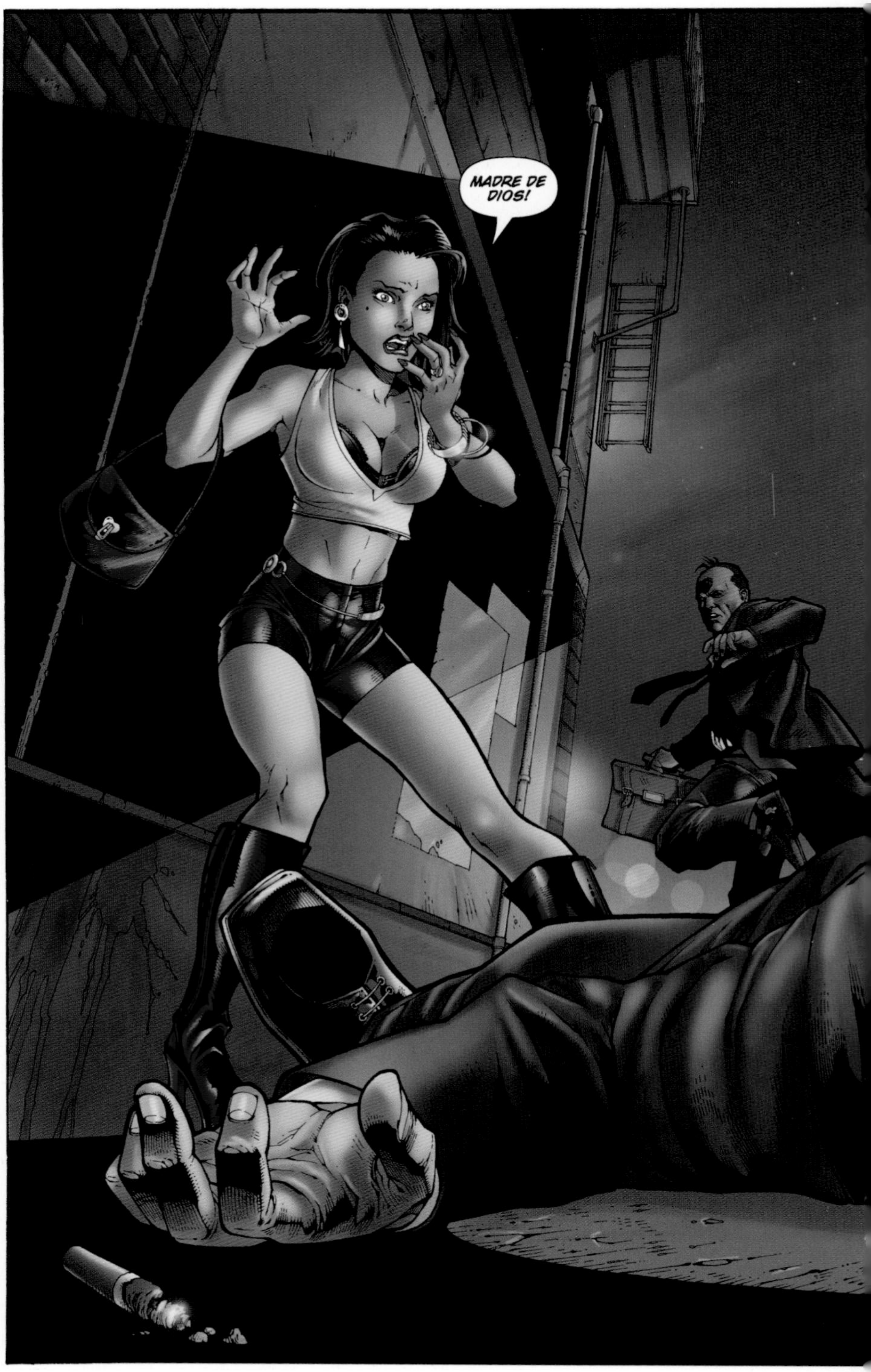
MADRE DE DIOS!

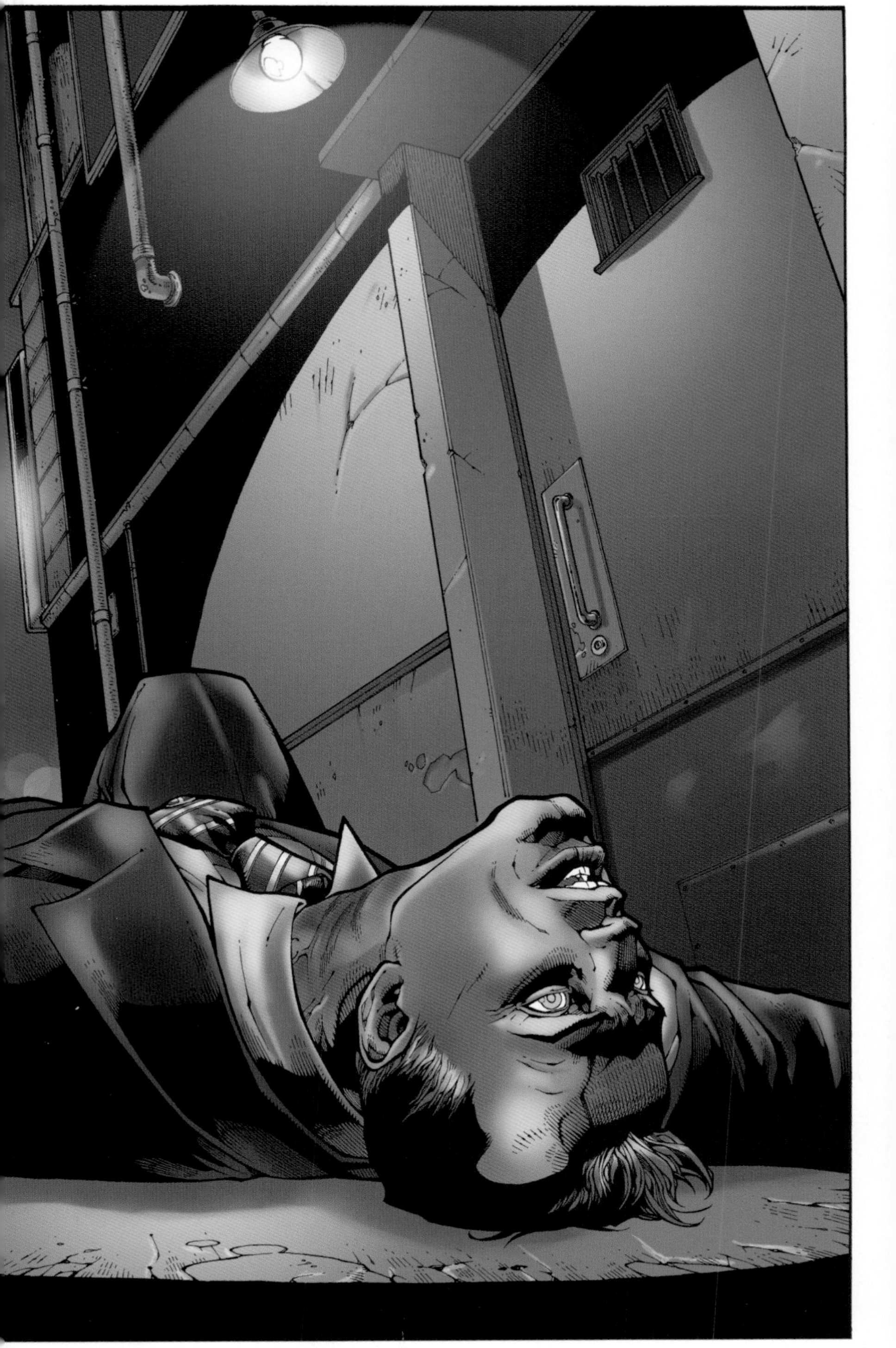

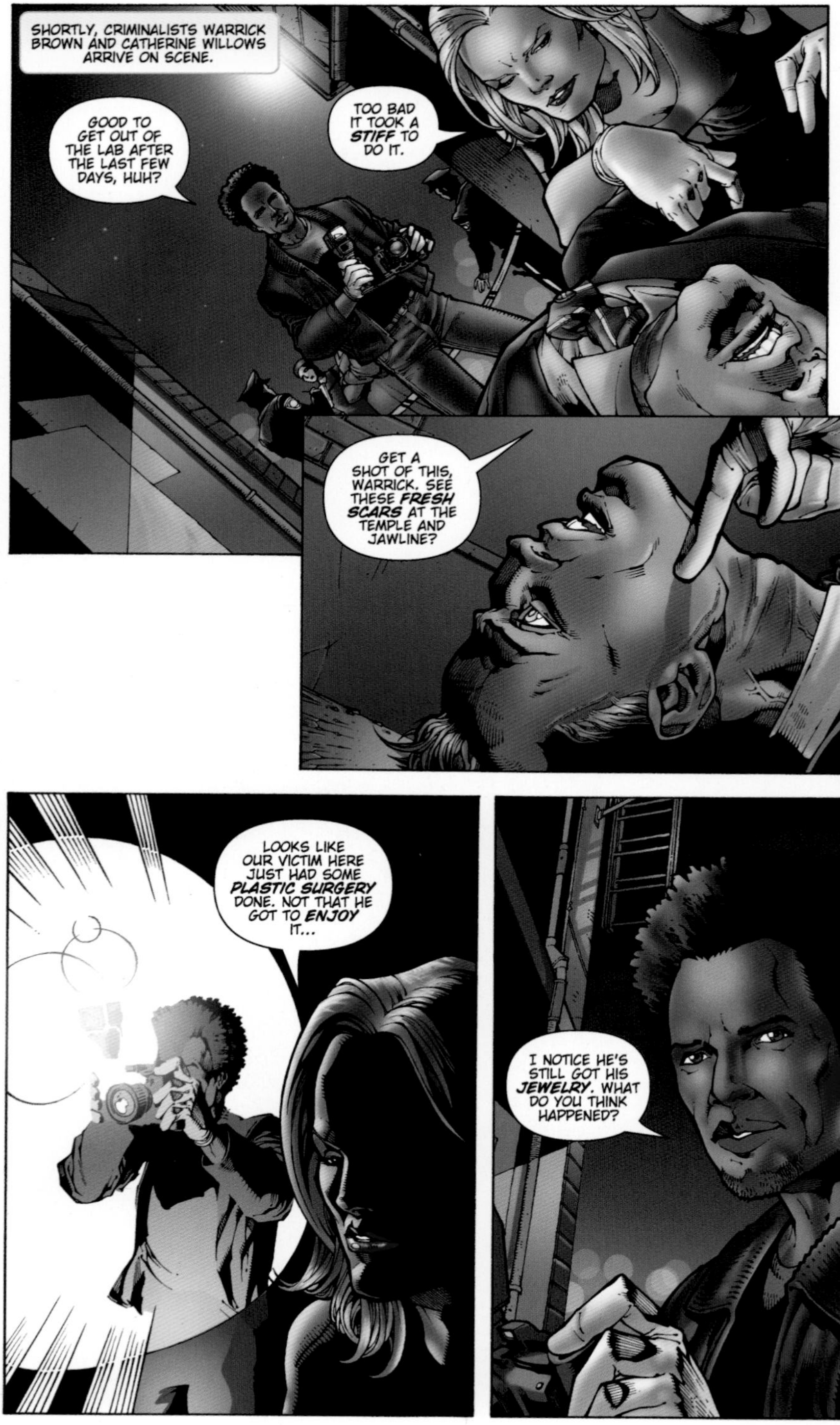
SHORTLY, CRIMINALISTS WARRICK BROWN AND CATHERINE WILLOWS ARRIVE ON SCENE.
GOOD TO GET OUT OF THE LAB AFTER THE LAST FEW DAYS, HUH?
TOO BAD IT TOOK A STIFF TO DO IT.
GET A SHOT OF THIS, WARRICK. SEE THESE FRESH SCARS AT THE TEMPLE AND JAWLINE?
LOOKS LIKE OUR VICTIM HERE JUST HAD SOME PLASTIC SURGERY DONE. NOT THAT HE GOT TO ENJOY IT...
I NOTICE HE'S STILL GOT HIS JEWELRY. WHAT DO YOU THINK HAPPENED?

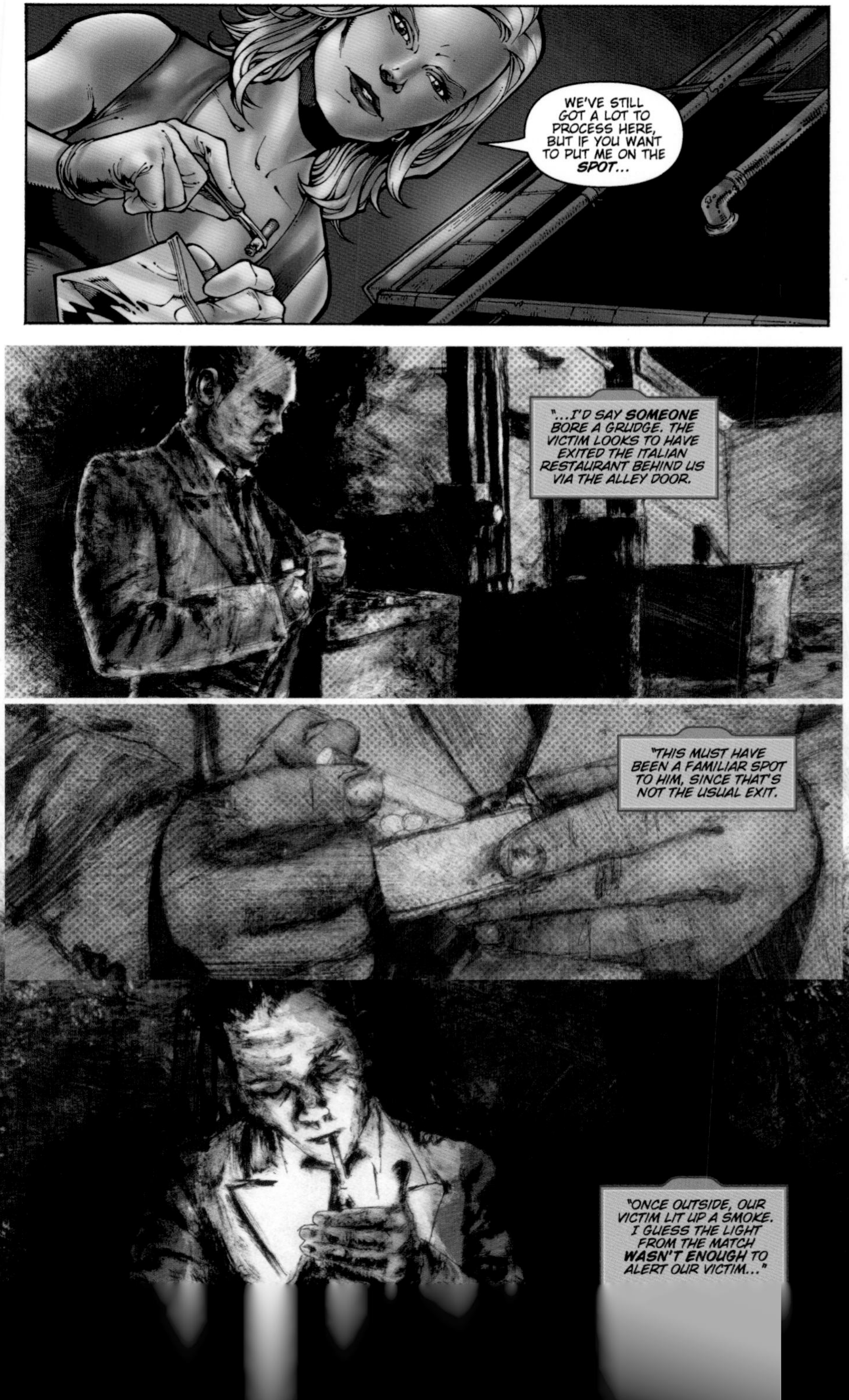

WE'VE STILL GOT A LOT TO PROCESS HERE, BUT IF YOU WANT TO PUT ME ON THE SPOT...
"...I'D SAY SOMEONE BORE A GRUDGE. THE VICTIM LOOKS TO HAVE EXITED THE ITALIAN RESTAURANT BEHIND US VIA THE ALLEY DOOR.
"THIS MUST HAVE BEEN A FAMILIAR SPOT TO HIM, SINCE THAT'S NOT THE USUAL EXIT.
"ONCE OUTSIDE, OUR VICTIM LIT UP A SMOKE. I GUESS THE LIGHT FROM THE MATCH WASN'T ENOUGH TO ALERT OUR VICTIM..."

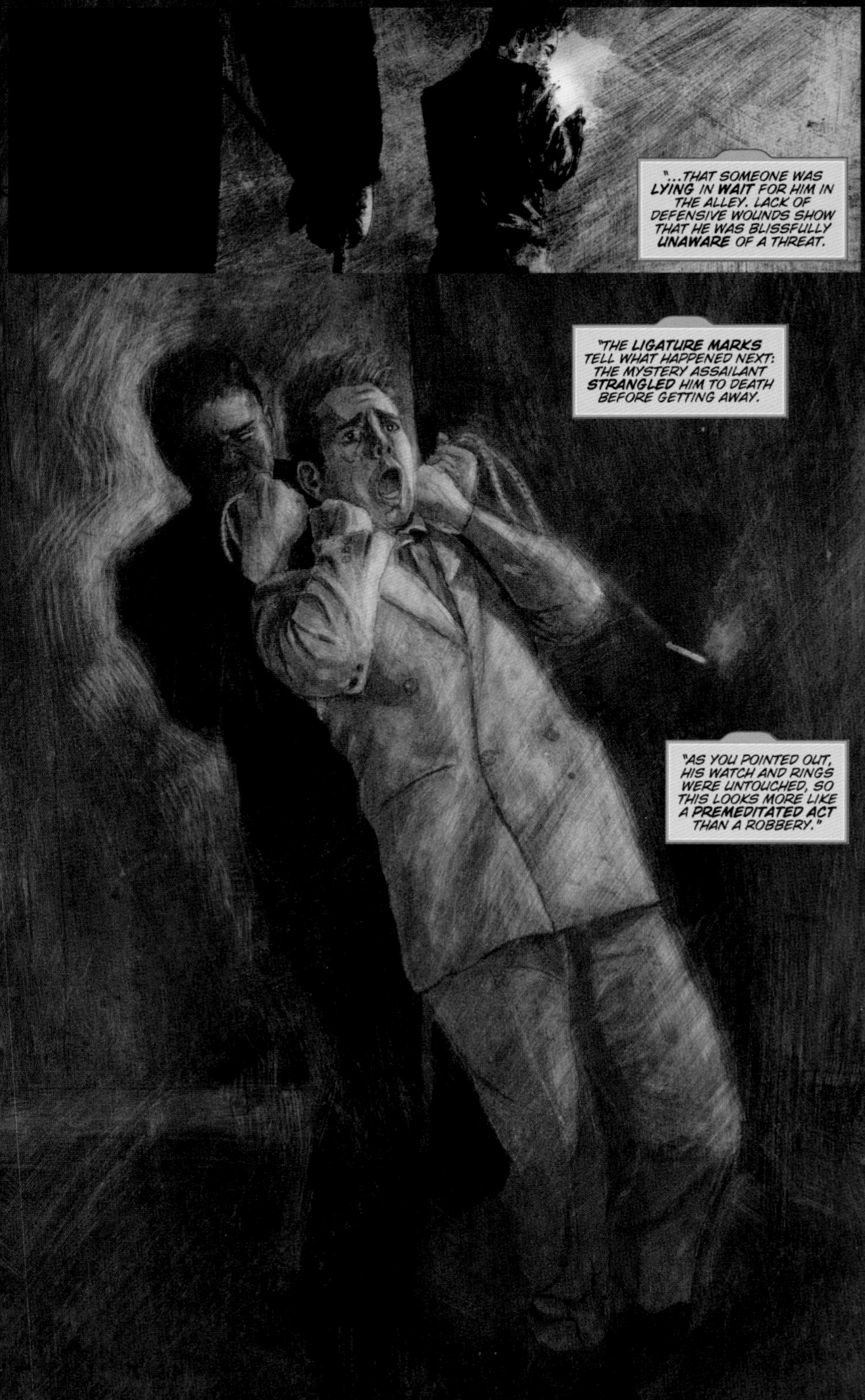
"...THAT SOMEONE WAS LYING IN WAIT FOR HIM IN THE ALLEY. LACK OF DEFENSIVE WOUNDS SHOW THAT HE WAS BLISSFULLY UNAWARE OF A THREAT.
"THE LIGATURE MARKS TELL WHAT HAPPENED NEXT: THE MYSTERY ASSAILANT STRANGLED HIM TO DEATH BEFORE GETTING AWAY.
"AS YOU POINTED OUT, HIS WATCH AND RINGS WERE UNTOUCHED, SO THIS LOOKS MORE LIKE A PREMEDITATED ACT THAN A ROBBERY."

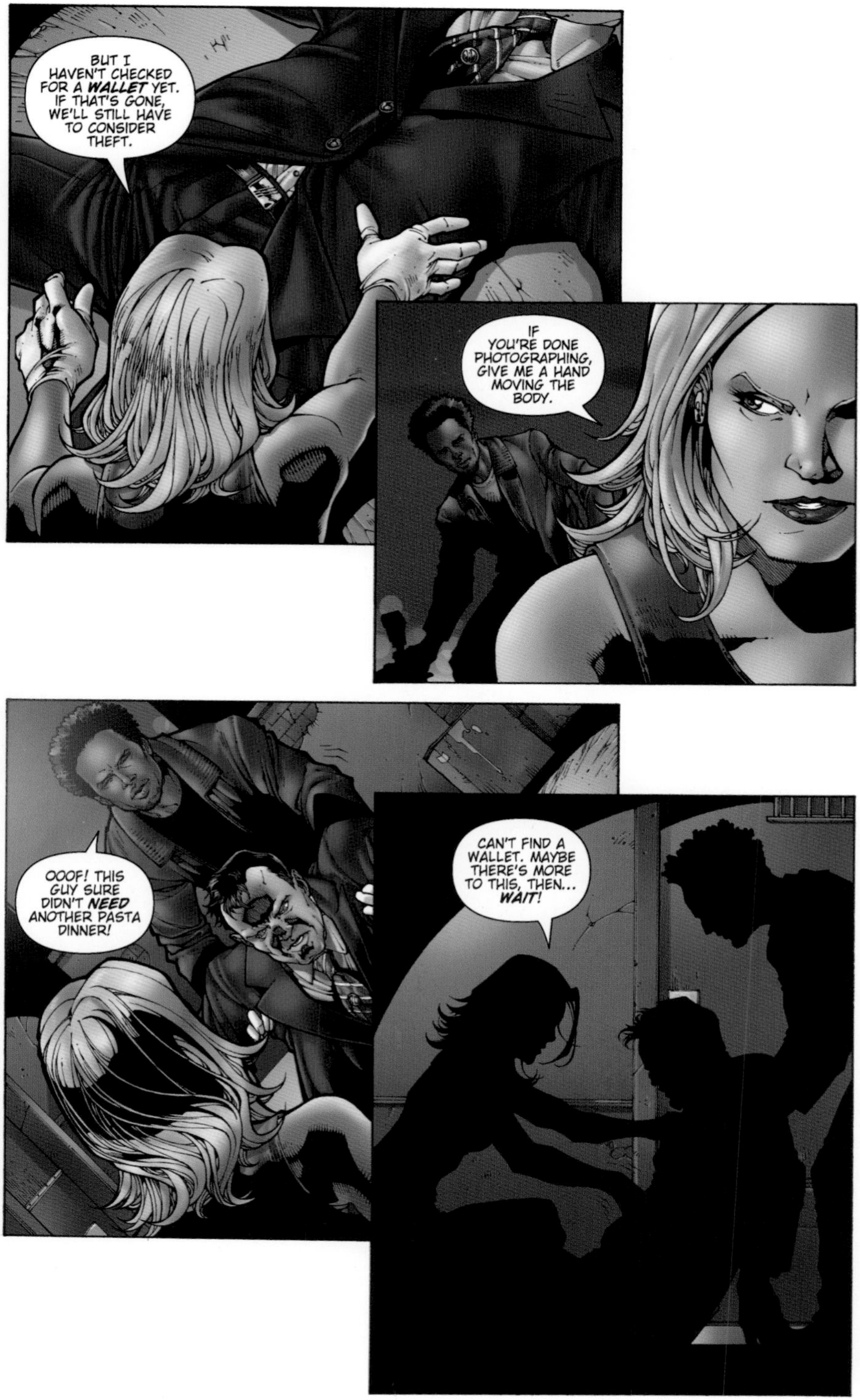
BUT I HAVEN'T CHECKED FOR A WALLET YET. IF THAT'S GONE, WE'LL STILL HAVE TO CONSIDER THEFT.
IF YOU'RE DONE PHOTOGRAPHING, GIVE ME A HAND MOVING THE BODY.
OOOF! THIS GUY SURE DIDN'T NEED ANOTHER PASTA DINNER!
CAN'T FIND A WALLET. MAYBE THERE'S MORE TO THIS, THEN... WAIT!

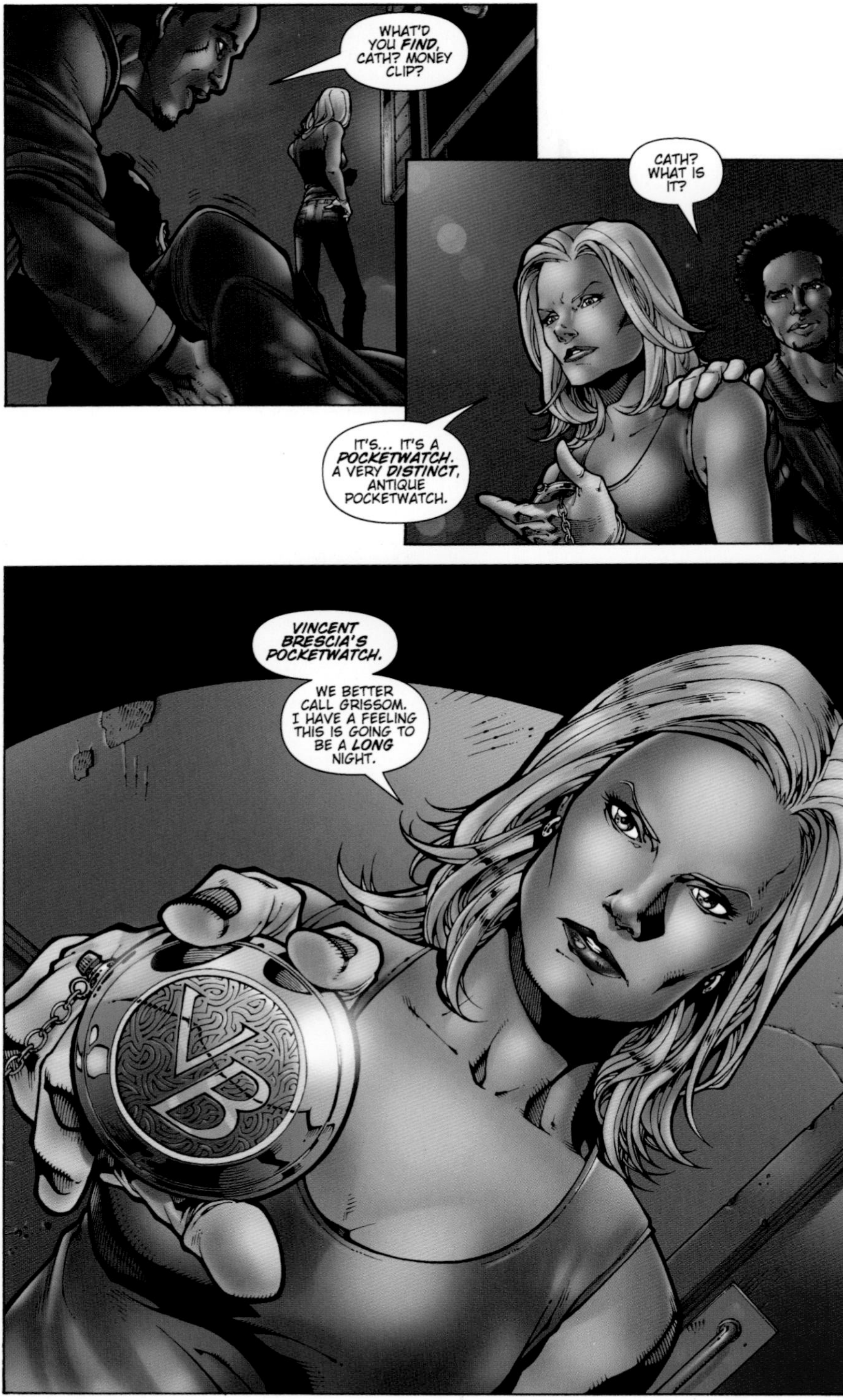
WHAT'D YOU FIND, CATH? MONEY CLIP?
CATH? WHAT IS IT?
IT'S... IT'S A POCKETWATCH. A VERY DISTINCT, ANTIQUE POCKETWATCH.
VINCENT BRESCIA'S POCKETWATCH.
WE BETTER CALL GRISSOM. I HAVE A FEELING THIS IS GOING TO BE A LONG NIGHT.

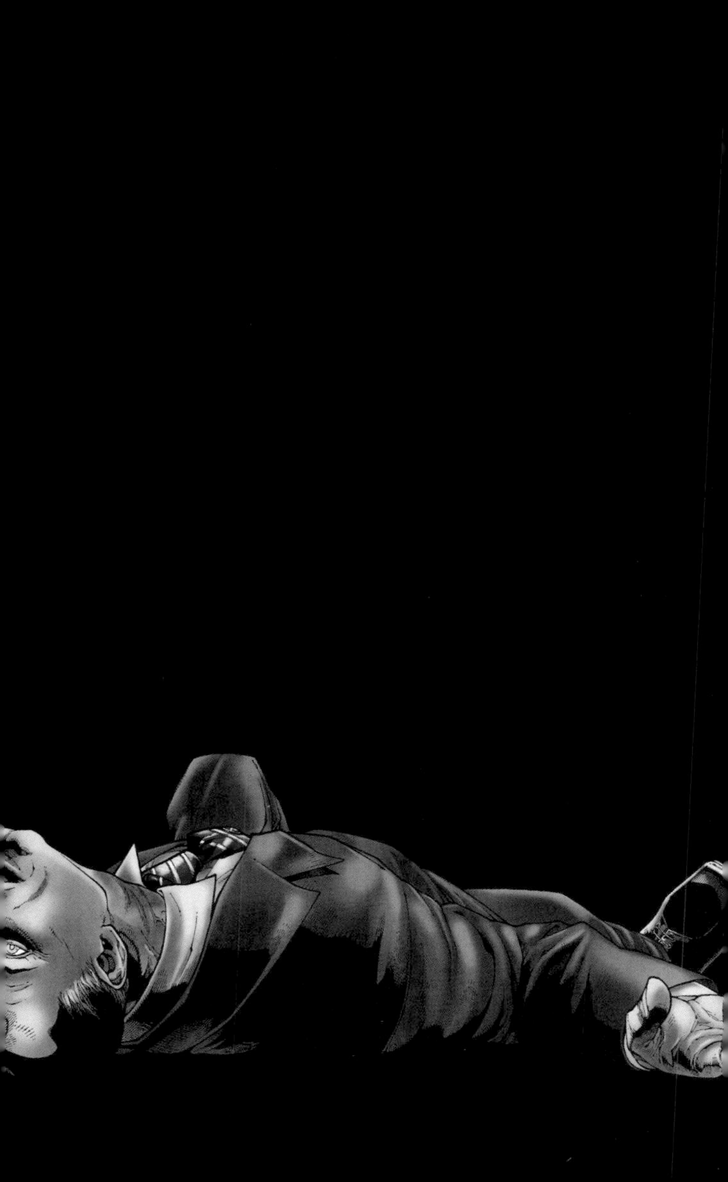

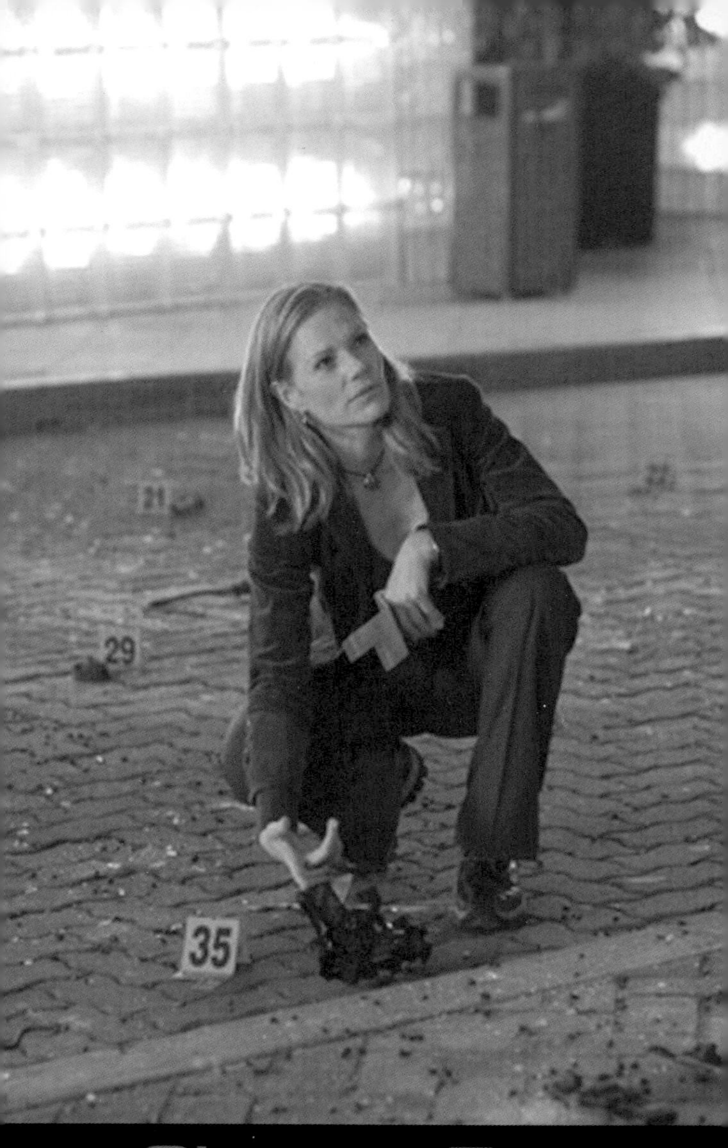

Chapter Two

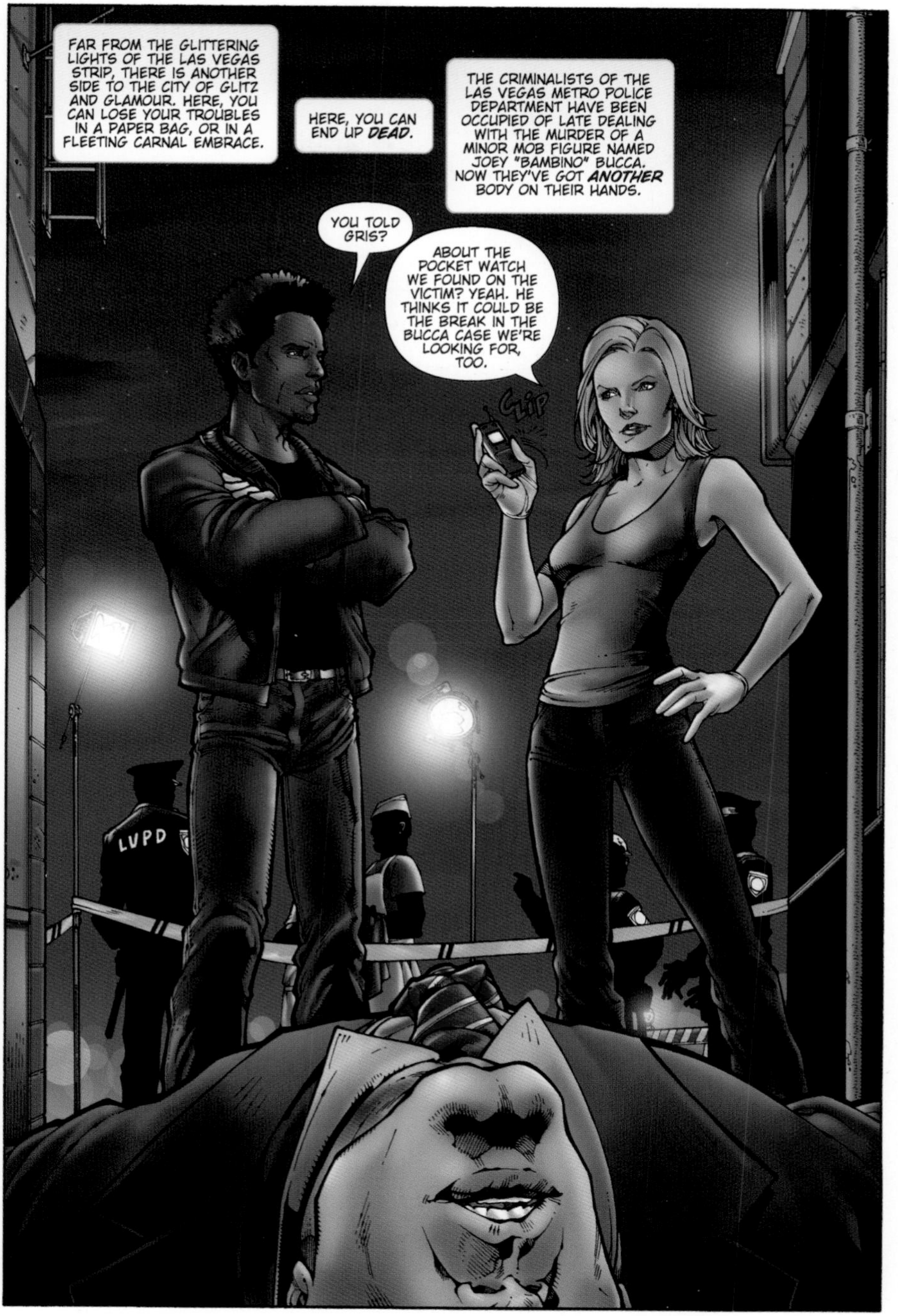
FAR FROM THE GLITTERING LIGHTS OF THE LAS VEGAS STRIP, THERE IS ANOTHER SIDE TO THE CITY OF GLITZ AND GLAMOUR. HERE, YOU CAN LOSE YOUR TROUBLES IN A PAPER BAG, OR IN A FLEETING CARNAL EMBRACE.
HERE, YOU CAN END UP DEAD.
THE CRIMINALISTS OF THE LAS VEGAS METRO POLICE DEPARTMENT HAVE BEEN OCCUPIED OF LATE DEALING WITH THE MURDER OF A MINOR MOB FIGURE NAMED JOEY "BAMBINO" BUCCA. NOW THEY'VE GOT ANOTHER BODY ON THEIR HANDS.
YOU TOLD GRIS?
ABOUT THE POCKET WATCH WE FOUND ON THE VICTIM? YEAH. HE THINKS IT COULD BE THE BREAK IN THE BUCCA CASE WE'RE LOOKING FOR, TOO.
CLIP
LVPD

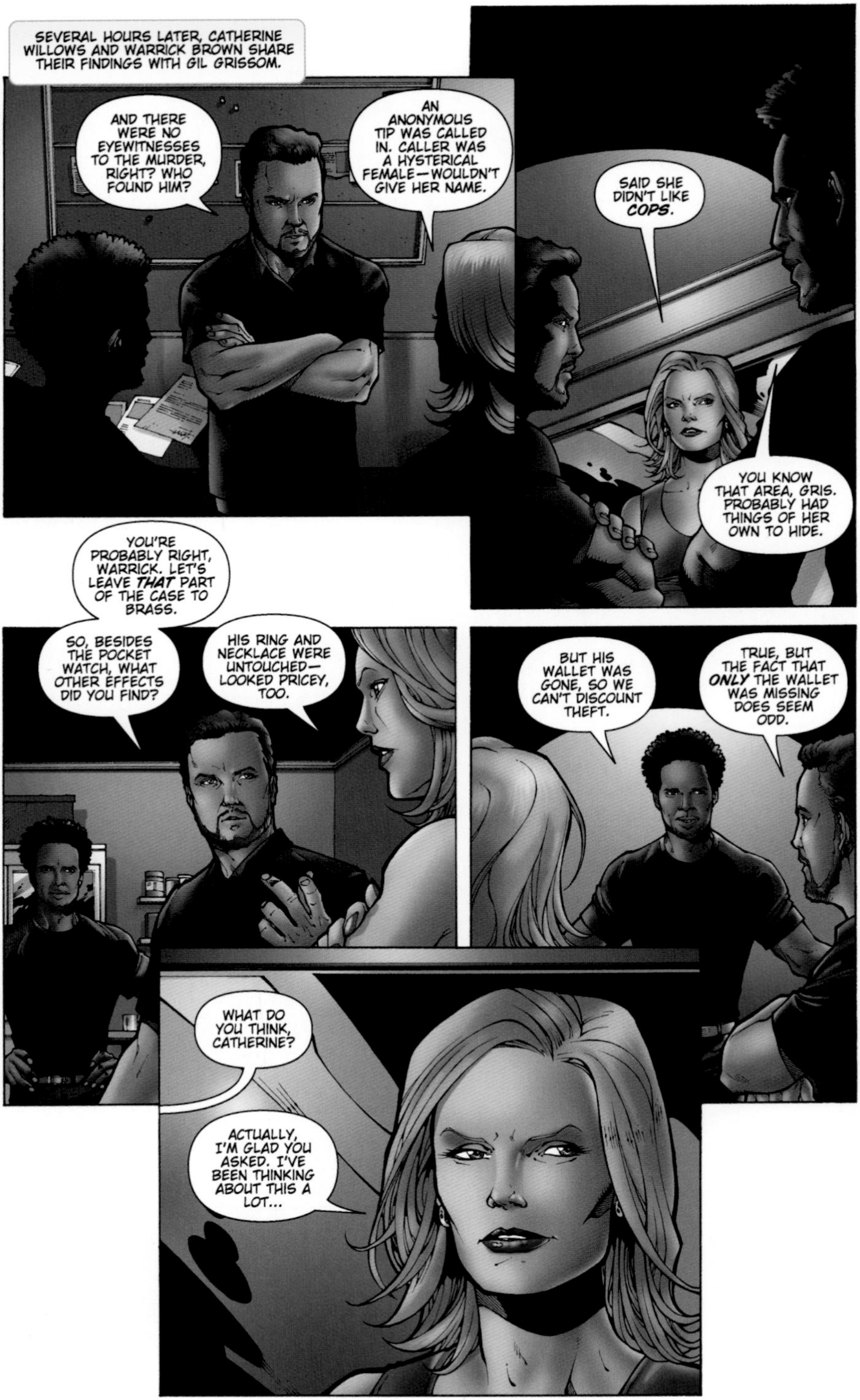

SEVERAL HOURS LATER, CATHERINE WILLOWS AND WARRICK BROWN SHARE THEIR FINDINGS WITH GIL GRISSOM.
AND THERE WERE NO EYEWITNESSES TO THE MURDER, RIGHT? WHO FOUND HIM?
AN ANONYMOUS TIP WAS CALLED IN. CALLER WAS A HYSTERICAL FEMALE—WOULDN'T GIVE HER NAME.
SAID SHE DIDN'T LIKE **COPS**.
YOU KNOW THAT AREA, GRIS. PROBABLY HAD THINGS OF HER OWN TO HIDE.
YOU'RE PROBABLY RIGHT, WARRICK. LET'S LEAVE ***THAT*** PART OF THE CASE TO BRASS.
SO, BESIDES THE POCKET WATCH, WHAT OTHER EFFECTS DID YOU FIND?
HIS RING AND NECKLACE WERE UNTOUCHED—LOOKED PRICEY, TOO.
BUT HIS WALLET WAS GONE, SO WE CAN'T DISCOUNT THEFT.
TRUE, BUT THE FACT THAT ***ONLY*** THE WALLET WAS MISSING DOES SEEM ODD.
WHAT DO YOU THINK, CATHERINE?
ACTUALLY, I'M GLAD YOU ASKED. I'VE BEEN THINKING ABOUT THIS A LOT...

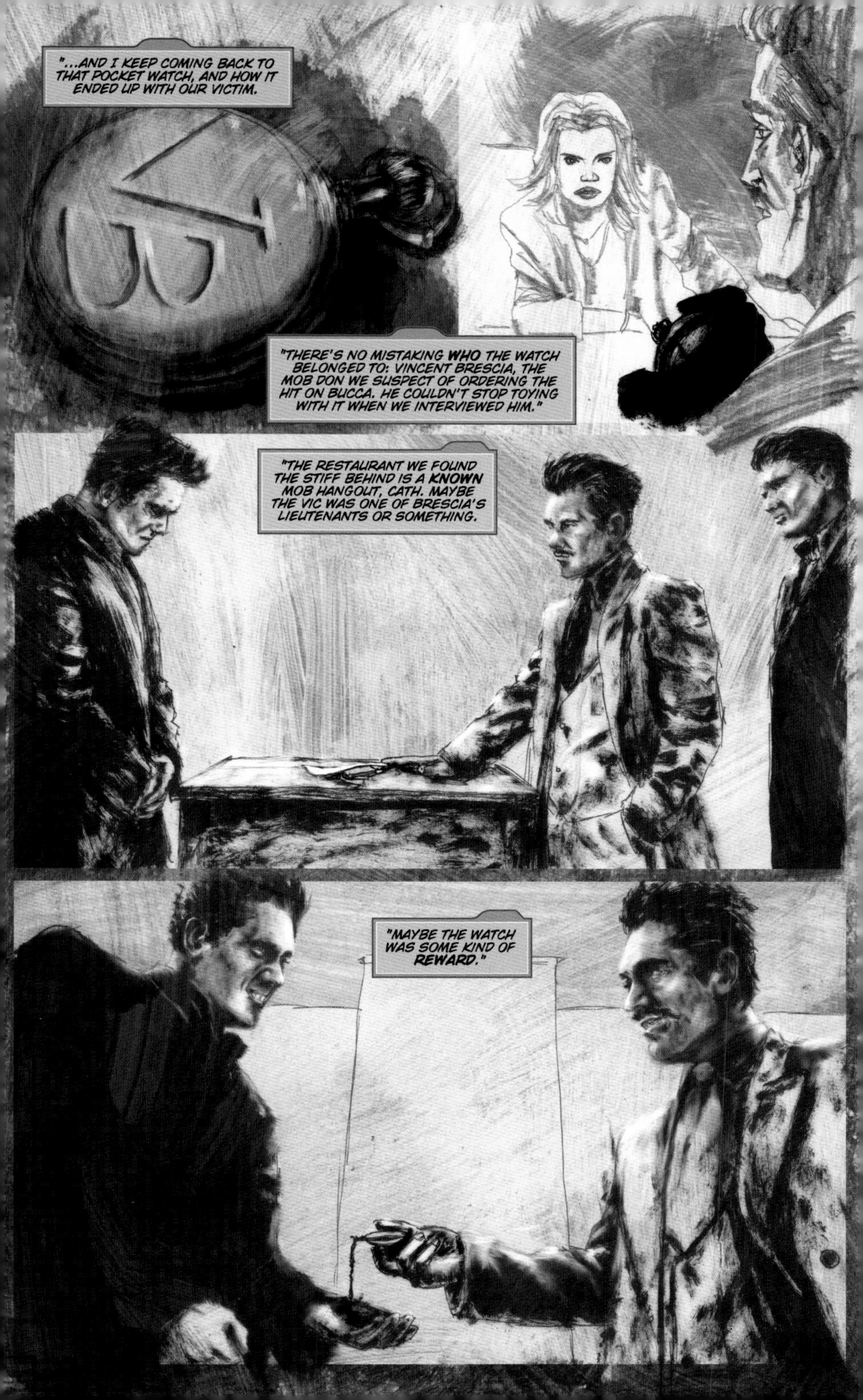
"...AND I KEEP COMING BACK TO THAT POCKET WATCH, AND HOW IT ENDED UP WITH OUR VICTIM.
"THERE'S NO MISTAKING WHO THE WATCH BELONGED TO: VINCENT BRESCIA, THE MOB DON WE SUSPECT OF ORDERING THE HIT ON BUCCA. HE COULDN'T STOP TOYING WITH IT WHEN WE INTERVIEWED HIM."
"THE RESTAURANT WE FOUND THE STIFF BEHIND IS A KNOWN MOB HANGOUT, CATH. MAYBE THE VIC WAS ONE OF BRESCIA'S LIEUTENANTS OR SOMETHING.
"MAYBE THE WATCH WAS SOME KIND OF REWARD."

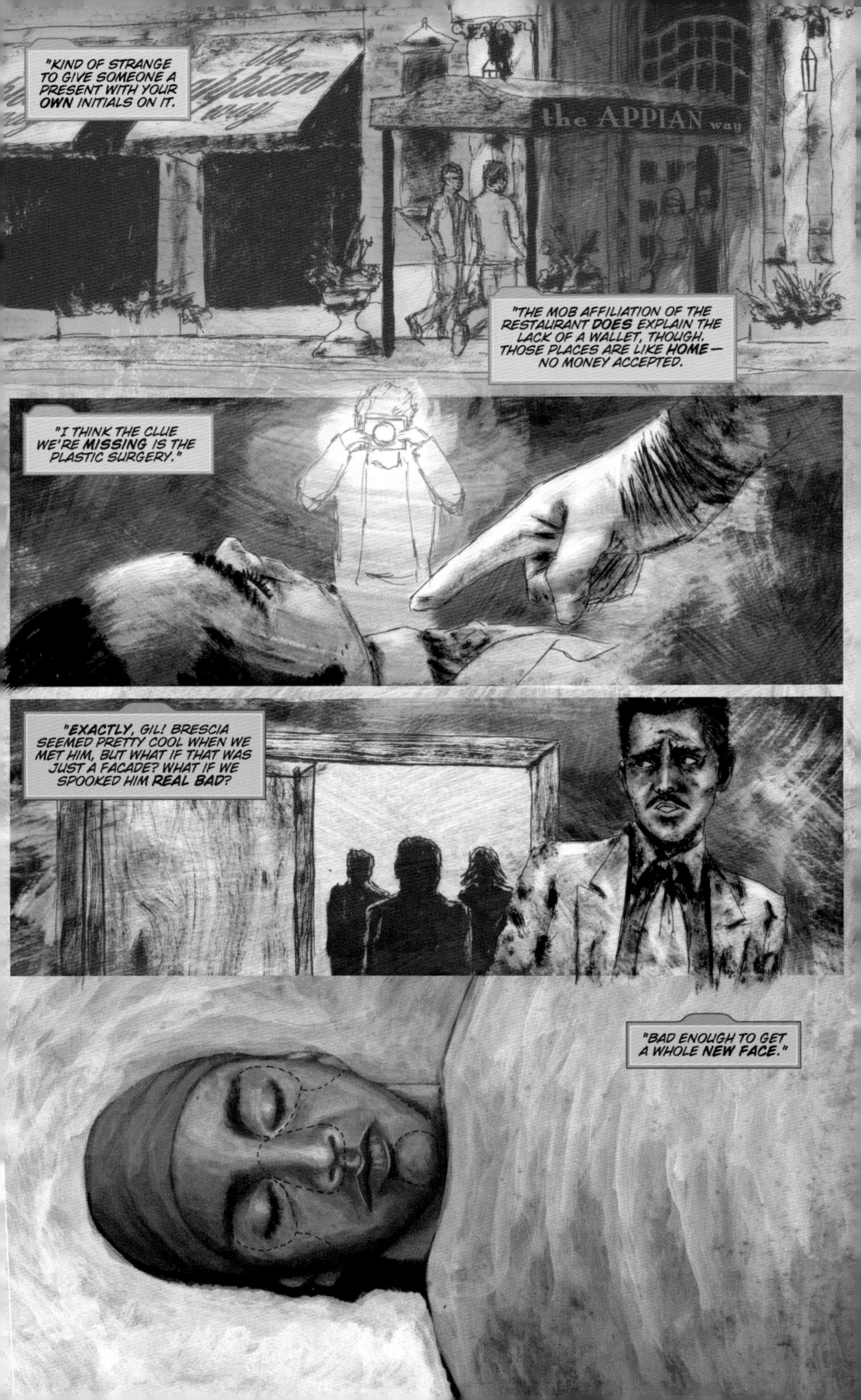
"KIND OF STRANGE TO GIVE SOMEONE A PRESENT WITH YOUR OWN INITIALS ON IT.
the APPIAN way
"THE MOB AFFILIATION OF THE RESTAURANT DOES EXPLAIN THE LACK OF A WALLET, THOUGH. THOSE PLACES ARE LIKE HOME— NO MONEY ACCEPTED.
"I THINK THE CLUE WE'RE MISSING IS THE PLASTIC SURGERY."
"EXACTLY, GIL! BRESCIA SEEMED PRETTY COOL WHEN WE MET HIM, BUT WHAT IF THAT WAS JUST A FACADE? WHAT IF WE SPOOKED HIM REAL BAD?
"BAD ENOUGH TO GET A WHOLE NEW FACE."

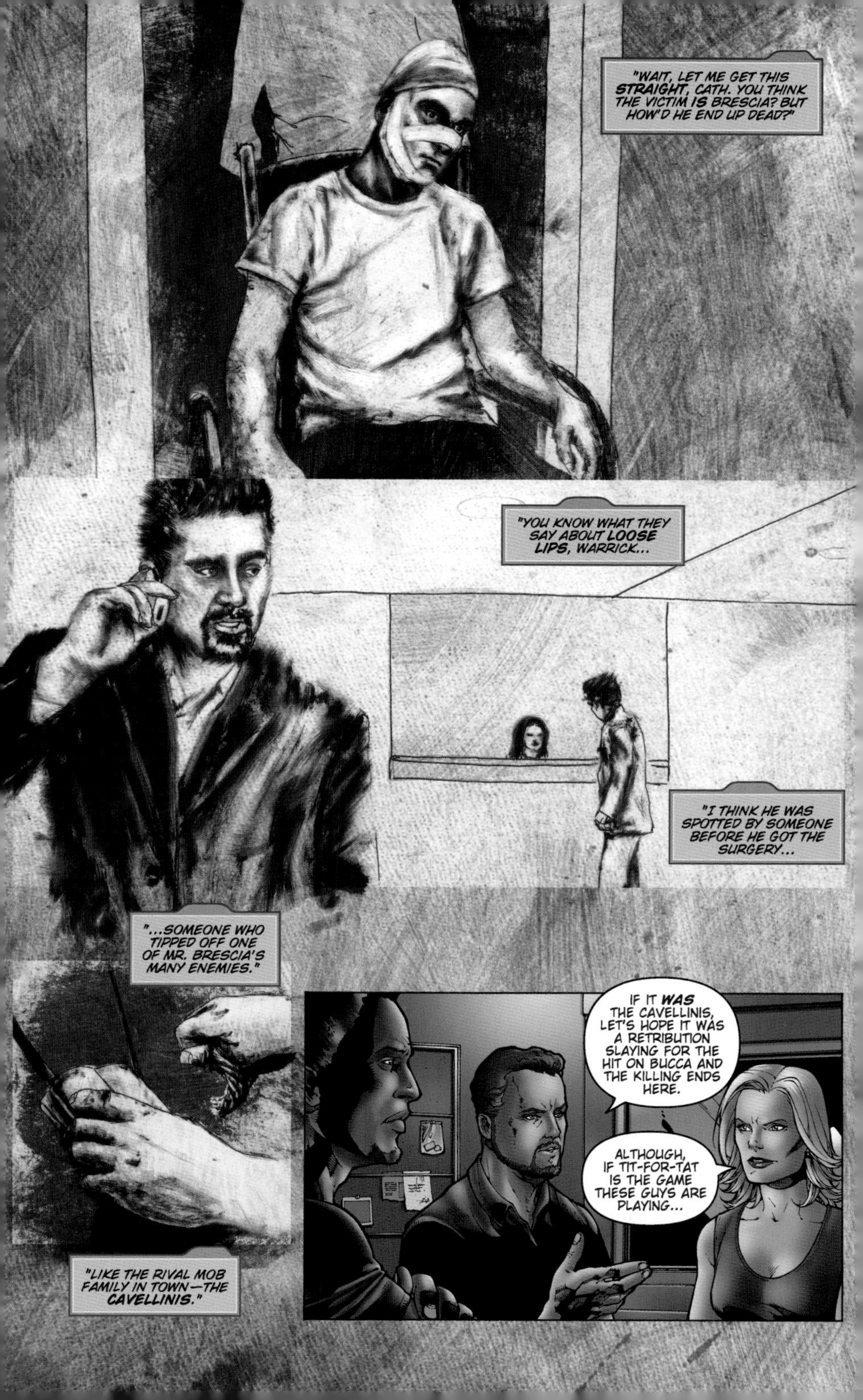
"WAIT, LET ME GET THIS STRAIGHT, CATH. YOU THINK THE VICTIM IS BRESCIA? BUT HOW'D HE END UP DEAD?"
"YOU KNOW WHAT THEY SAY ABOUT LOOSE LIPS, WARRICK...
"I THINK HE WAS SPOTTED BY SOMEONE BEFORE HE GOT THE SURGERY...
"...SOMEONE WHO TIPPED OFF ONE OF MR. BRESCIA'S MANY ENEMIES."
"LIKE THE RIVAL MOB FAMILY IN TOWN—THE CAVELLINIS."
IF IT WAS THE CAVELLINIS, LET'S HOPE IT WAS A RETRIBUTION SLAYING FOR THE HIT ON BUCCA AND THE KILLING ENDS HERE.
ALTHOUGH, IF TIT-FOR-TAT IS THE GAME THESE GUYS ARE PLAYING...

"...LET'S NOT FORGET THERE WAS A *SECOND* TARGET IN THE *BUCCA* SLAYING, ONE THAT SEEMED TO HAVE GOT UP AND WALKED AWAY."

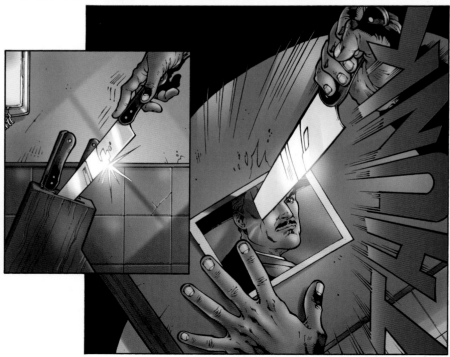

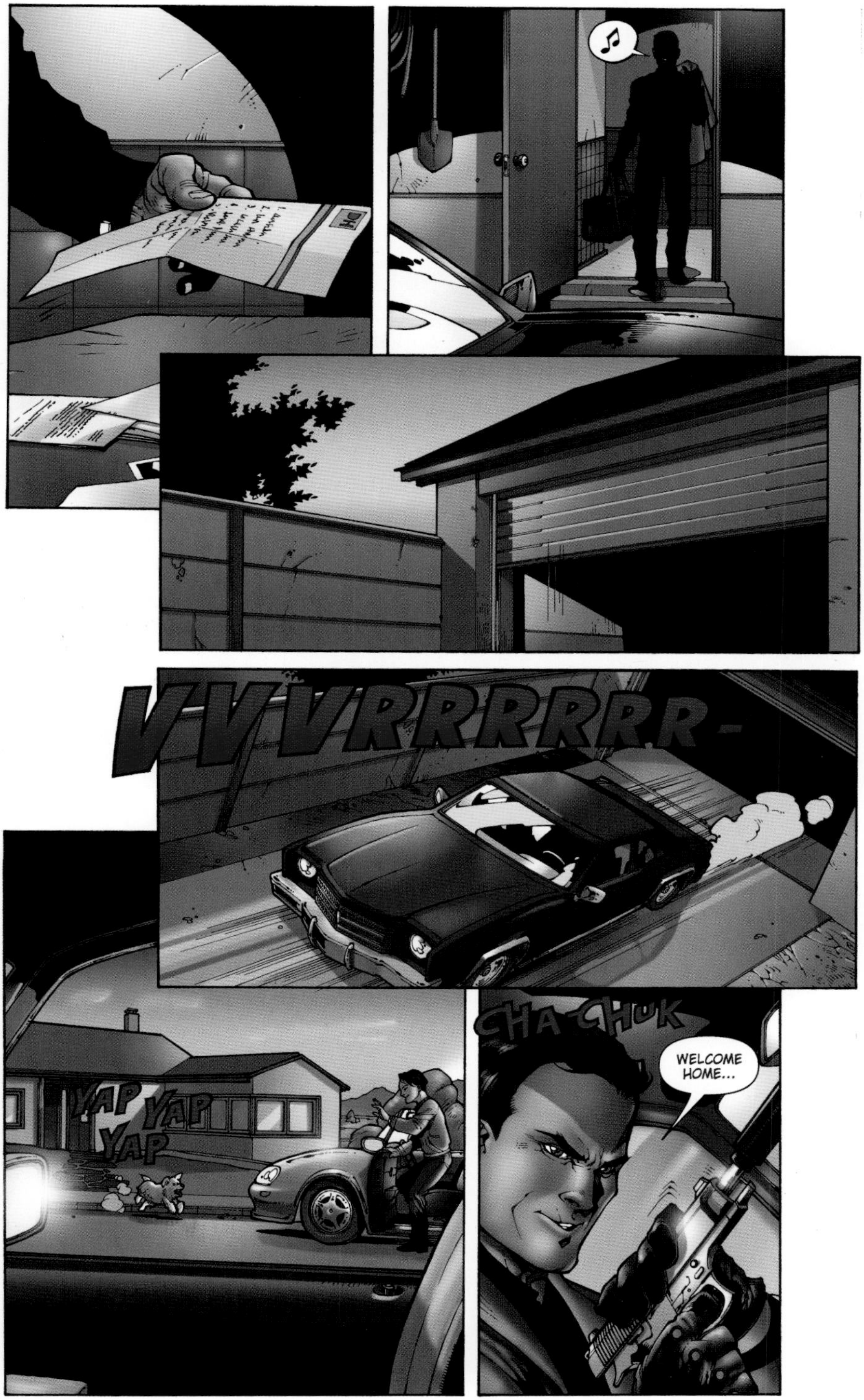
♫
VVVRRRRRR-
YAP YAP YAP
CHA CHUK
WELCOME HOME...

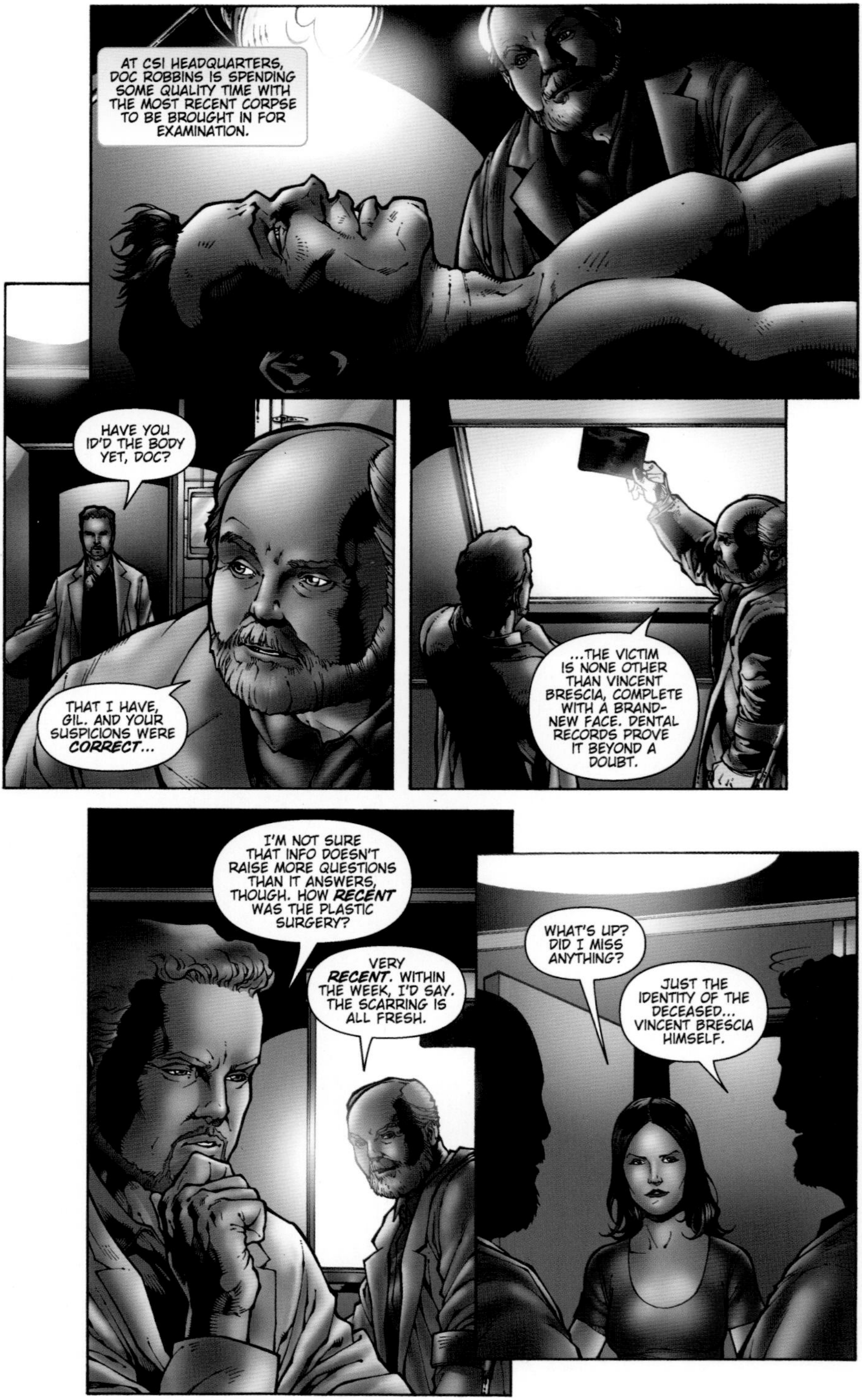
AT CSI HEADQUARTERS, DOC ROBBINS IS SPENDING SOME QUALITY TIME WITH THE MOST RECENT CORPSE TO BE BROUGHT IN FOR EXAMINATION.
HAVE YOU ID'D THE BODY YET, DOC?
THAT I HAVE, GIL. AND YOUR SUSPICIONS WERE CORRECT...
...THE VICTIM IS NONE OTHER THAN VINCENT BRESCIA, COMPLETE WITH A BRAND-NEW FACE. DENTAL RECORDS PROVE IT BEYOND A DOUBT.
I'M NOT SURE THAT INFO DOESN'T RAISE MORE QUESTIONS THAN IT ANSWERS, THOUGH. HOW RECENT WAS THE PLASTIC SURGERY?
VERY RECENT. WITHIN THE WEEK, I'D SAY. THE SCARRING IS ALL FRESH.
WHAT'S UP? DID I MISS ANYTHING?
JUST THE IDENTITY OF THE DECEASED... VINCENT BRESCIA HIMSELF.

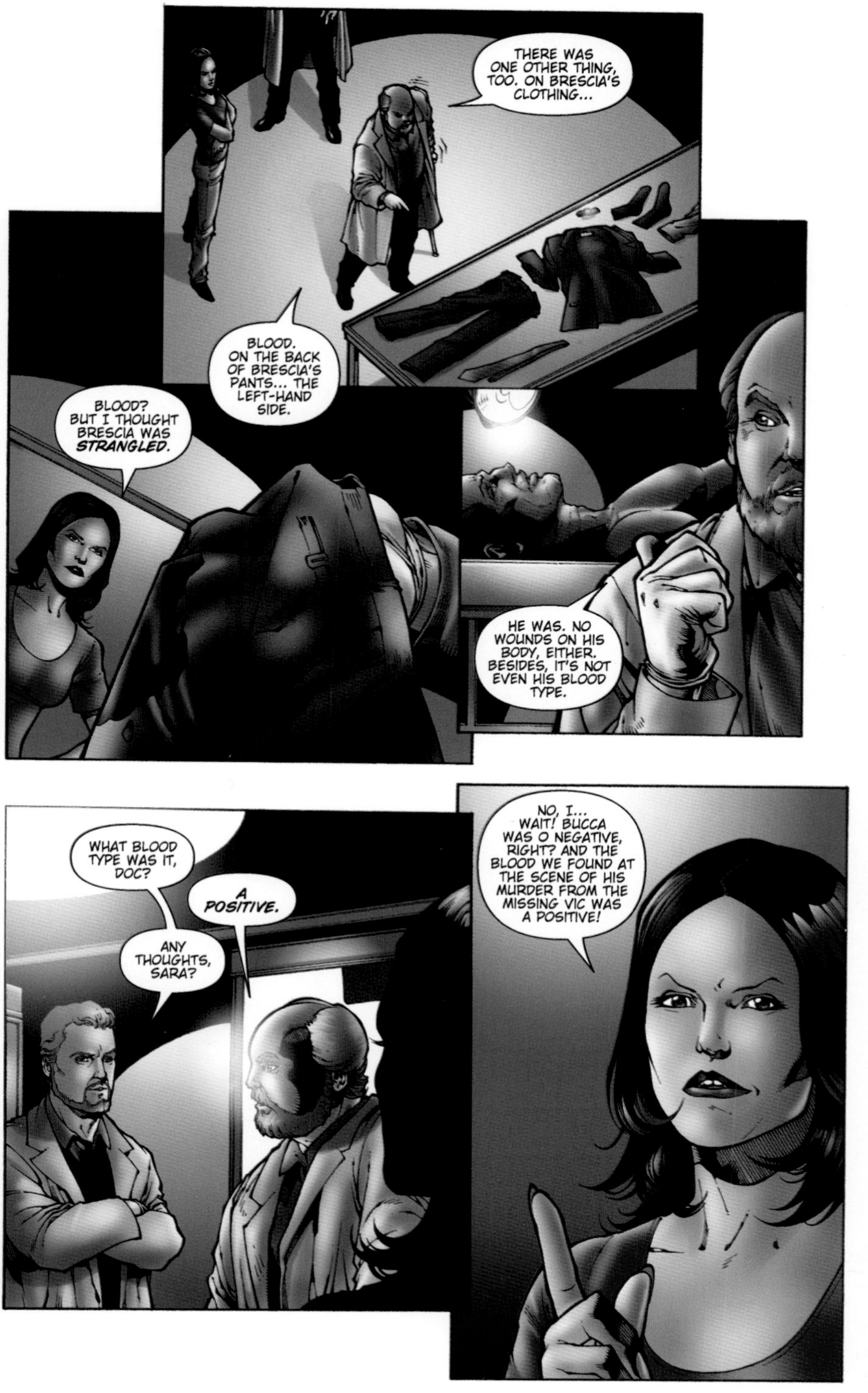
THERE WAS ONE OTHER THING, TOO. ON BRESCIA'S CLOTHING...
BLOOD. ON THE BACK OF BRESCIA'S PANTS... THE LEFT-HAND SIDE.
BLOOD? BUT I THOUGHT BRESCIA WAS *STRANGLED*.
HE WAS. NO WOUNDS ON HIS BODY, EITHER. BESIDES, IT'S NOT EVEN HIS BLOOD TYPE.
WHAT BLOOD TYPE WAS IT, DOC?
A POSITIVE.
ANY THOUGHTS, SARA?
NO, I... WAIT! BUCCA WAS O NEGATIVE, RIGHT? AND THE BLOOD WE FOUND AT THE SCENE OF HIS MURDER FROM THE MISSING VIC WAS A POSITIVE!

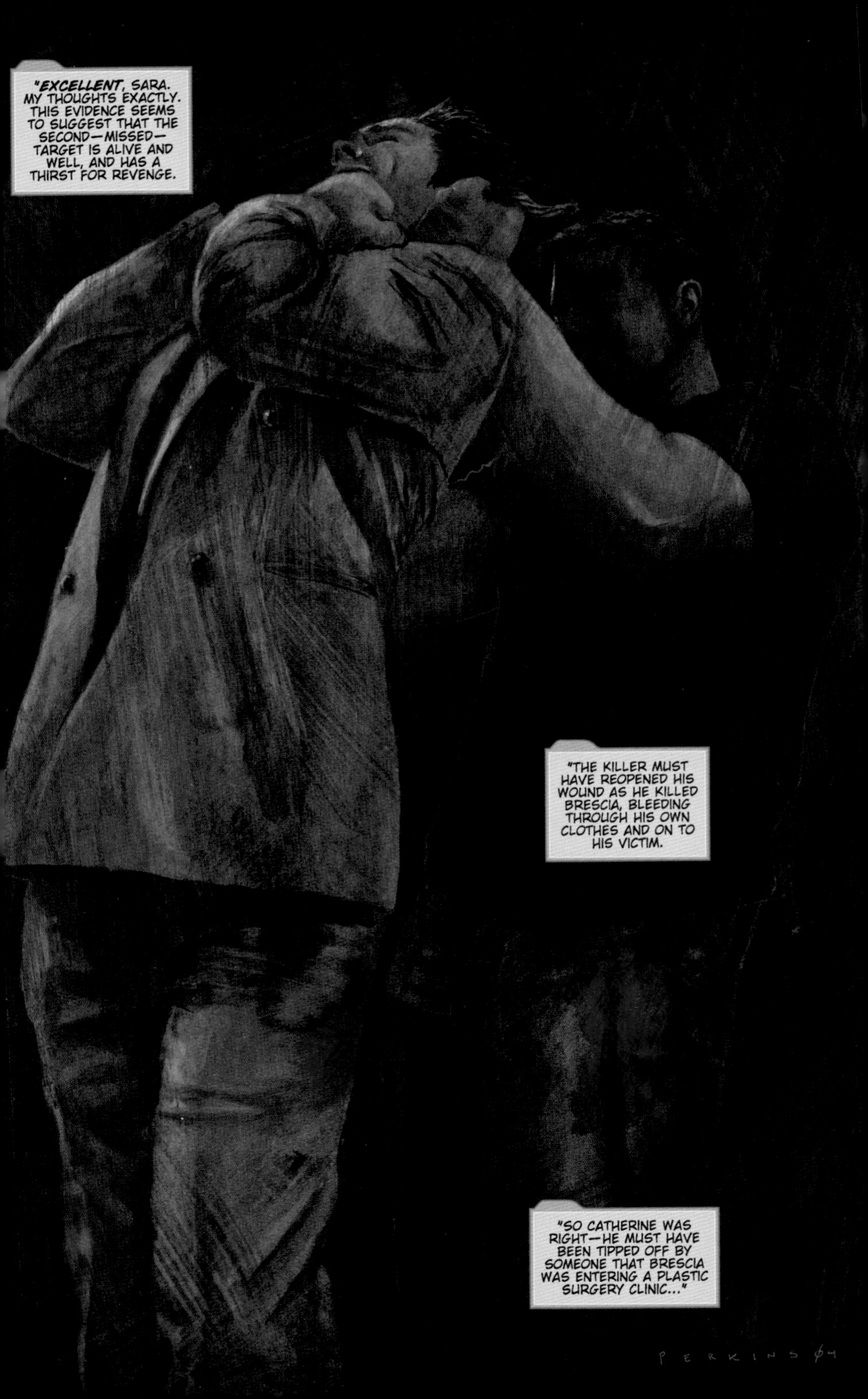
"EXCELLENT, SARA. MY THOUGHTS EXACTLY. THIS EVIDENCE SEEMS TO SUGGEST THAT THE SECOND—MISSED—TARGET IS ALIVE AND WELL, AND HAS A THIRST FOR REVENGE.
"THE KILLER MUST HAVE REOPENED HIS WOUND AS HE KILLED BRESCIA, BLEEDING THROUGH HIS OWN CLOTHES AND ON TO HIS VICTIM.
"SO CATHERINE WAS RIGHT—HE MUST HAVE BEEN TIPPED OFF BY SOMEONE THAT BRESCIA WAS ENTERING A PLASTIC SURGERY CLINIC..."
PERKINS 04

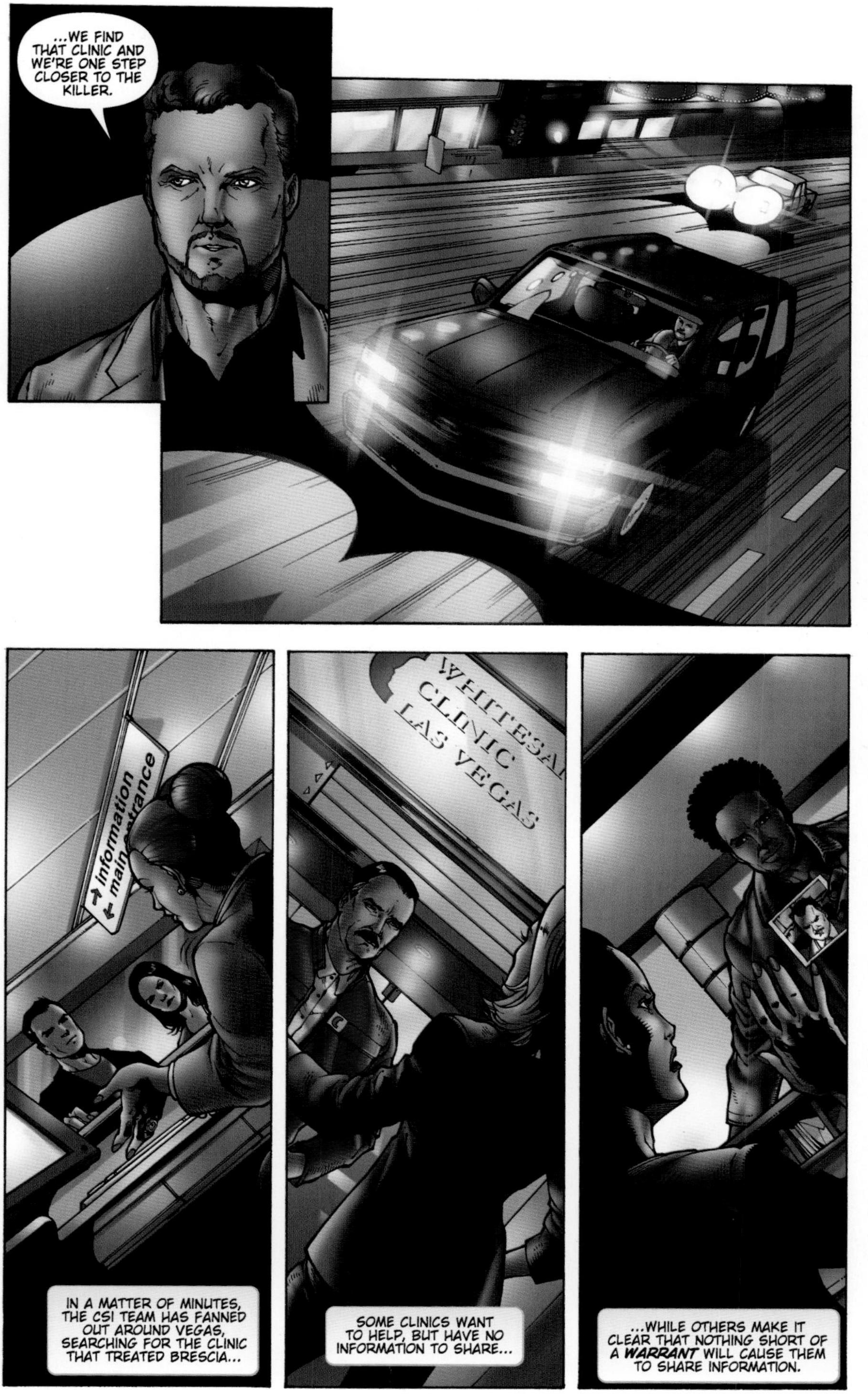
...WE FIND THAT CLINIC AND WE'RE ONE STEP CLOSER TO THE KILLER.
information
CLINIC
LAS VEGAS
IN A MATTER OF MINUTES, THE CSI TEAM HAS FANNED OUT AROUND VEGAS, SEARCHING FOR THE CLINIC THAT TREATED BRESCIA...
SOME CLINICS WANT TO HELP, BUT HAVE NO INFORMATION TO SHARE...
...WHILE OTHERS MAKE IT CLEAR THAT NOTHING SHORT OF A *WARRANT* WILL CAUSE THEM TO SHARE INFORMATION.

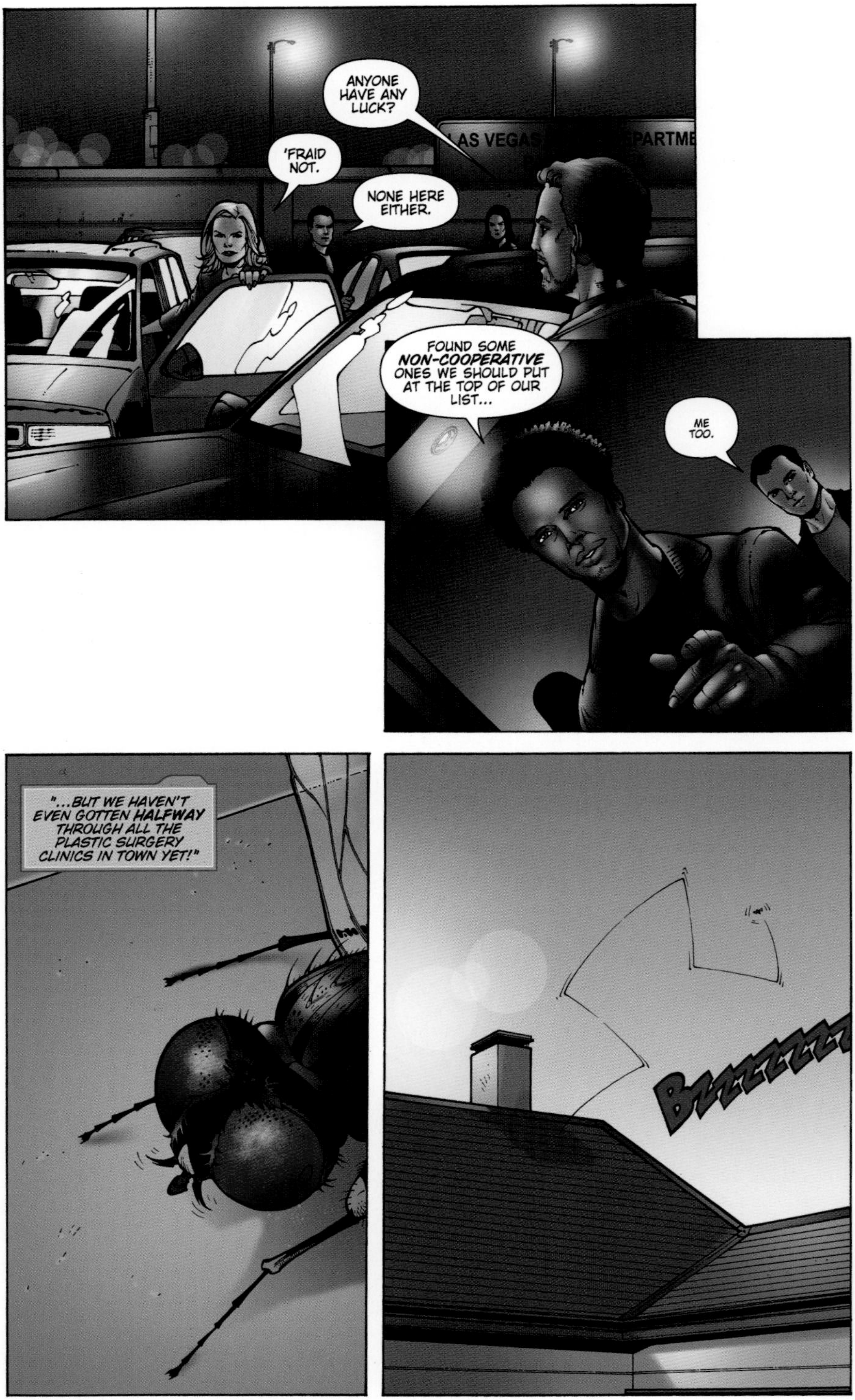
ANYONE HAVE ANY LUCK?
'FRAID NOT.
NONE HERE EITHER.
FOUND SOME **NON-COOPERATIVE** ONES WE SHOULD PUT AT THE TOP OF OUR LIST...
ME TOO.
"...BUT WE HAVEN'T EVEN GOTTEN **HALFWAY** THROUGH ALL THE PLASTIC SURGERY CLINICS IN TOWN YET!"

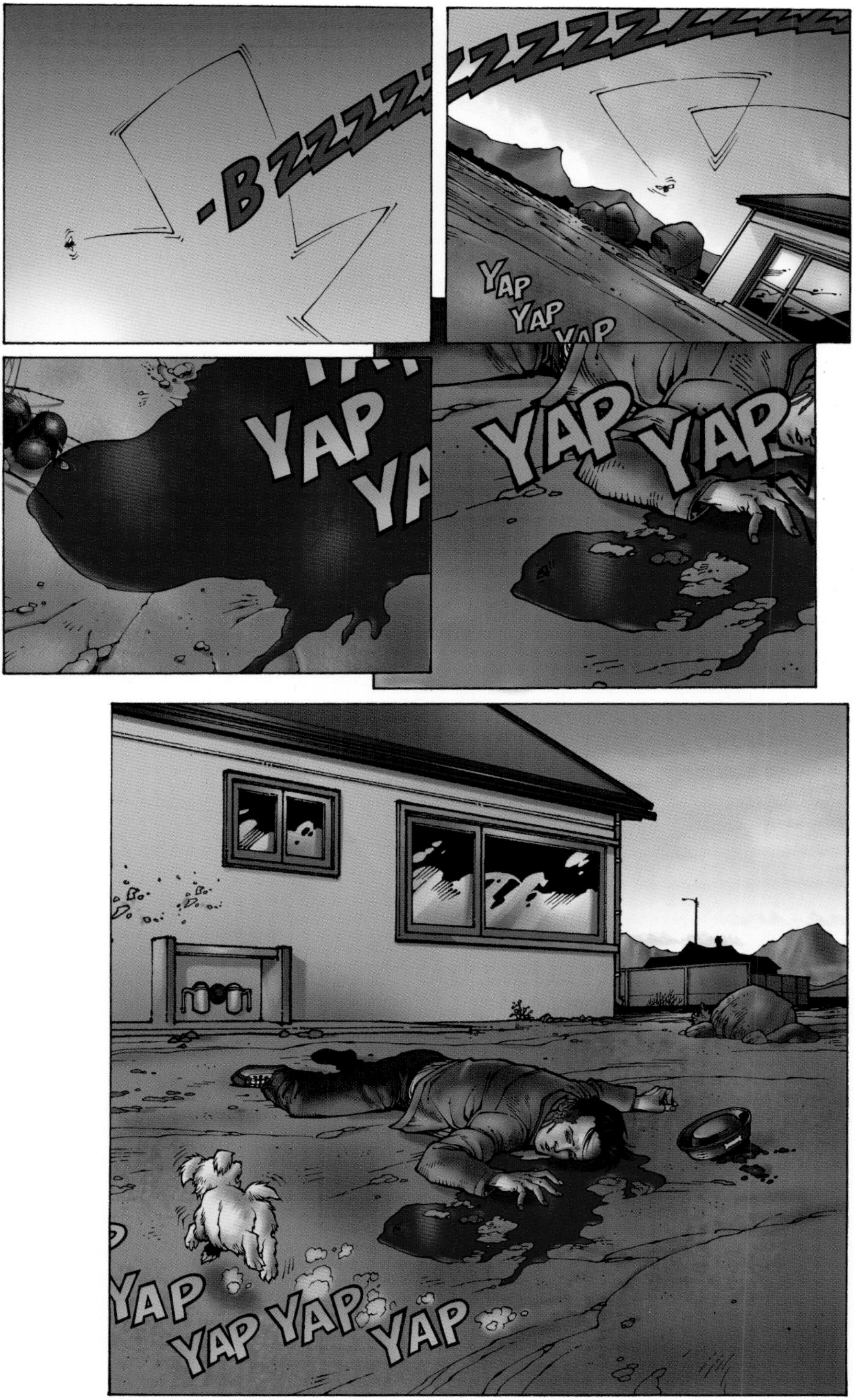
-BZZZZZZZZZZZZZZ
YAP
YAP
YAP
YAP
YAP
YAP
YAP
YAP
YAP
YAP
YAP

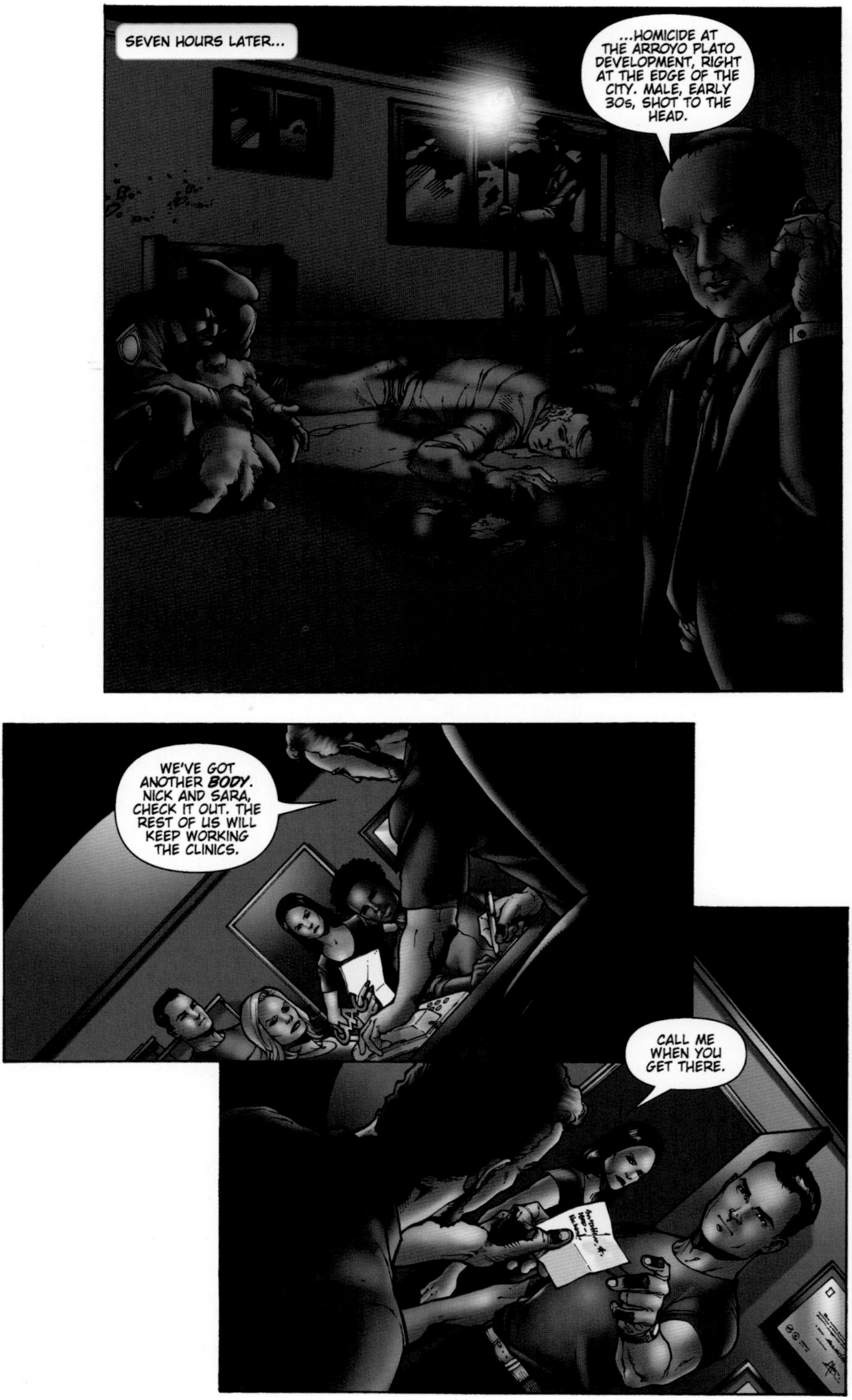
SEVEN HOURS LATER...
...HOMICIDE AT THE ARROYO PLATO DEVELOPMENT, RIGHT AT THE EDGE OF THE CITY. MALE, EARLY 30s, SHOT TO THE HEAD.
WE'VE GOT ANOTHER BODY. NICK AND SARA, CHECK IT OUT. THE REST OF US WILL KEEP WORKING THE CLINICS.
CALL ME WHEN YOU GET THERE.

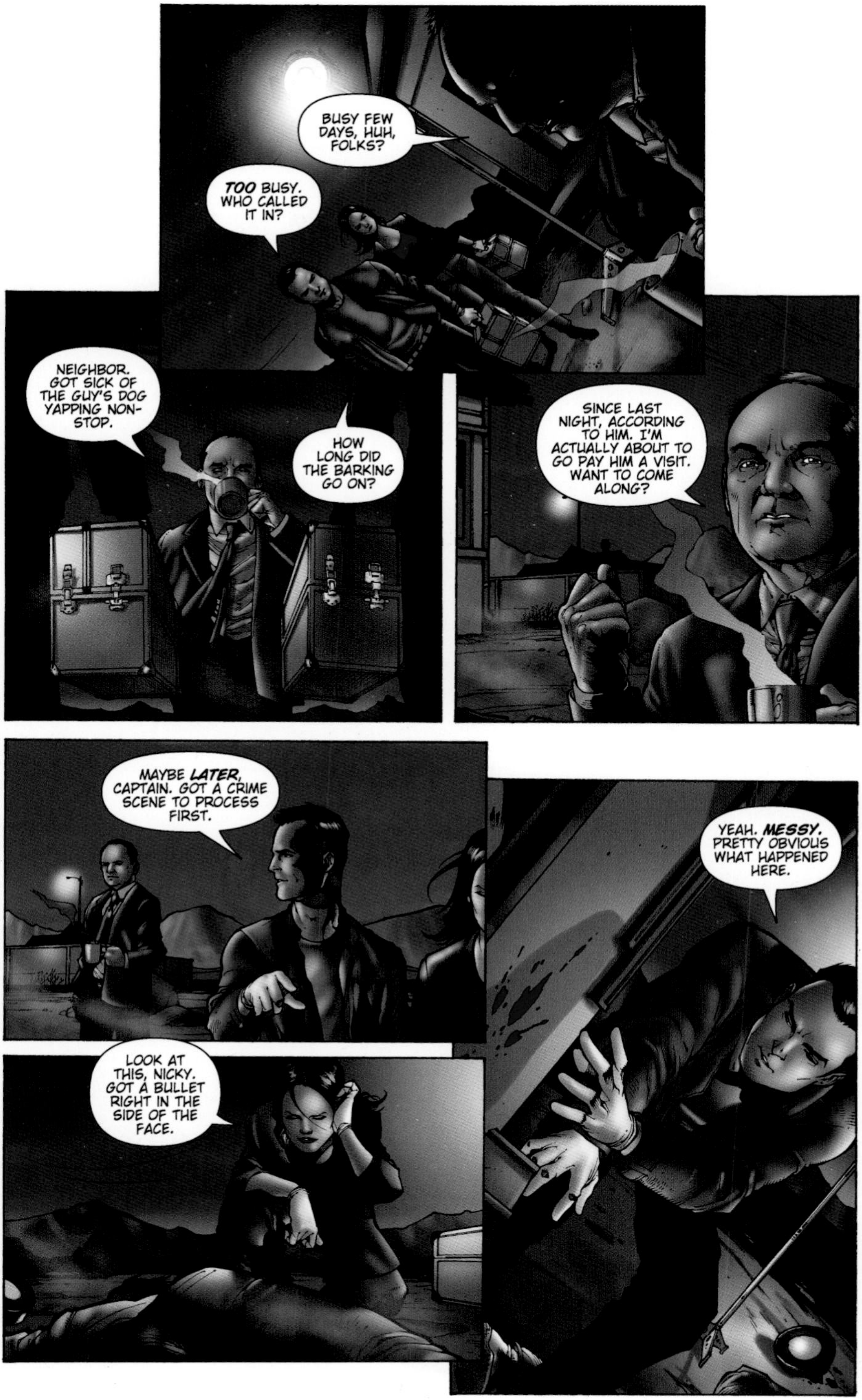
BUSY FEW DAYS, HUH, FOLKS?
TOO BUSY. WHO CALLED IT IN?
NEIGHBOR. GOT SICK OF THE GUY'S DOG YAPPING NON-STOP.
HOW LONG DID THE BARKING GO ON?
SINCE LAST NIGHT, ACCORDING TO HIM. I'M ACTUALLY ABOUT TO GO PAY HIM A VISIT. WANT TO COME ALONG?
MAYBE LATER, CAPTAIN. GOT A CRIME SCENE TO PROCESS FIRST.
YEAH. MESSY. PRETTY OBVIOUS WHAT HAPPENED HERE.
LOOK AT THIS, NICKY. GOT A BULLET RIGHT IN THE SIDE OF THE FACE.

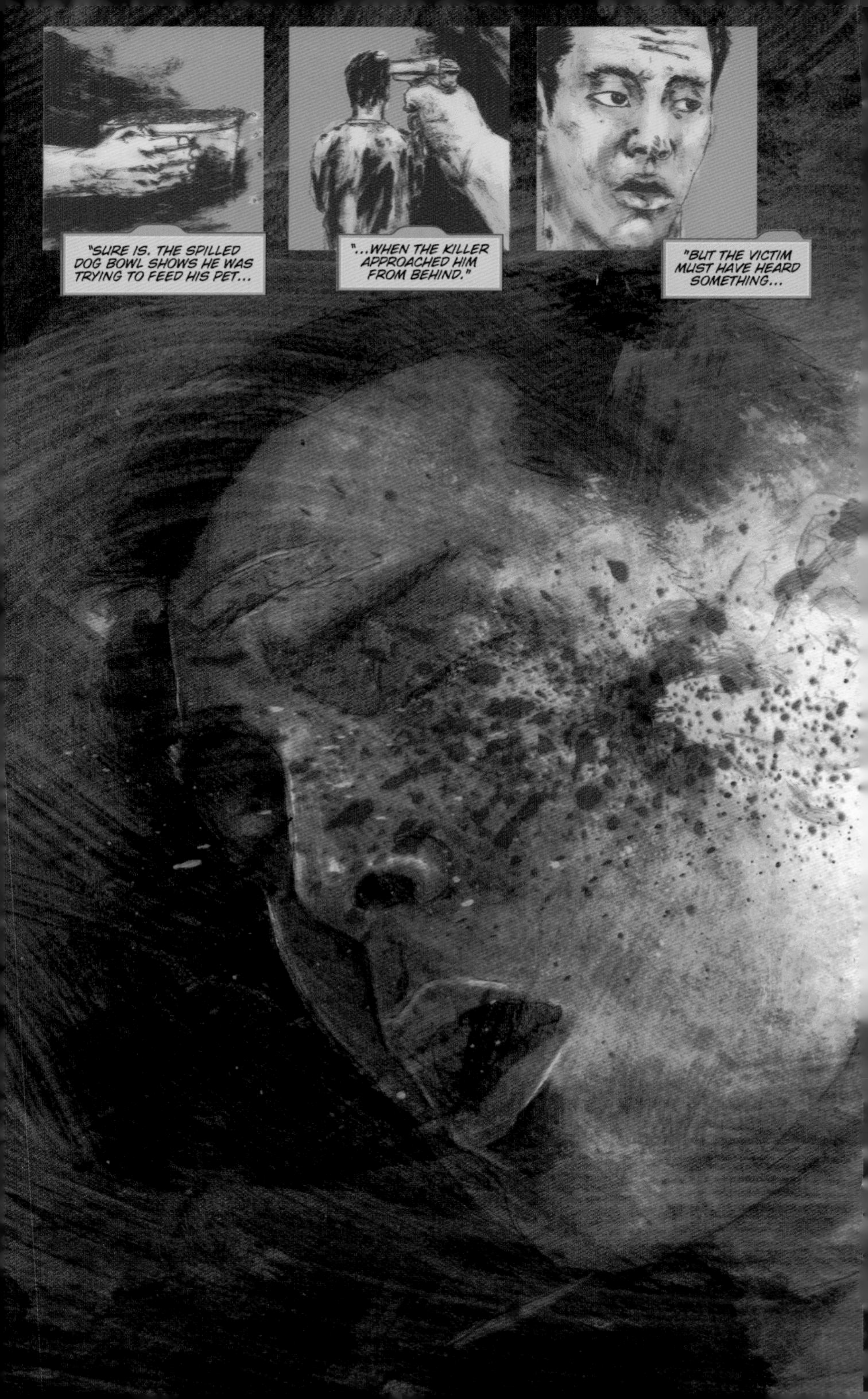
"SURE IS. THE SPILLED DOG BOWL SHOWS HE WAS TRYING TO FEED HIS PET...
"...WHEN THE KILLER APPROACHED HIM FROM BEHIND."
"BUT THE VICTIM MUST HAVE HEARD SOMETHING...

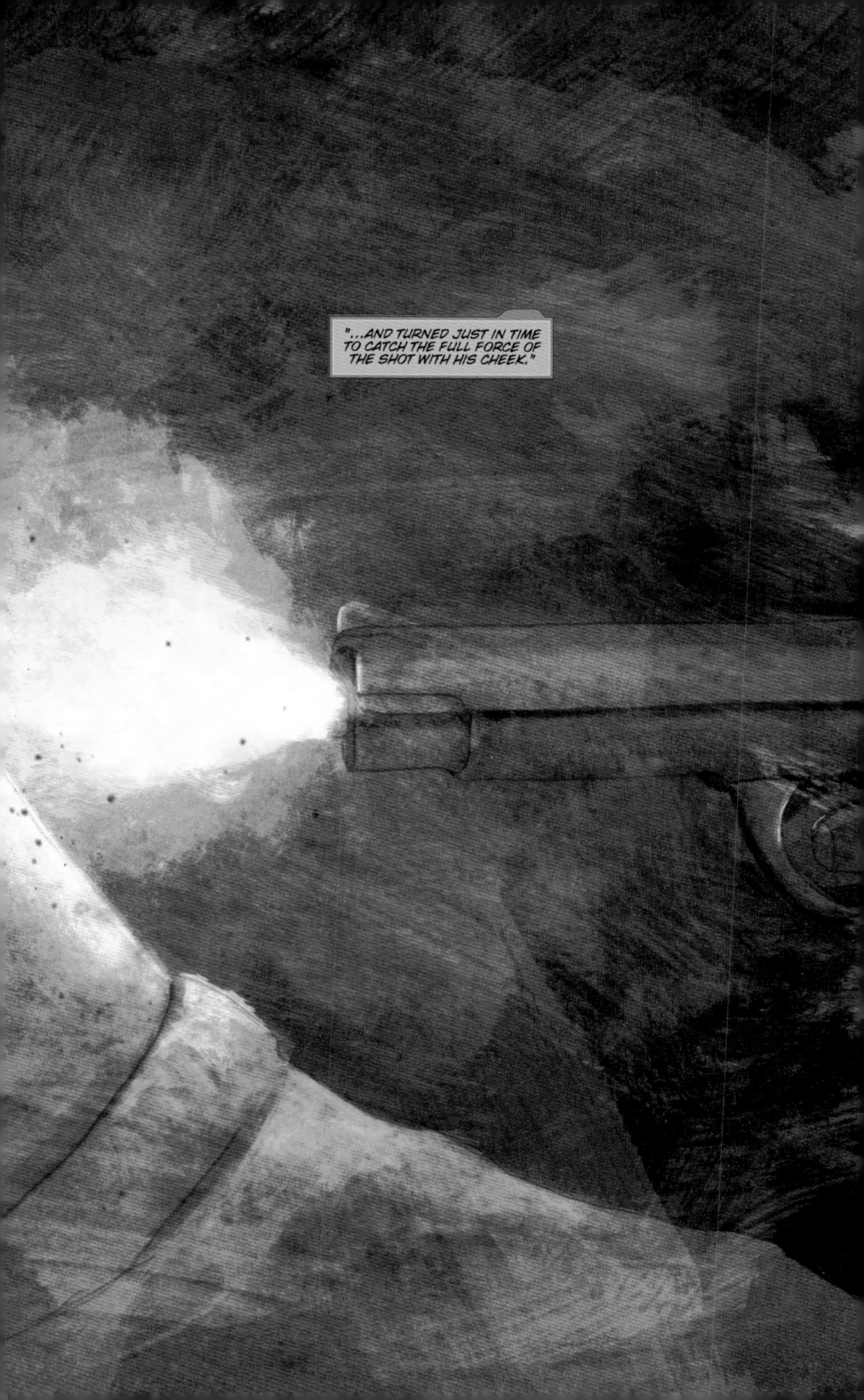
"...AND TURNED JUST IN TIME TO CATCH THE FULL FORCE OF THE SHOT WITH HIS CHEEK."

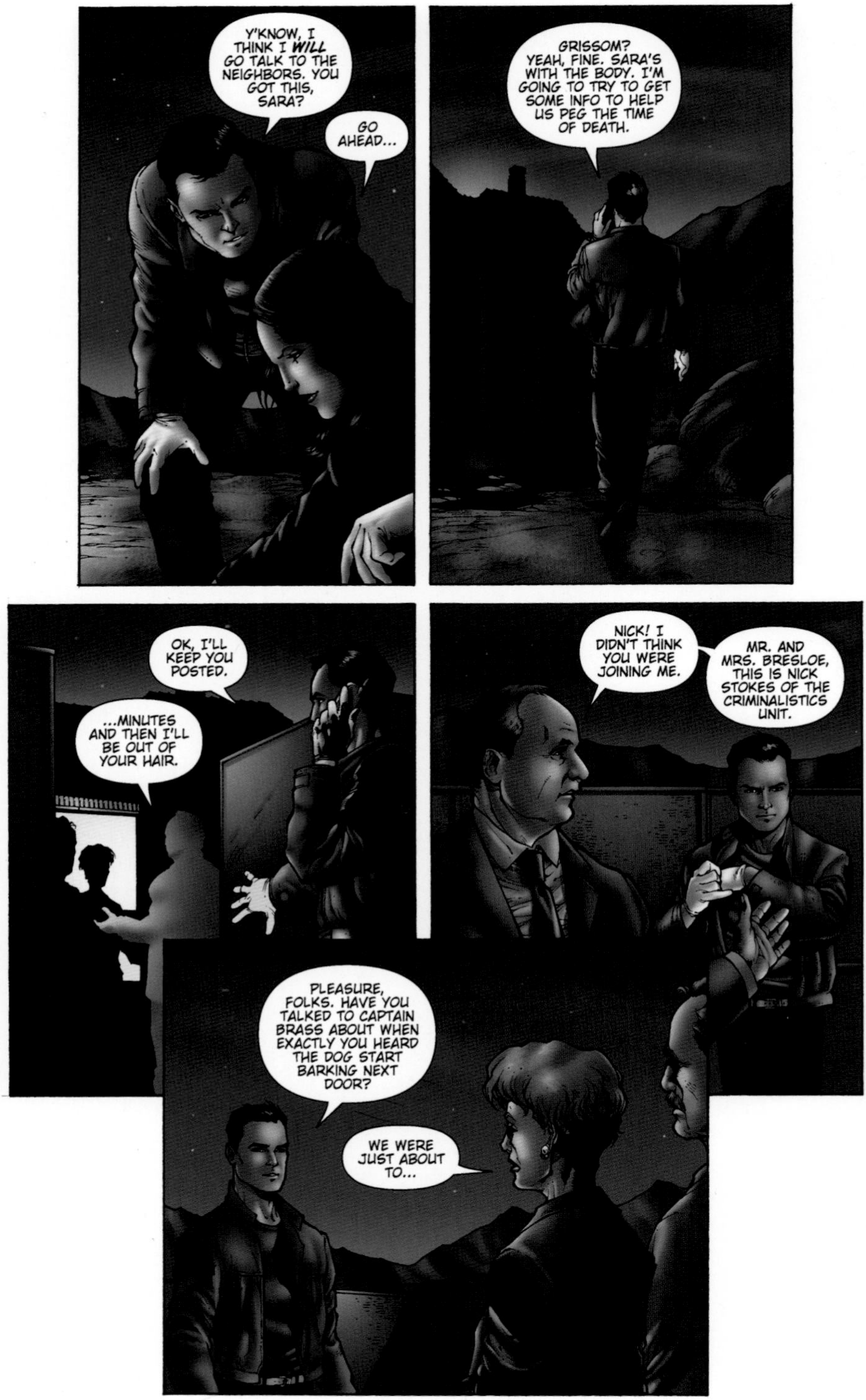
Y'KNOW, I THINK I *WILL* GO TALK TO THE NEIGHBORS. YOU GOT THIS, SARA?
GO AHEAD...
GRISSOM? YEAH, FINE. SARA'S WITH THE BODY. I'M GOING TO TRY TO GET SOME INFO TO HELP US PEG THE TIME OF DEATH.
OK, I'LL KEEP YOU POSTED.
...MINUTES AND THEN I'LL BE OUT OF YOUR HAIR.
NICK! I DIDN'T THINK YOU WERE JOINING ME.
MR. AND MRS. BRESLOE, THIS IS NICK STOKES OF THE CRIMINALISTICS UNIT.
PLEASURE, FOLKS. HAVE YOU TALKED TO CAPTAIN BRASS ABOUT WHEN EXACTLY YOU HEARD THE DOG START BARKING NEXT DOOR?
WE WERE JUST ABOUT TO...

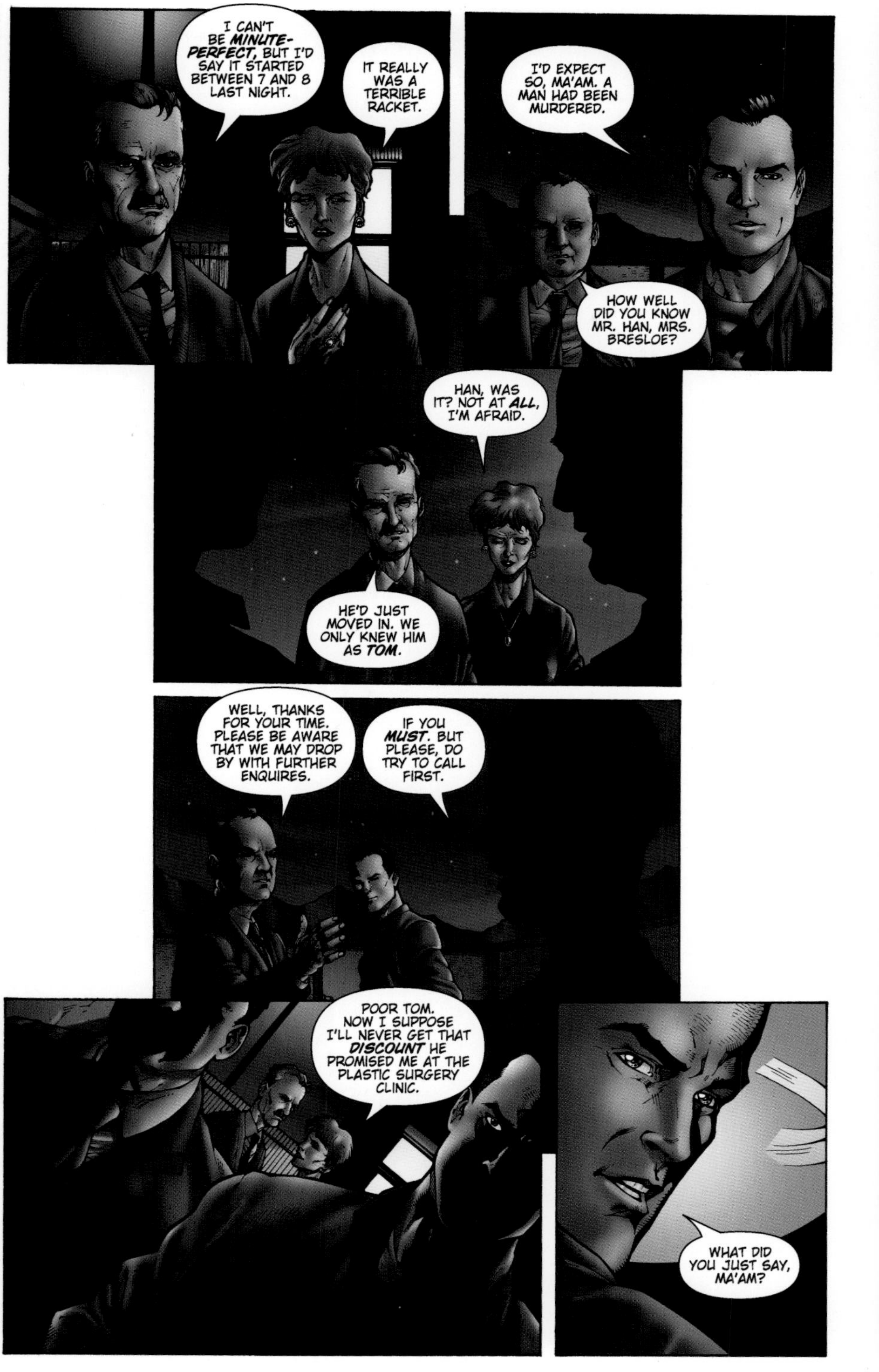
I CAN'T BE MINUTE-PERFECT, BUT I'D SAY IT STARTED BETWEEN 7 AND 8 LAST NIGHT.
IT REALLY WAS A TERRIBLE RACKET.
I'D EXPECT SO, MA'AM. A MAN HAD BEEN MURDERED.
HOW WELL DID YOU KNOW MR. HAN, MRS. BRESLOE?
HAN, WAS IT? NOT AT ALL, I'M AFRAID.
HE'D JUST MOVED IN. WE ONLY KNEW HIM AS TOM.
WELL, THANKS FOR YOUR TIME. PLEASE BE AWARE THAT WE MAY DROP BY WITH FURTHER ENQUIRES.
IF YOU MUST. BUT PLEASE, DO TRY TO CALL FIRST.
POOR TOM. NOW I SUPPOSE I'LL NEVER GET THAT DISCOUNT HE PROMISED ME AT THE PLASTIC SURGERY CLINIC.
WHAT DID YOU JUST SAY, MA'AM?

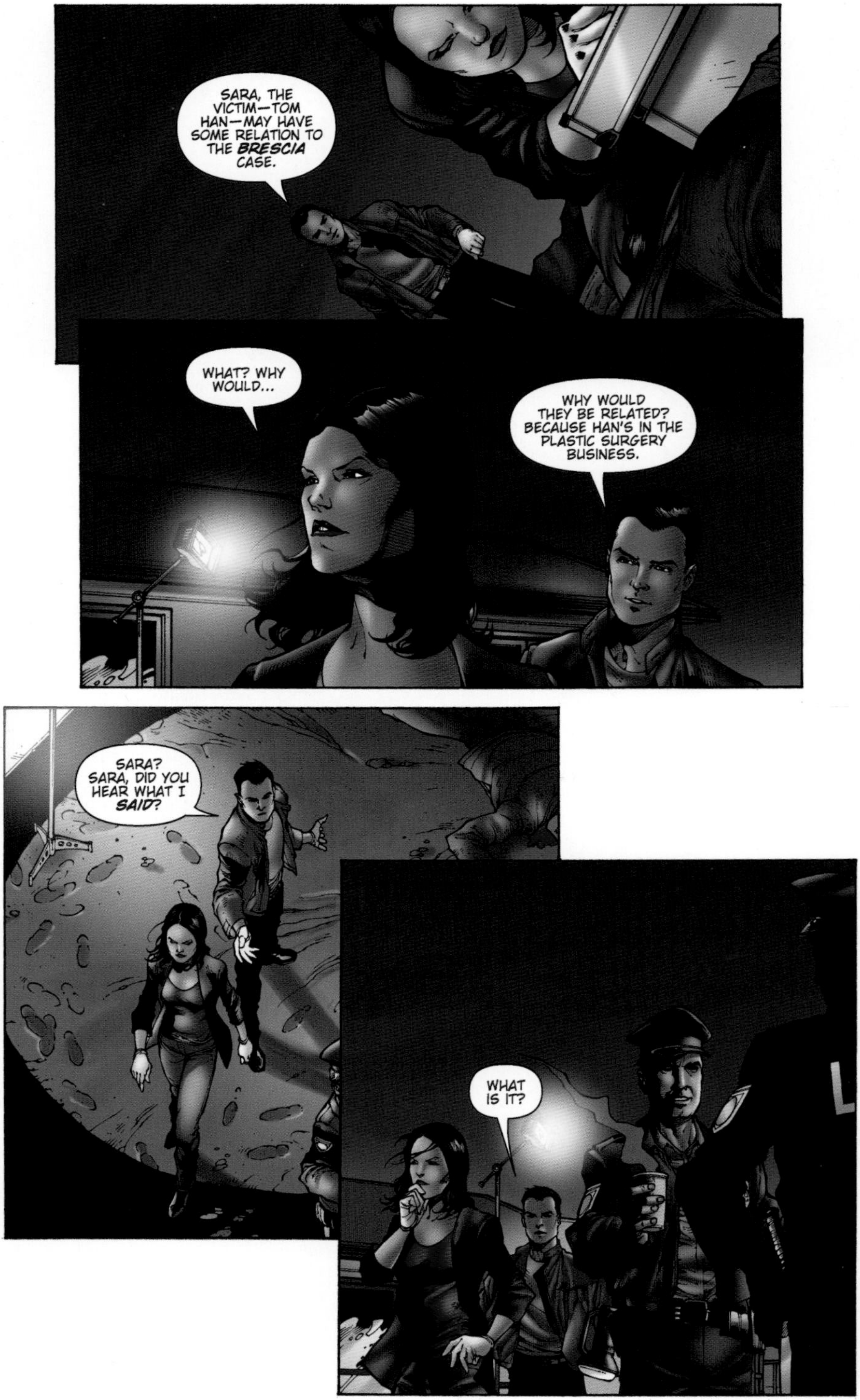
SARA, THE VICTIM—TOM HAN—MAY HAVE SOME RELATION TO THE BRESCIA CASE.
WHAT? WHY WOULD...
WHY WOULD THEY BE RELATED? BECAUSE HAN'S IN THE PLASTIC SURGERY BUSINESS.
SARA? SARA, DID YOU HEAR WHAT I SAID?
WHAT IS IT?

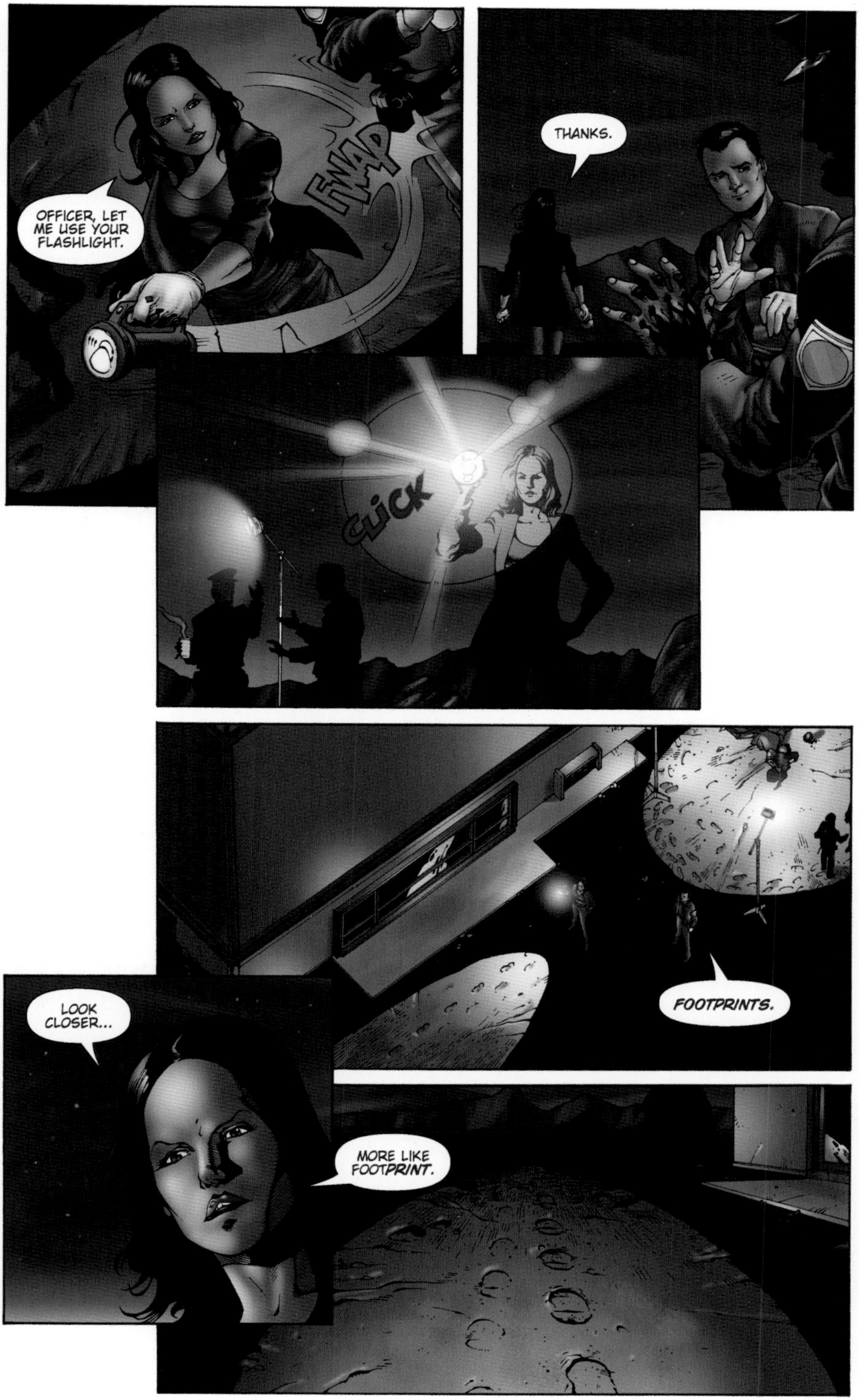
OFFICER, LET ME USE YOUR FLASHLIGHT.
FWAP
THANKS.
CLICK
FOOTPRINTS.
LOOK CLOSER...
MORE LIKE FOOTPRINT.

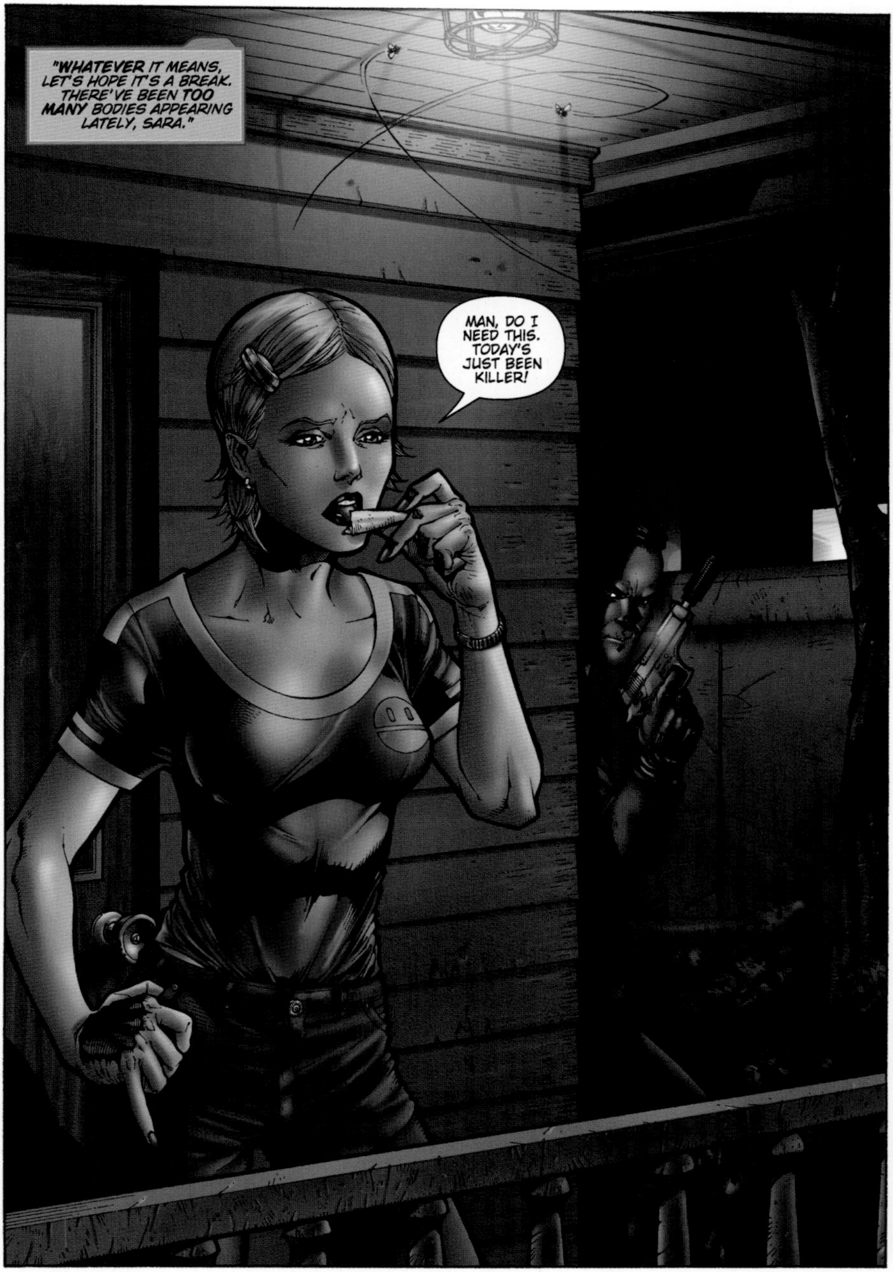
"WHATEVER IT MEANS, LET'S HOPE IT'S A BREAK. THERE'VE BEEN TOO MANY BODIES APPEARING LATELY, SARA."
MAN, DO I NEED THIS. TODAY'S JUST BEEN KILLER!

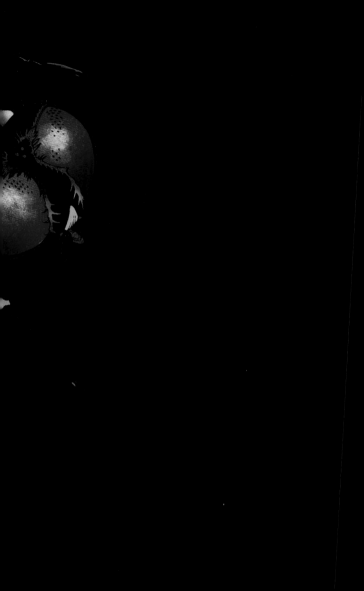

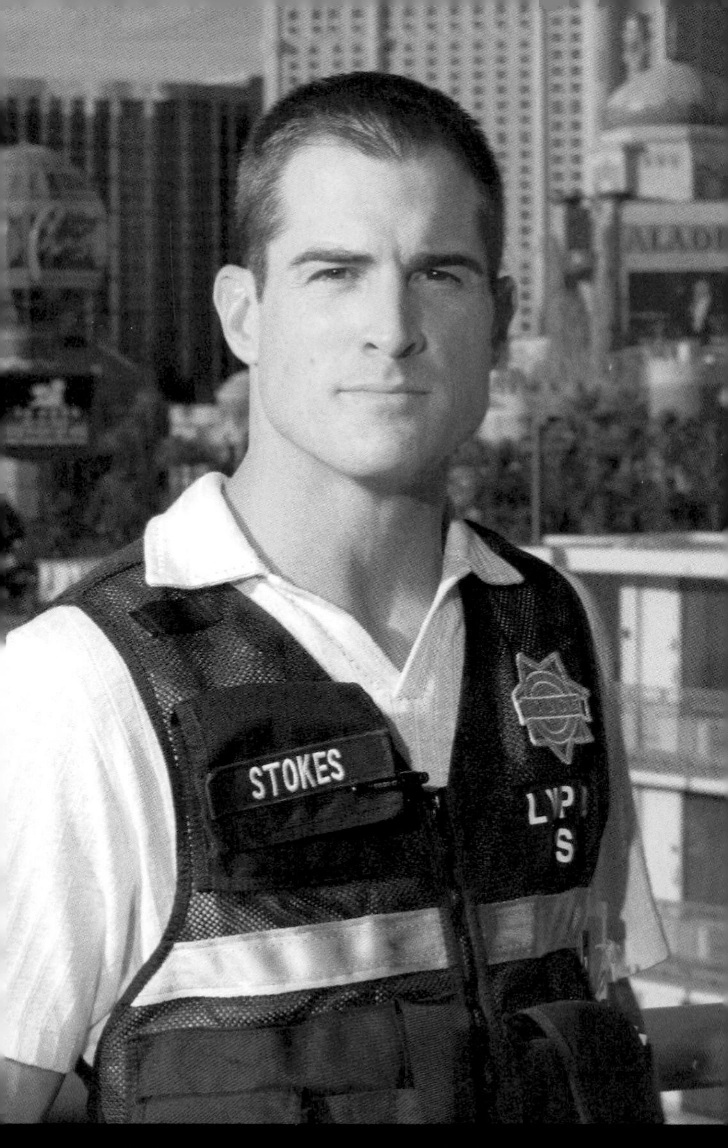
STOKES

Chapter Three

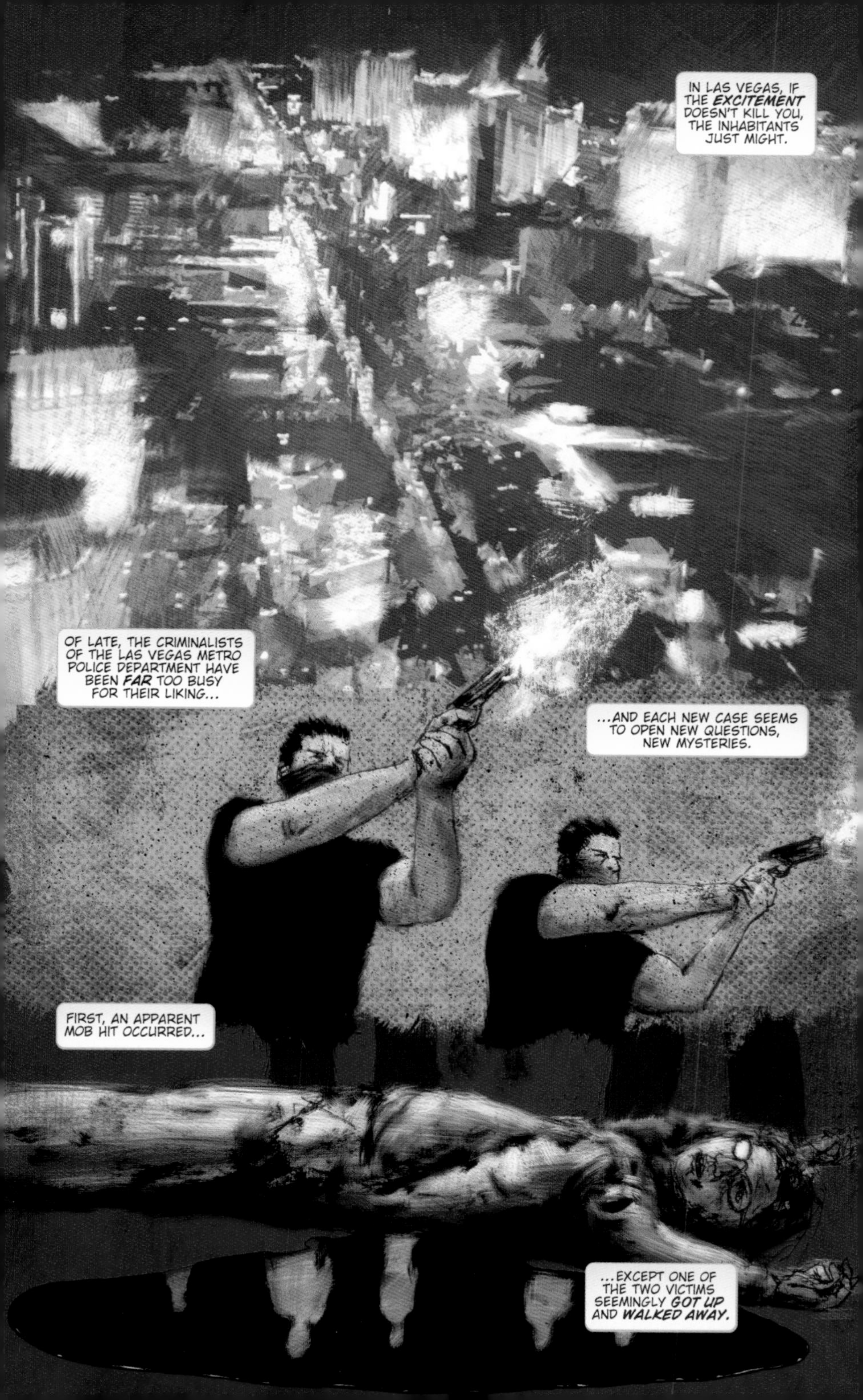
IN LAS VEGAS, IF THE EXCITEMENT DOESN'T KILL YOU, THE INHABITANTS JUST MIGHT.
OF LATE, THE CRIMINALISTS OF THE LAS VEGAS METRO POLICE DEPARTMENT HAVE BEEN FAR TOO BUSY FOR THEIR LIKING...
...AND EACH NEW CASE SEEMS TO OPEN NEW QUESTIONS, NEW MYSTERIES.
FIRST, AN APPARENT MOB HIT OCCURRED...
...EXCEPT ONE OF THE TWO VICTIMS SEEMINGLY GOT UP AND WALKED AWAY.

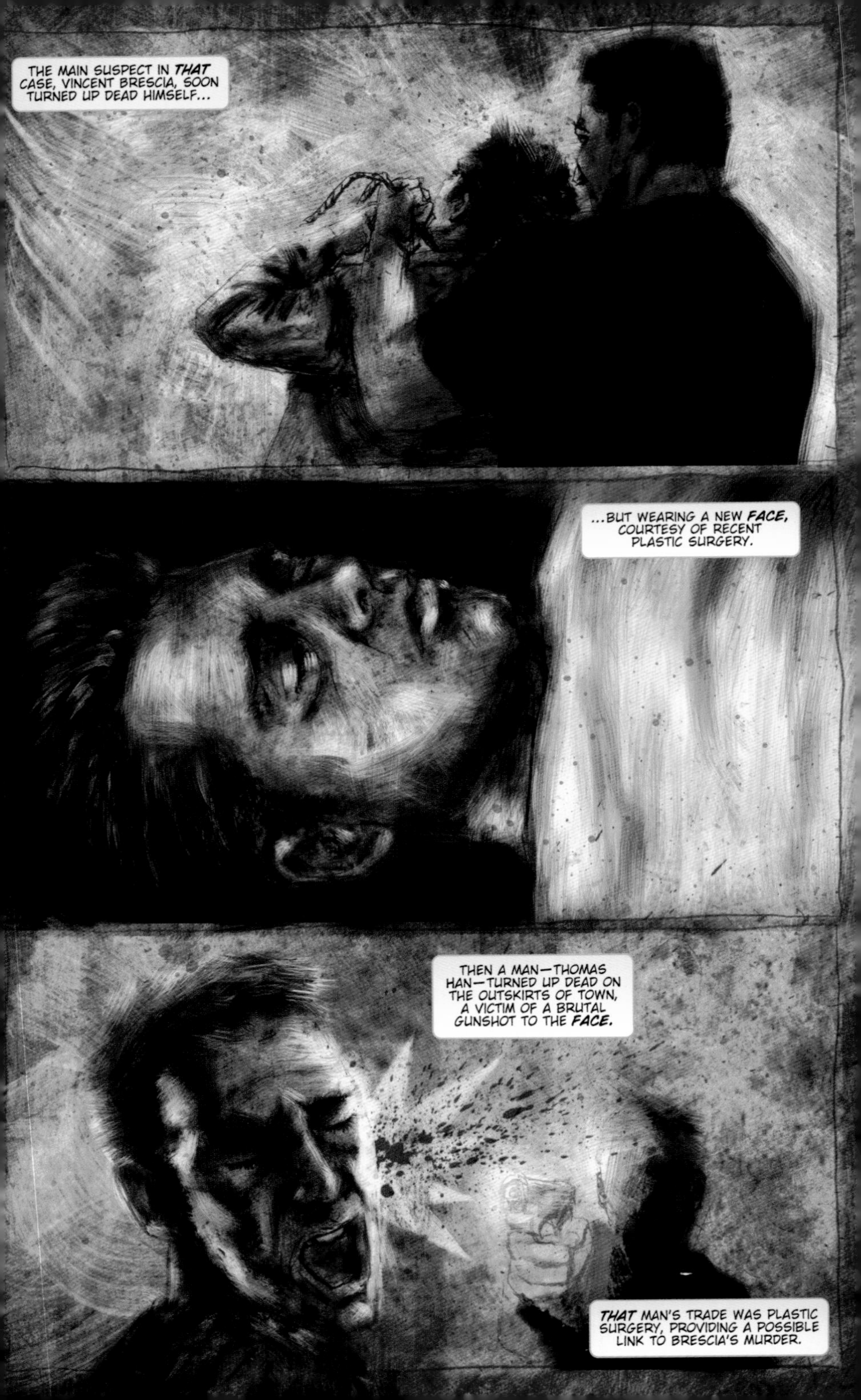
THE MAIN SUSPECT IN THAT CASE, VINCENT BRESCIA, SOON TURNED UP DEAD HIMSELF...
...BUT WEARING A NEW FACE, COURTESY OF RECENT PLASTIC SURGERY.
THEN A MAN—THOMAS HAN—TURNED UP DEAD ON THE OUTSKIRTS OF TOWN, A VICTIM OF A BRUTAL GUNSHOT TO THE FACE.
THAT MAN'S TRADE WAS PLASTIC SURGERY, PROVIDING A POSSIBLE LINK TO BRESCIA'S MURDER.

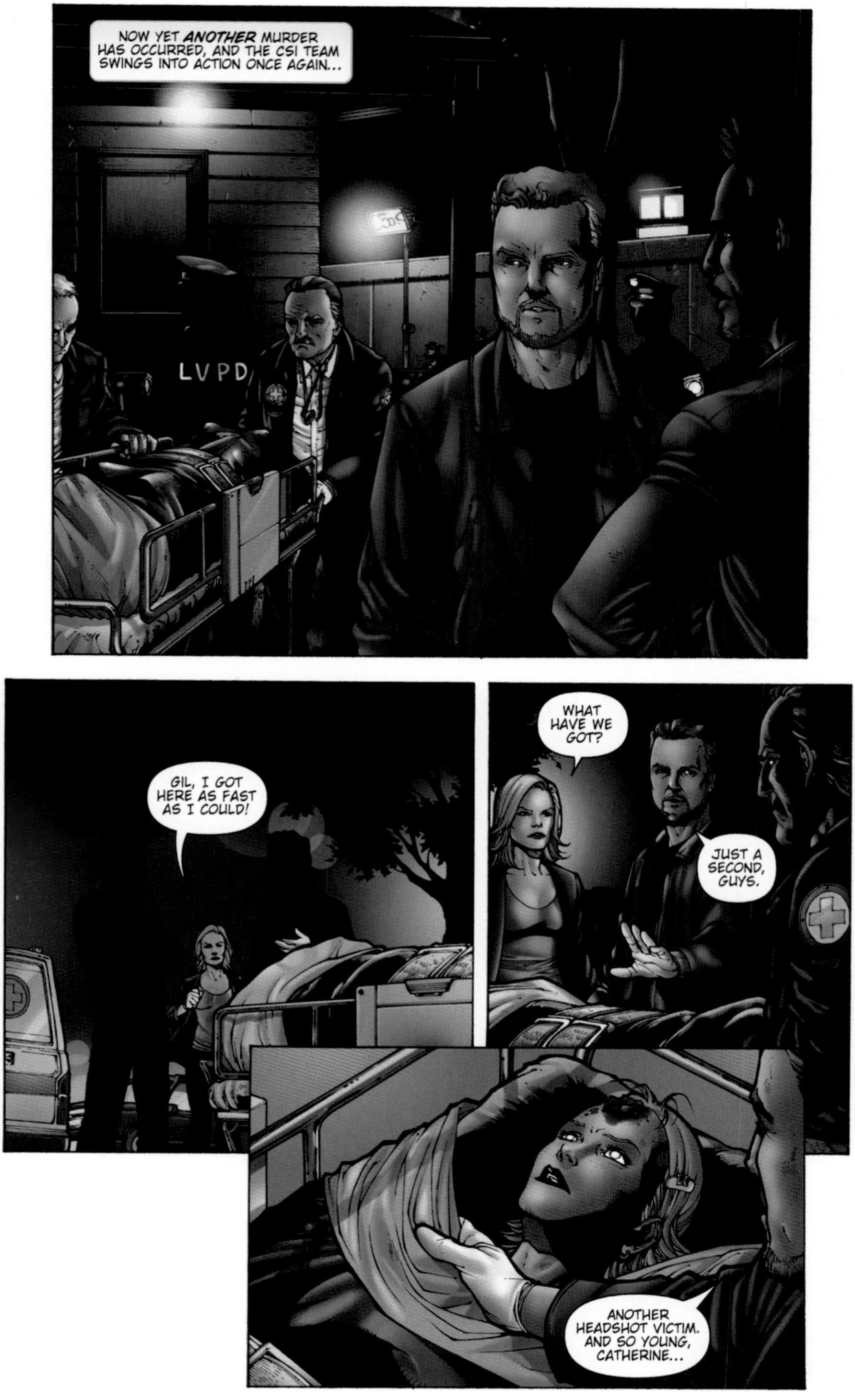
NOW YET ANOTHER MURDER HAS OCCURRED, AND THE CSI TEAM SWINGS INTO ACTION ONCE AGAIN...
LVPD
GIL, I GOT HERE AS FAST AS I COULD!
WHAT HAVE WE GOT?
JUST A SECOND, GUYS.
ANOTHER HEADSHOT VICTIM. AND SO YOUNG, CATHERINE...

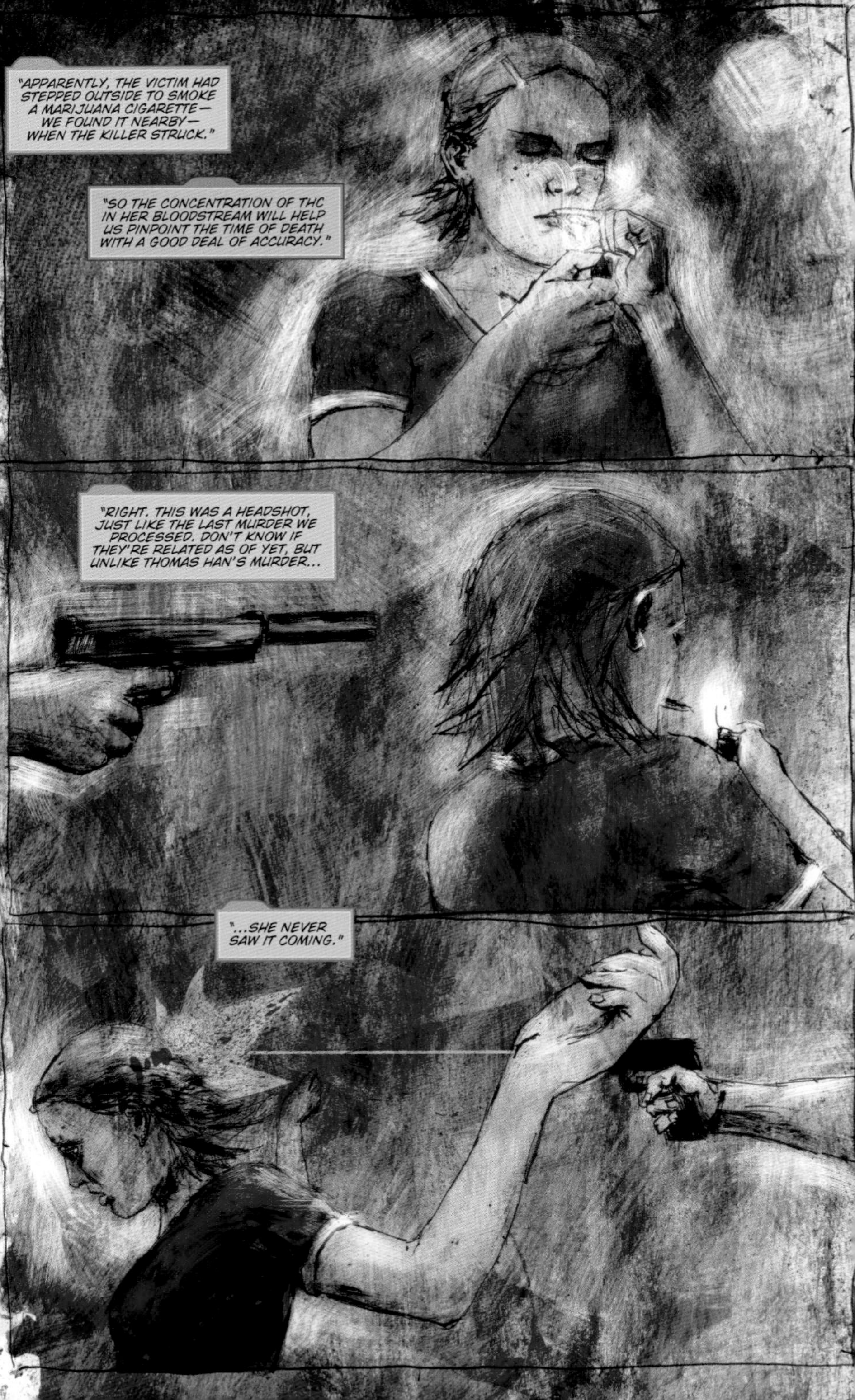
"APPARENTLY, THE VICTIM HAD STEPPED OUTSIDE TO SMOKE A MARIJUANA CIGARETTE— WE FOUND IT NEARBY— WHEN THE KILLER STRUCK."
"SO THE CONCENTRATION OF THC IN HER BLOODSTREAM WILL HELP US PINPOINT THE TIME OF DEATH WITH A GOOD DEAL OF ACCURACY."
"RIGHT. THIS WAS A HEADSHOT, JUST LIKE THE LAST MURDER WE PROCESSED. DON'T KNOW IF THEY'RE RELATED AS OF YET, BUT UNLIKE THOMAS HAN'S MURDER...
"...SHE NEVER SAW IT COMING."

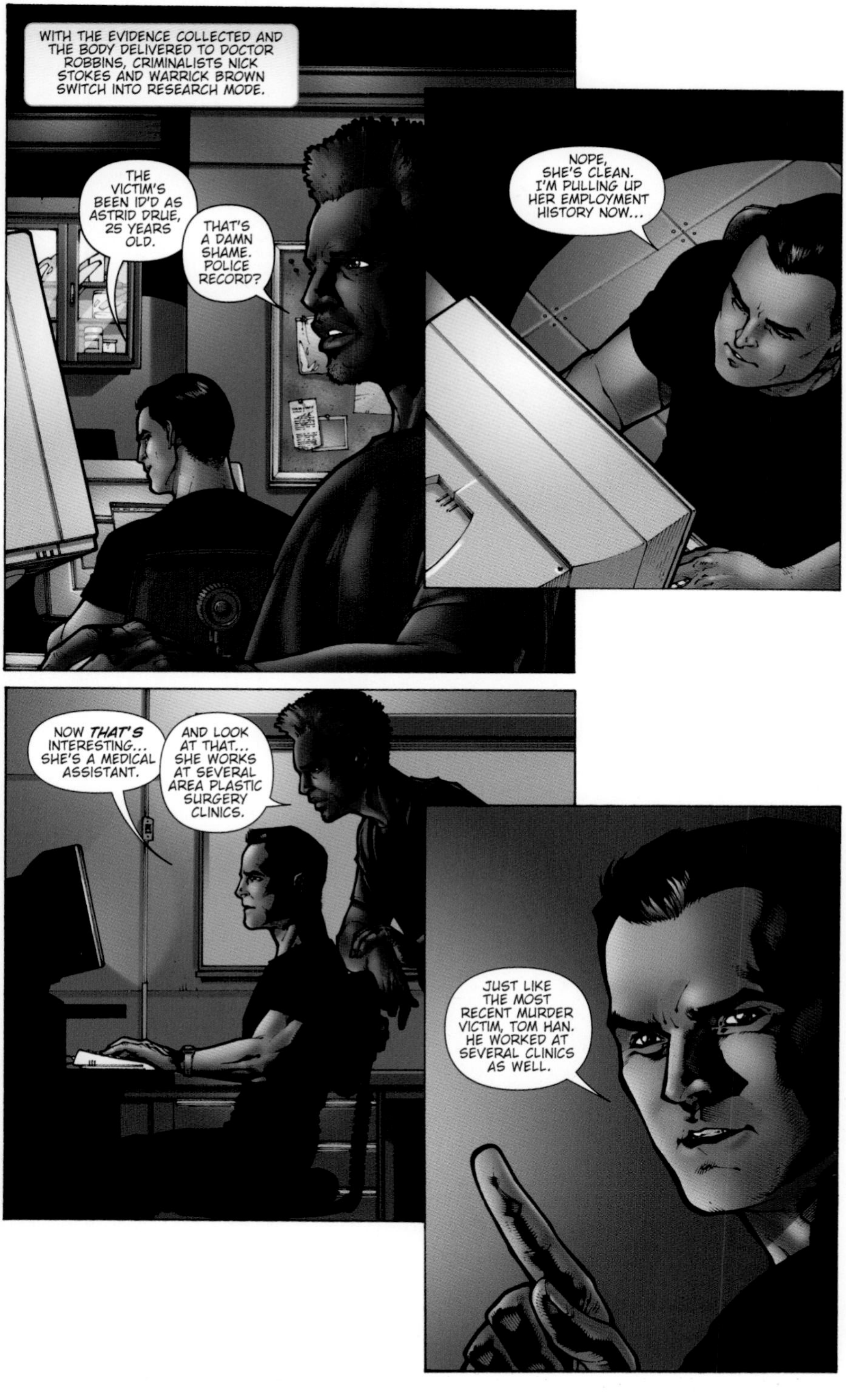
WITH THE EVIDENCE COLLECTED AND THE BODY DELIVERED TO DOCTOR ROBBINS, CRIMINALISTS NICK STOKES AND WARRICK BROWN SWITCH INTO RESEARCH MODE.
THE VICTIM'S BEEN ID'D AS ASTRID DRUE, 25 YEARS OLD.
THAT'S A DAMN SHAME. POLICE RECORD?
NOPE, SHE'S CLEAN. I'M PULLING UP HER EMPLOYMENT HISTORY NOW...
NOW *THAT'S* INTERESTING... SHE'S A MEDICAL ASSISTANT.
AND LOOK AT THAT... SHE WORKS AT SEVERAL AREA PLASTIC SURGERY CLINICS.
JUST LIKE THE MOST RECENT MURDER VICTIM, TOM HAN. HE WORKED AT SEVERAL CLINICS AS WELL.

I'LL CROSS-REFERENCE DRUE'S LIST AGAINST HAN'S. LET'S SEE IF THEY SHARED A COMMON EMPLOYER.

TWO MATCHES: DESERT HEARTS AND HOPE/MYERS.

NOW WE'RE IN BUSINESS.

THEY'RE WITHIN A FEW BLOCKS OF EACH OTHER AS WELL. DESERT HEARTS IS ON MONROE AND HOPE/MYERS IS ON VAN BUREN.

COOL. IF YOU KEEP DIGGING, I'LL HIT BOTH AND SEE IF HAN AND DRUE'S WORK SCHEDULES COINCIDED...

"MAYBE THIS'LL FINALLY BE THE BREAK WE'VE BEEN LOOKING FOR."

LAS VEGAS POLICE PARKING

EXIT

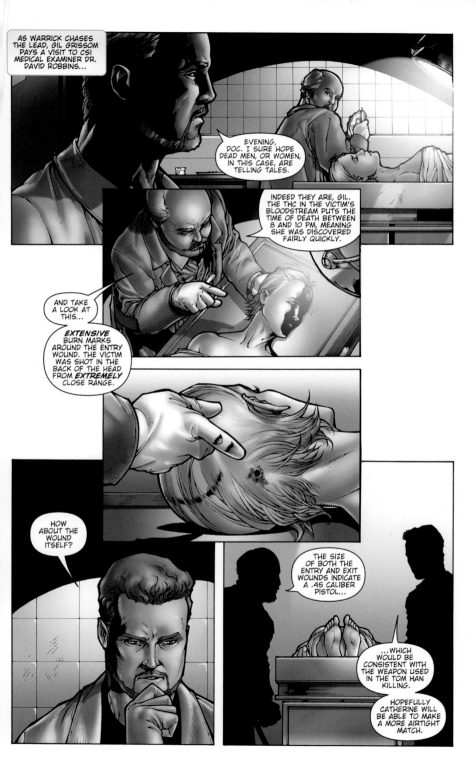

AS WARRICK CHASES THE LEAD, GIL GRISSOM PAYS A VISIT TO CSI MEDICAL EXAMINER DR. DAVID ROBBINS...

EVENING, DOC. I SURE HOPE DEAD MEN, OR WOMEN, IN THIS CASE, ARE TELLING TALES.

INDEED THEY ARE, GIL. THE THC IN THE VICTIM'S BLOODSTREAM PUTS THE TIME OF DEATH BETWEEN 8 AND 10 PM, MEANING SHE WAS DISCOVERED FAIRLY QUICKLY.

AND TAKE A LOOK AT THIS...

EXTENSIVE BURN MARKS AROUND THE ENTRY WOUND. THE VICTIM WAS SHOT IN THE BACK OF THE HEAD FROM *EXTREMELY* CLOSE RANGE.

HOW ABOUT THE WOUND ITSELF?

THE SIZE OF BOTH THE ENTRY AND EXIT WOUNDS INDICATE A .45 CALIBER PISTOL...

...WHICH WOULD BE CONSISTENT WITH THE WEAPON USED IN THE TOM HAN KILLING.

HOPEFULLY CATHERINE WILL BE ABLE TO MAKE A MORE AIRTIGHT MATCH.

59

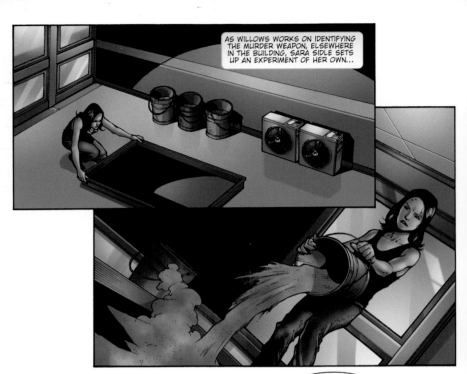

AS WILLOWS WORKS ON IDENTIFYING THE MURDER WEAPON, ELSEWHERE IN THE BUILDING, SARA SIDLE SETS UP AN EXPERIMENT OF HER OWN...

JUST TRYING A LITTLE *EXPERIMENT* TO SEE IF WE CAN FIGURE OUT THE DEAL WITH THOSE ODD FOOTPRINTS.

I RETRIEVED SAND FROM NEARBY THE CRIME SCENE AND ADJUSTED THE MOISTURE CONTENT TO MATCH CONDITIONS AT THOMAS HAN'S TIME OF DEATH.

HEY, SARA, WHATCHA—

HOLD ON, NICK.

CONGRATULATIONS— YOU PROVED FOOTFALLS IN SAND LEAVE PRINTS!

HUSH, NICKY. JUST HELP ME GET THESE FANS IN PLACE.

NOW I JUST NEED TO MATCH THE WIND VELOCITY FROM THE NIGHT OF THE MURDER AND LET 'ER RIP!

WHHiRR

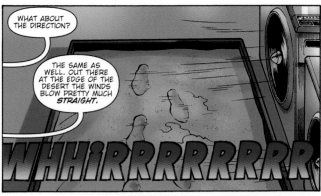

WHAT ABOUT THE DIRECTION?

THE SAME AS WELL. OUT THERE AT THE EDGE OF THE DESERT THE WINDS BLOW PRETTY MUCH **STRAIGHT.**

WHHiRRRRRRRR

OF COURSE, THE WIND BLEW THE FOOTPRINTS AT THE CRIME SCENE FOR A MUCH **LONGER** TIME PERIOD, BUT YOU CAN ALREADY SEE THE RESULTS OF THIS EXPERIMENT...

YEAH, NORMAL FOOTPRINTS. NOT THE STRANGE, ALMOST **SINGLE** FOOTPRINTS WE SAW THERE. GUESS YOUR EXPERIMENT WAS A FAILURE.

WHHiRRRRRRR

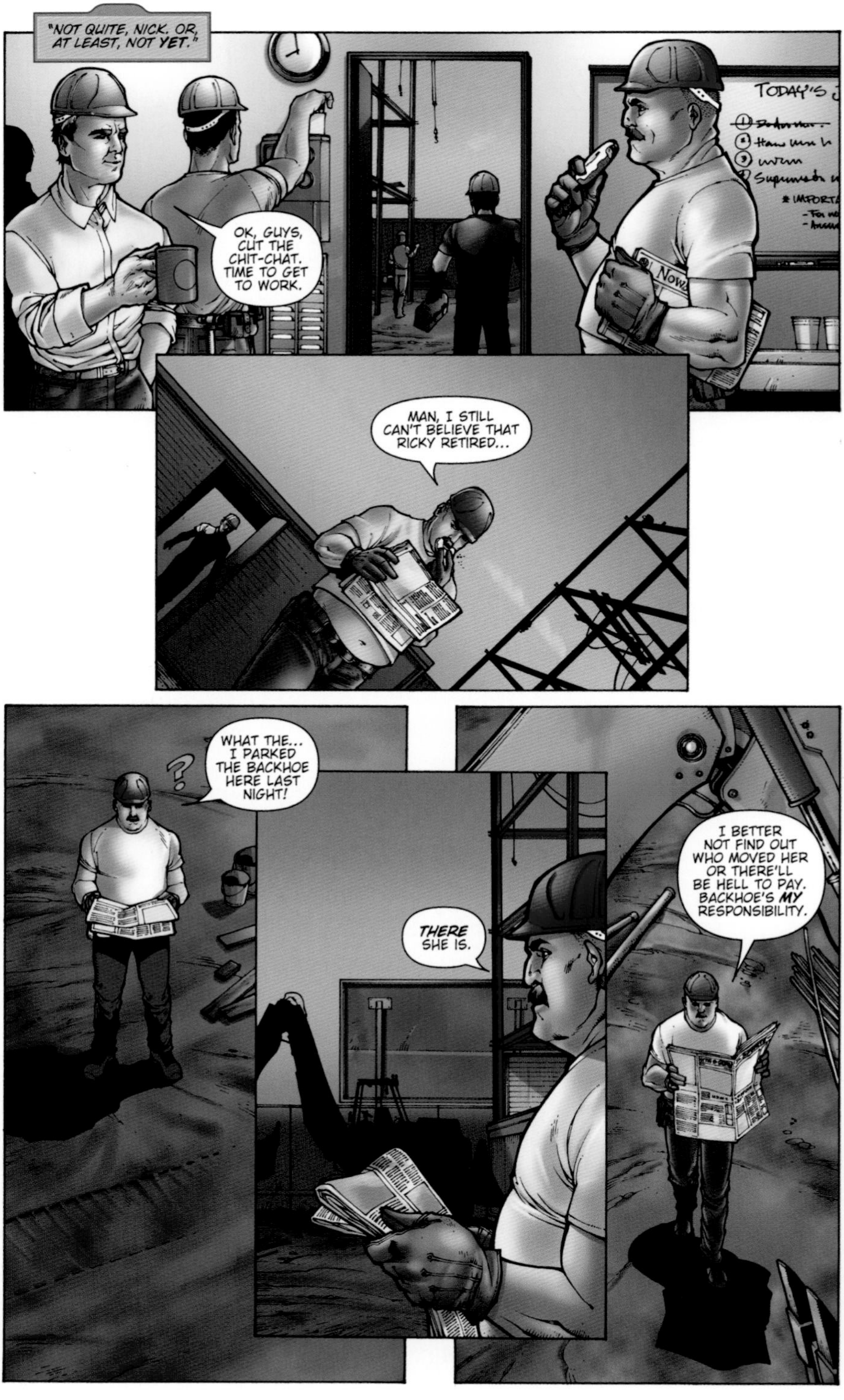
"NOT QUITE, NICK. OR, AT LEAST, NOT YET."
OK, GUYS, CUT THE CHIT-CHAT. TIME TO GET TO WORK.
TODAY'S
MAN, I STILL CAN'T BELIEVE THAT RICKY RETIRED...
WHAT THE... I PARKED THE BACKHOE HERE LAST NIGHT!
THERE SHE IS.
I BETTER NOT FIND OUT WHO MOVED HER OR THERE'LL BE HELL TO PAY. BACKHOE'S MY RESPONSIBILITY.

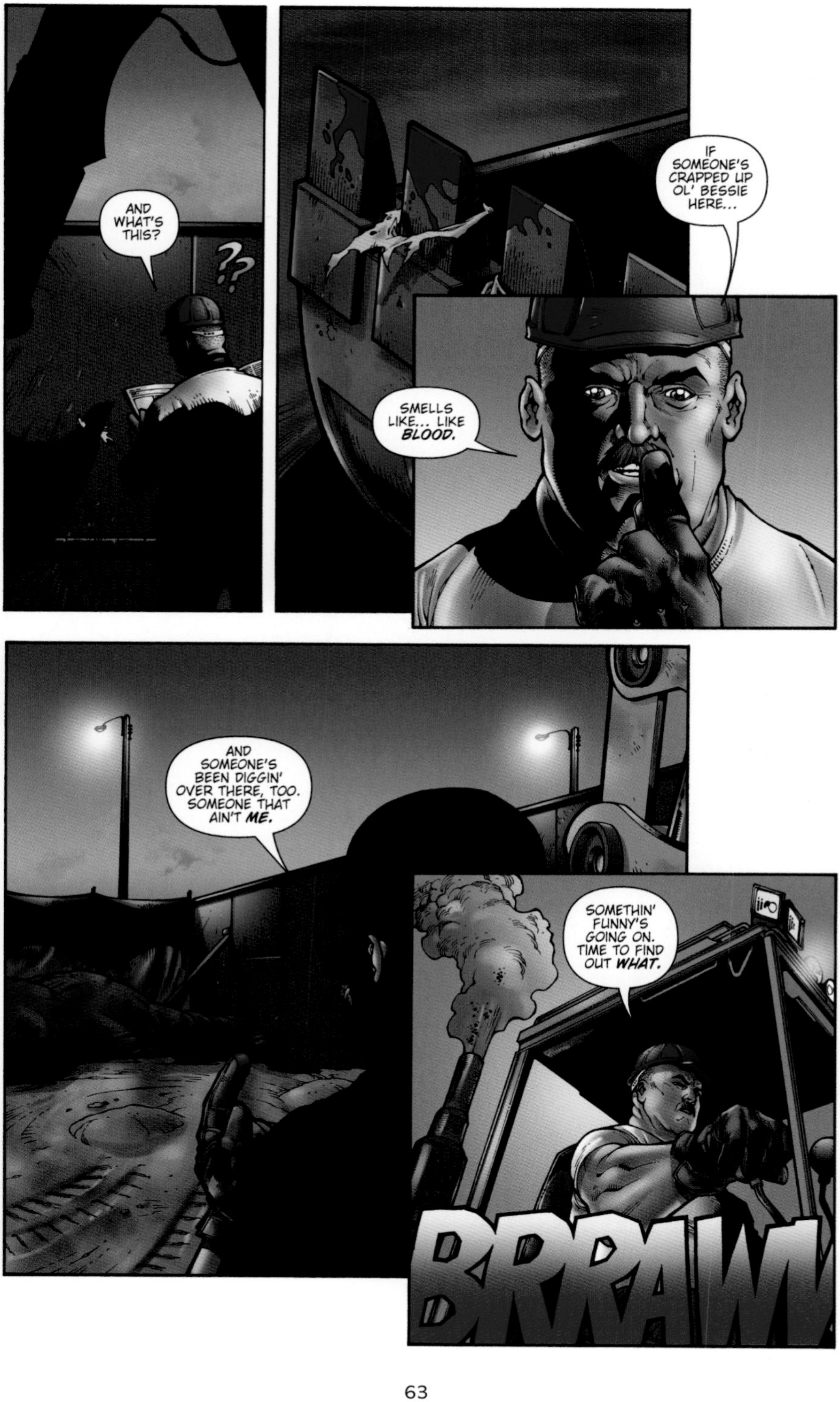
AND WHAT'S THIS?
??
IF SOMEONE'S CRAPPED UP OL' BESSIE HERE...
SMELLS LIKE... LIKE BLOOD.
AND SOMEONE'S BEEN DIGGIN' OVER THERE, TOO. SOMEONE THAT AIN'T ME.
SOMETHIN' FUNNY'S GOING ON. TIME TO FIND OUT WHAT.
BRRAWW

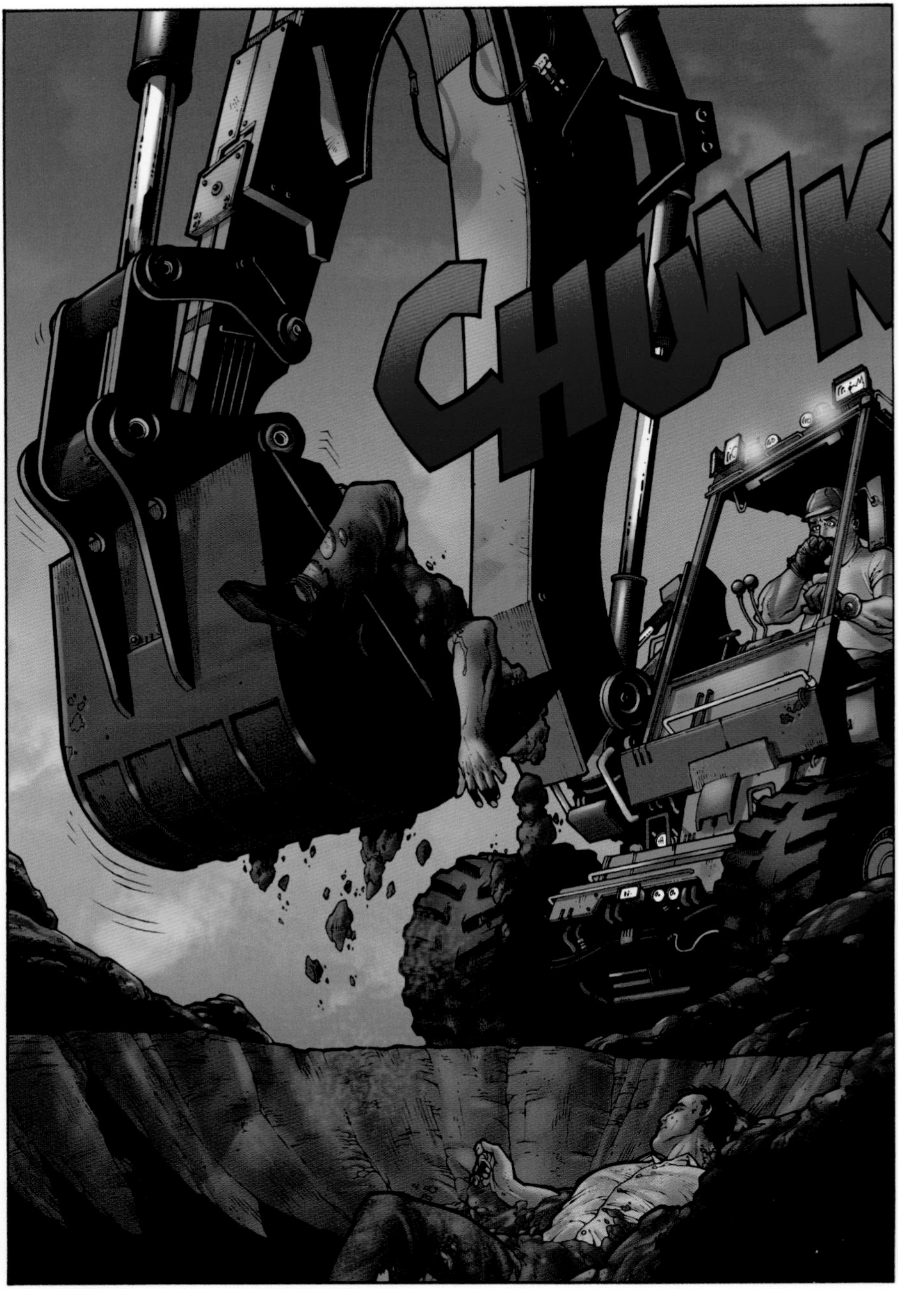
CHUNK

NOW FOR PART *TWO*...

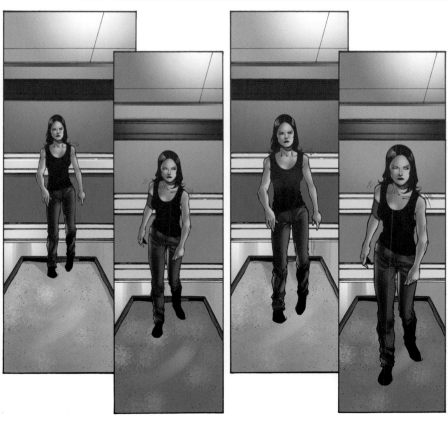

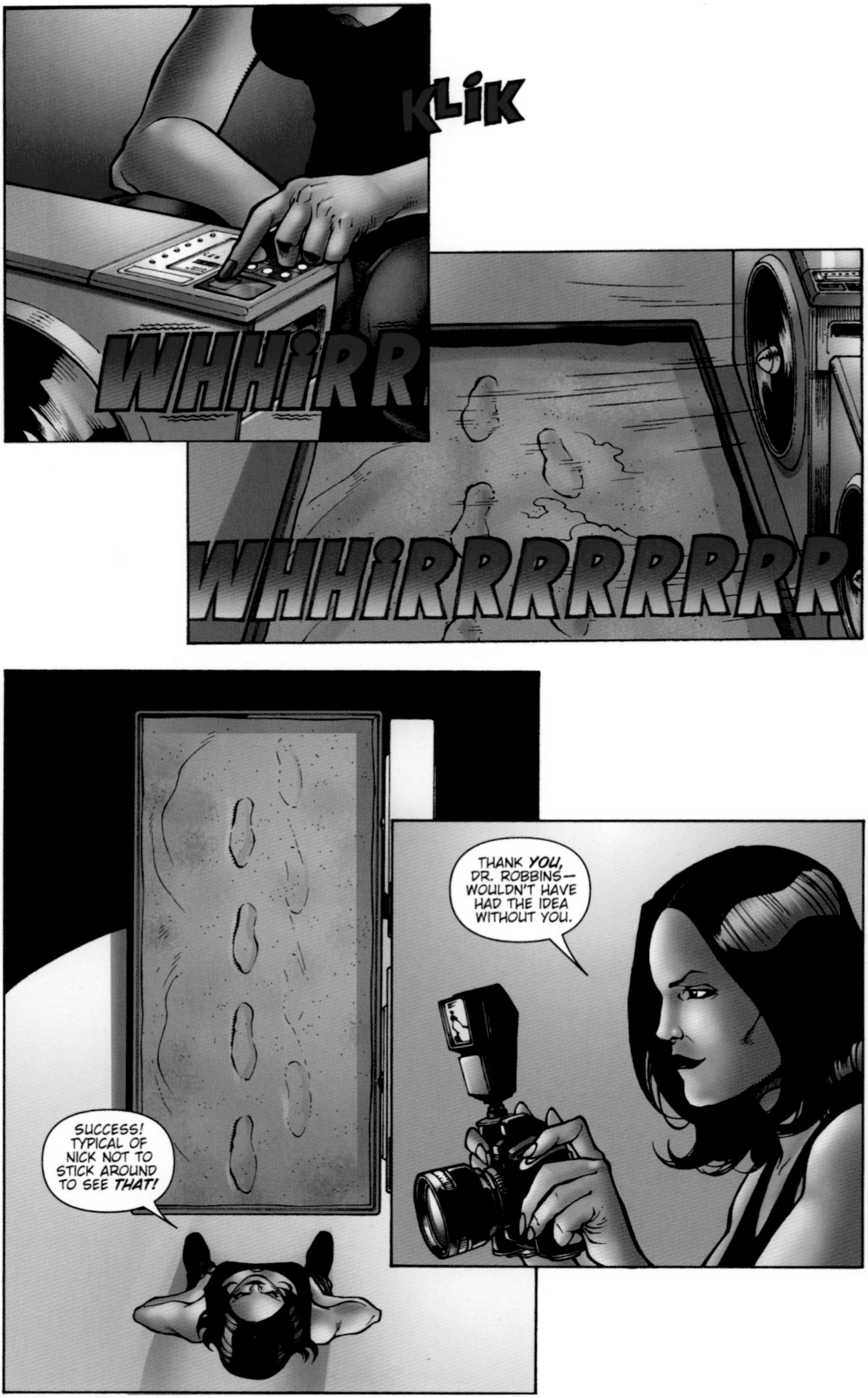
KLIK
WHHIRR
WHHIRRRRRRRR
THANK YOU, DR. ROBBINS—WOULDN'T HAVE HAD THE IDEA WITHOUT YOU.
SUCCESS! TYPICAL OF NICK NOT TO STICK AROUND TO SEE THAT!

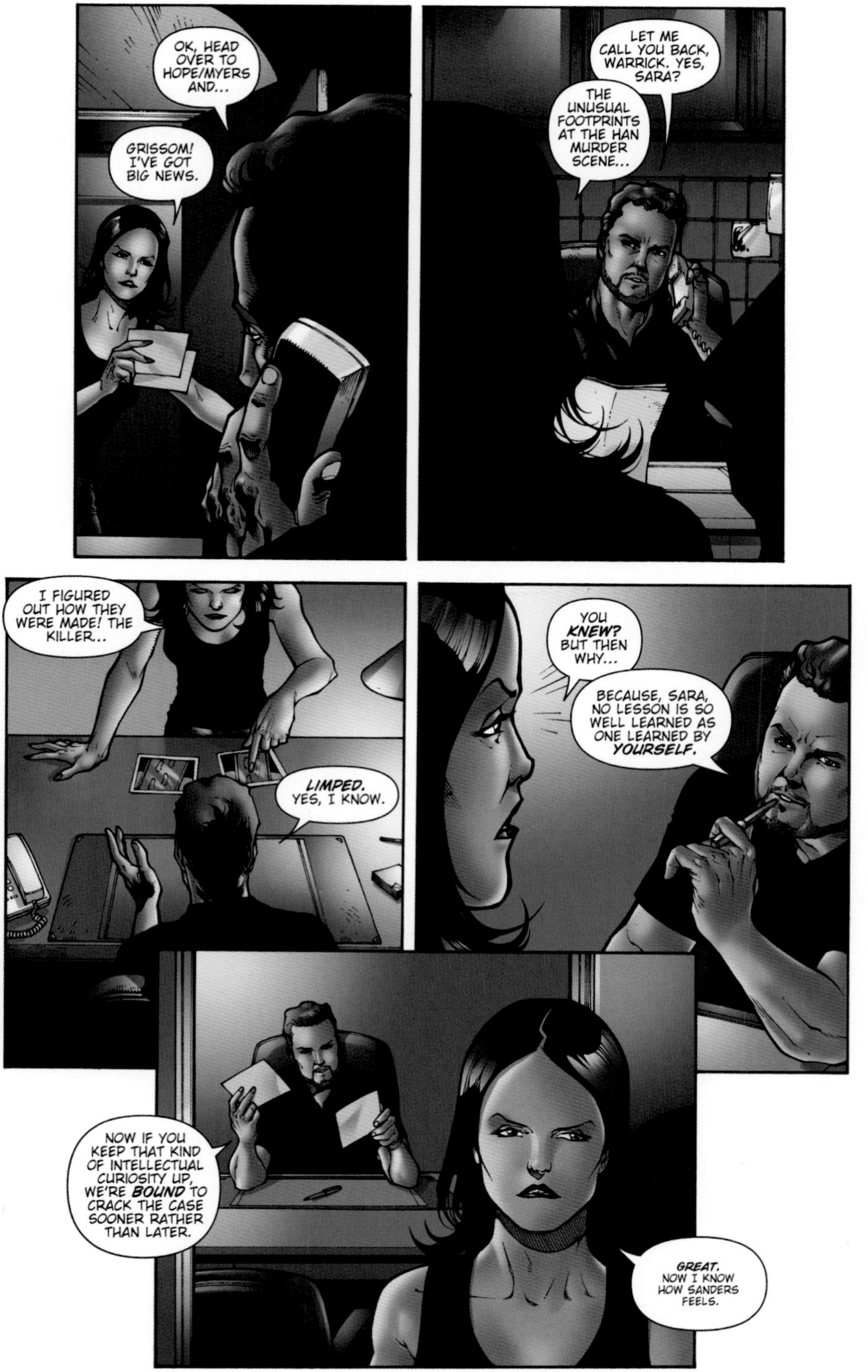
OK, HEAD OVER TO HOPE/MYERS AND...
GRISSOM! I'VE GOT BIG NEWS.
LET ME CALL YOU BACK, WARRICK. YES, SARA?
THE UNUSUAL FOOTPRINTS AT THE HAN MURDER SCENE...
I FIGURED OUT HOW THEY WERE MADE! THE KILLER...
LIMPED. YES, I KNOW.
YOU KNEW? BUT THEN WHY...
BECAUSE, SARA, NO LESSON IS SO WELL LEARNED AS ONE LEARNED BY YOURSELF.
NOW IF YOU KEEP THAT KIND OF INTELLECTUAL CURIOSITY UP, WE'RE BOUND TO CRACK THE CASE SOONER RATHER THAN LATER.
GREAT. NOW I KNOW HOW SANDERS FEELS.

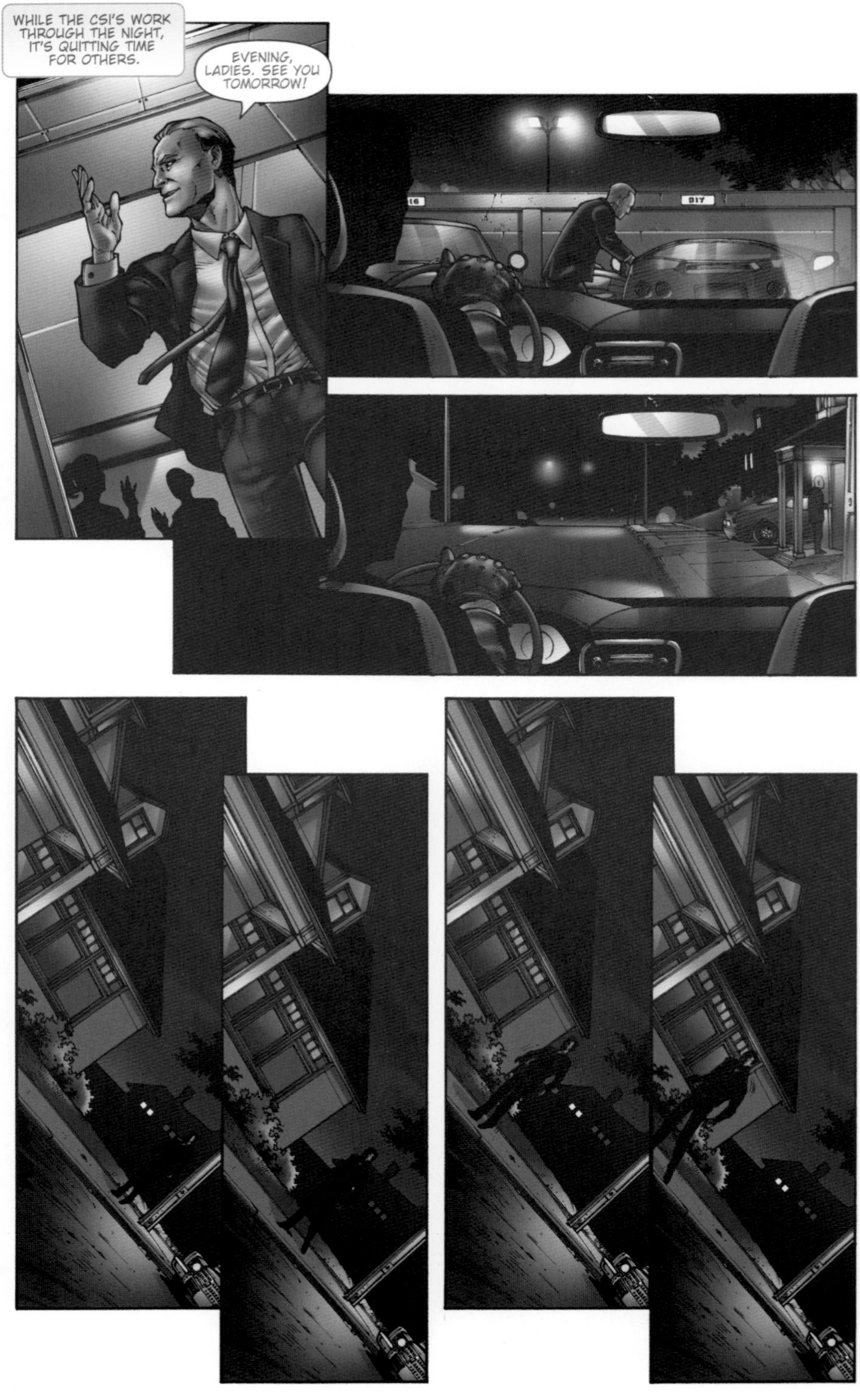
WHILE THE CSI'S WORK THROUGH THE NIGHT, IT'S QUITTING TIME FOR OTHERS.
EVENING, LADIES. SEE YOU TOMORROW!

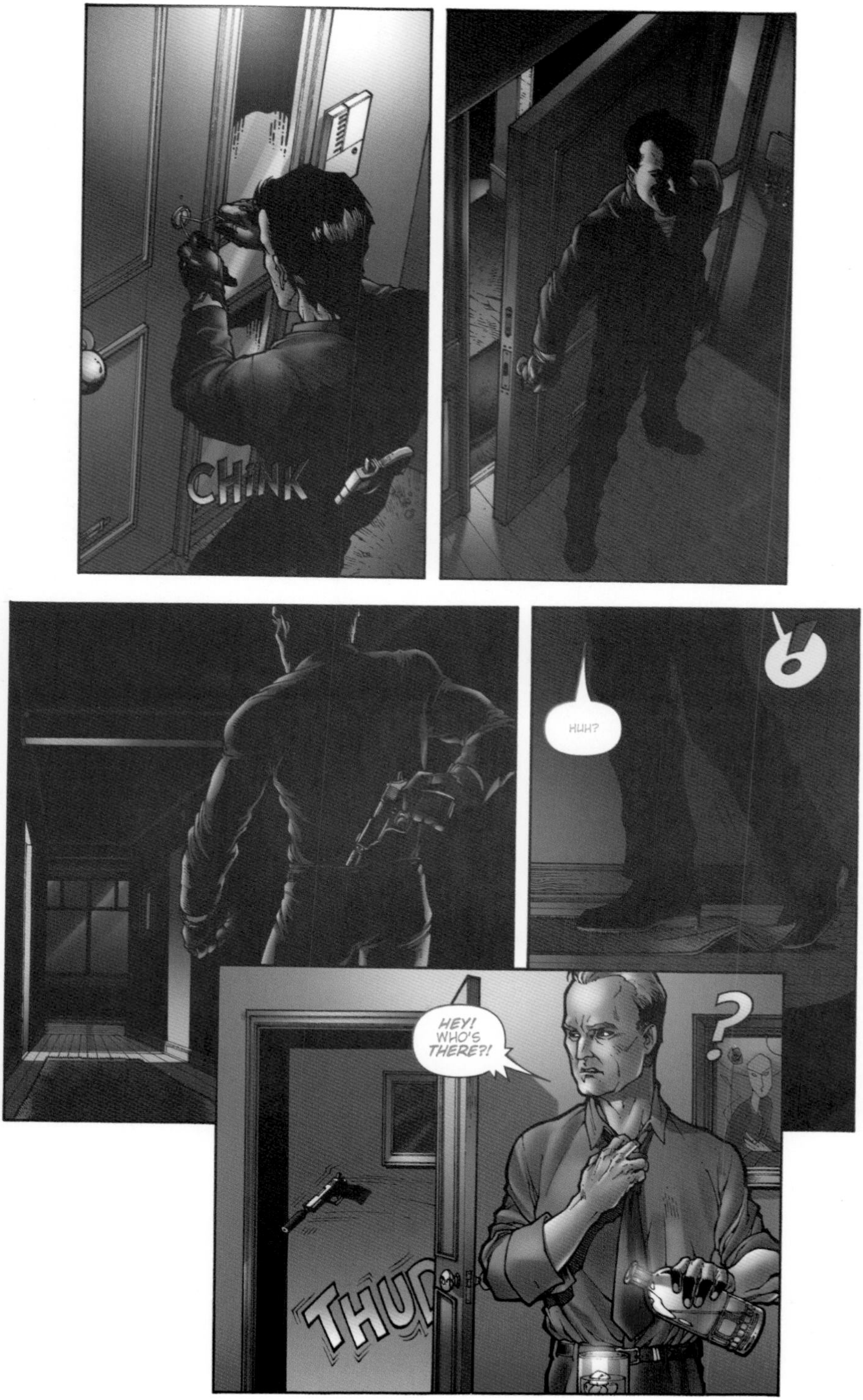
CHINK
HUH?
HEY! WHO'S THERE?!
THUD

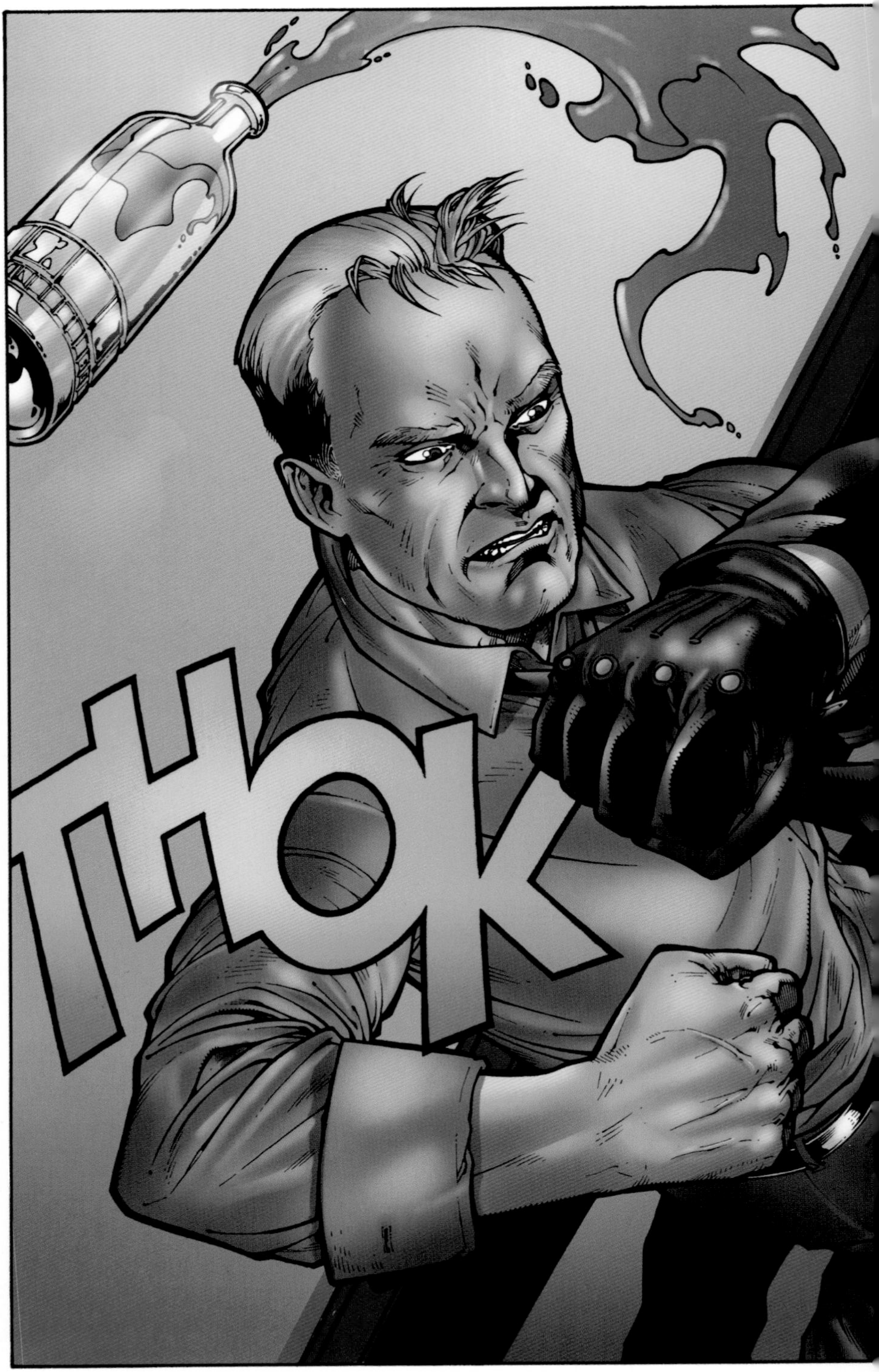
thok

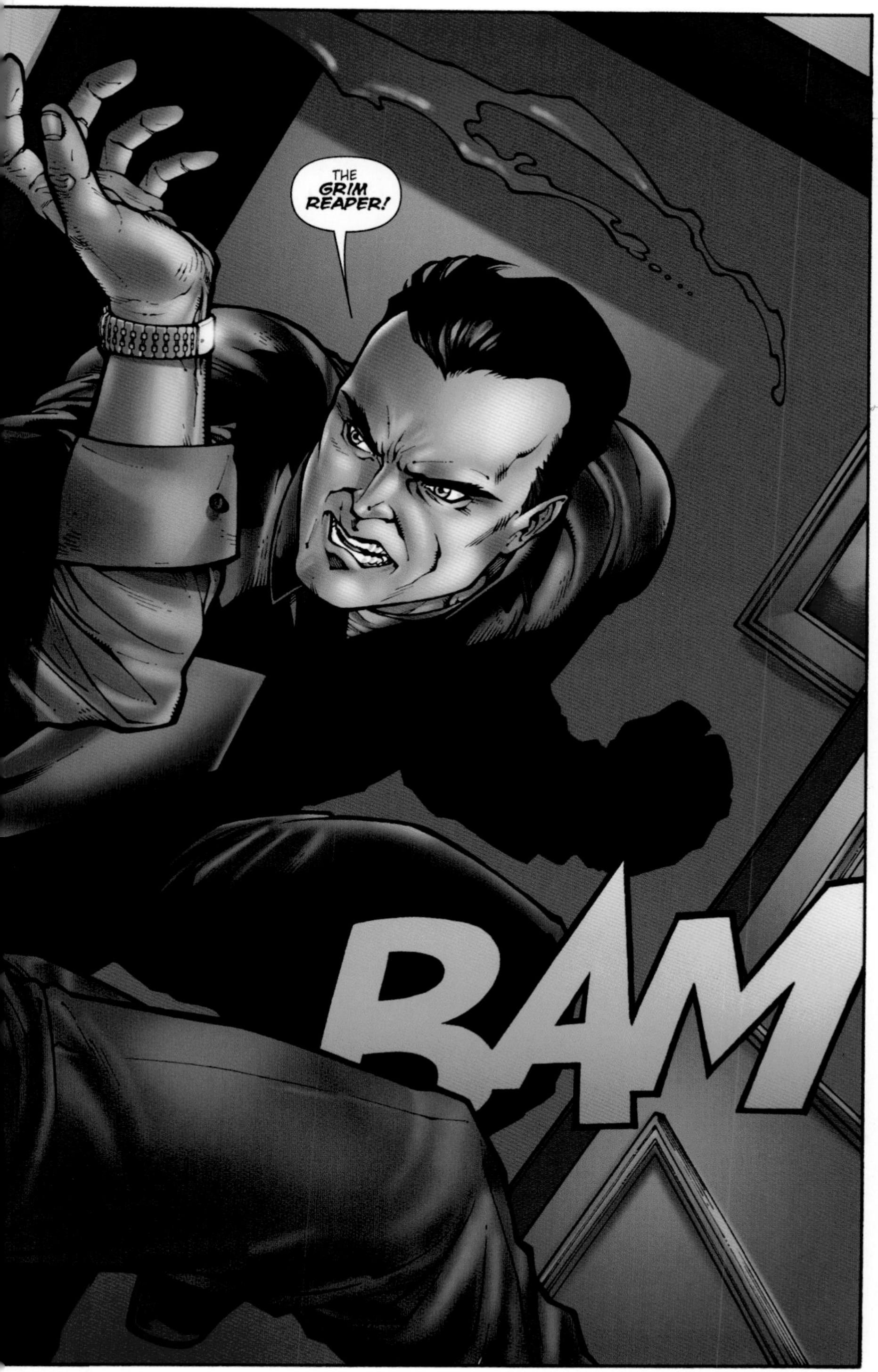
THE GRIM REAPER!
BAM

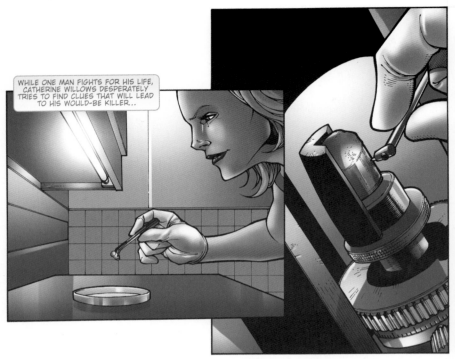

WHILE ONE MAN FIGHTS FOR HIS LIFE, CATHERINE WILLOWS DESPERATELY TRIES TO FIND CLUES THAT WILL LEAD TO HIS WOULD-BE KILLER...

WOULDN'T YOU KNOW IT?

GIL, I'VE JUST FINISHED TESTING THE *BULLET* FROM THE ASTRID DRUE MURDER. SHE WAS KILLED BY THE *SAME GUN* USED ON THOMAS HAN.

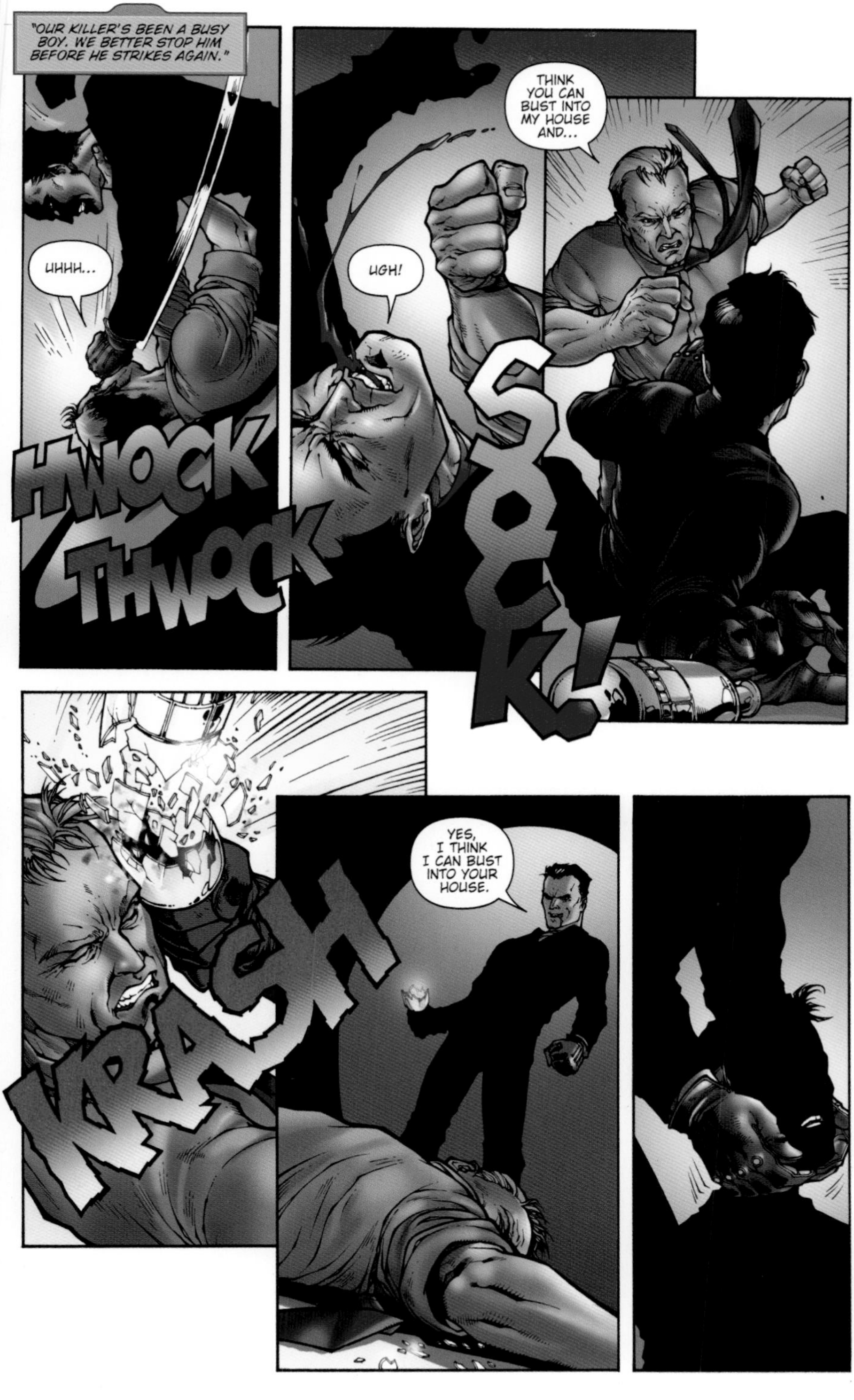
"OUR KILLER'S BEEN A BUSY BOY. WE BETTER STOP HIM BEFORE HE STRIKES AGAIN."
UHHH...
HWOCK
THWOCK
UGH!
THINK YOU CAN BUST INTO MY HOUSE AND...
SOCK!
KRASH
YES, I THINK I CAN BUST INTO YOUR HOUSE.

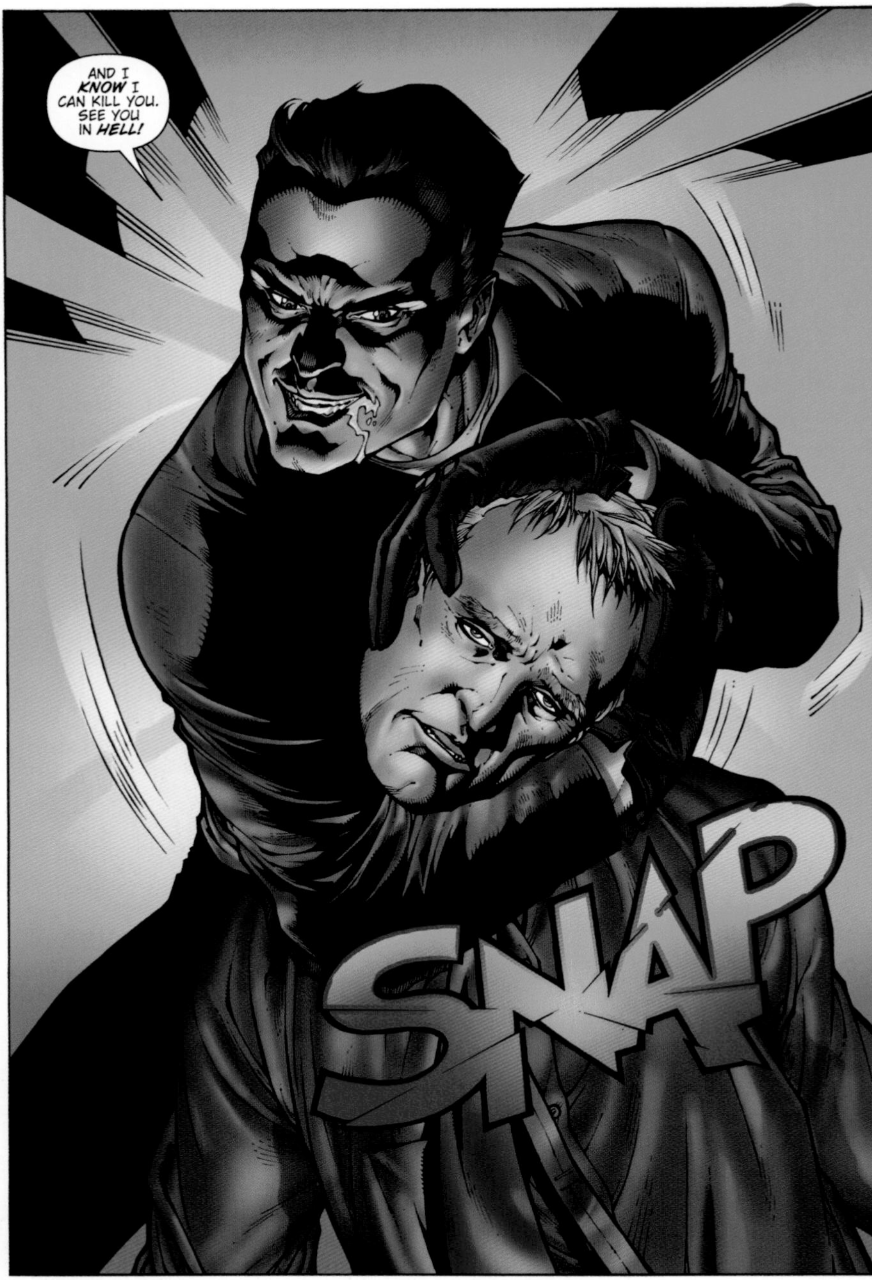
AND I KNOW I CAN KILL YOU. SEE YOU IN HELL!
SNAP

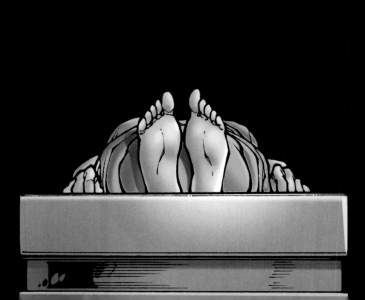

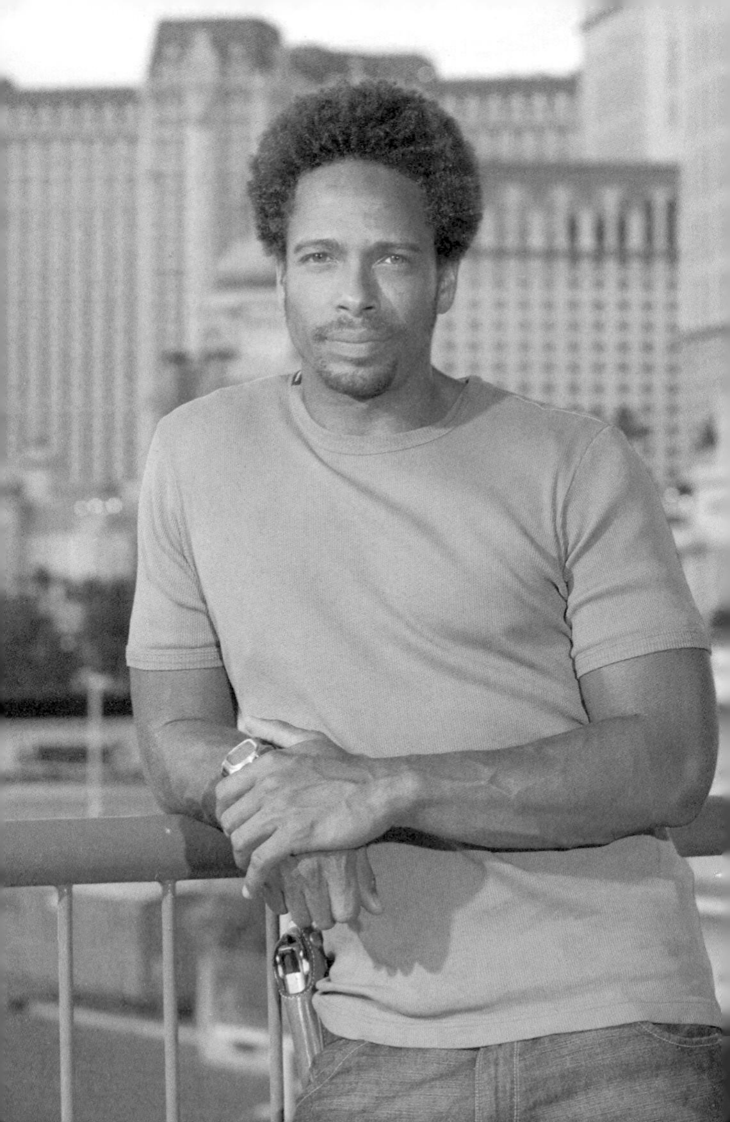

Chapter Four

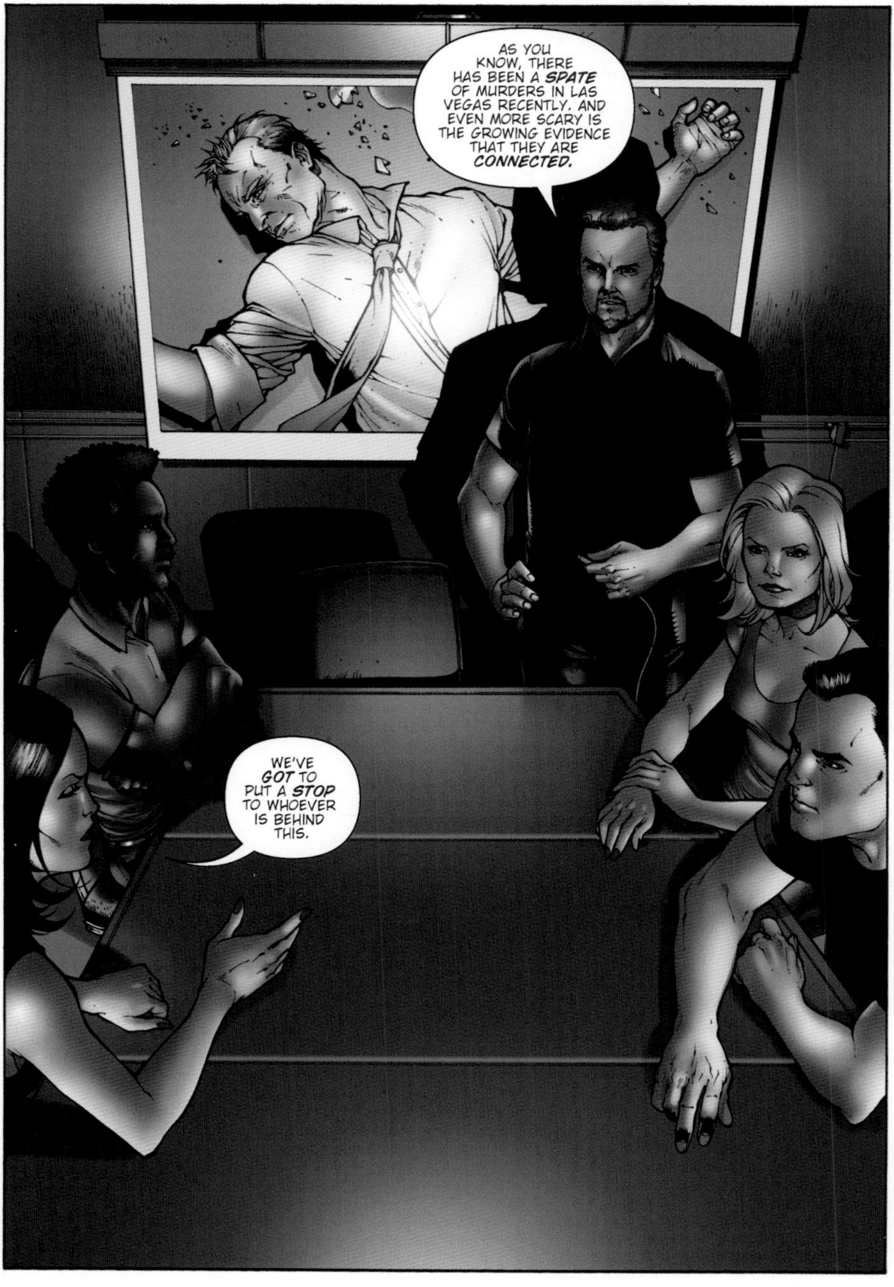
AS YOU KNOW, THERE HAS BEEN A SPATE OF MURDERS IN LAS VEGAS RECENTLY. AND EVEN MORE SCARY IS THE GROWING EVIDENCE THAT THEY ARE CONNECTED.
WE'VE GOT TO PUT A STOP TO WHOEVER IS BEHIND THIS.

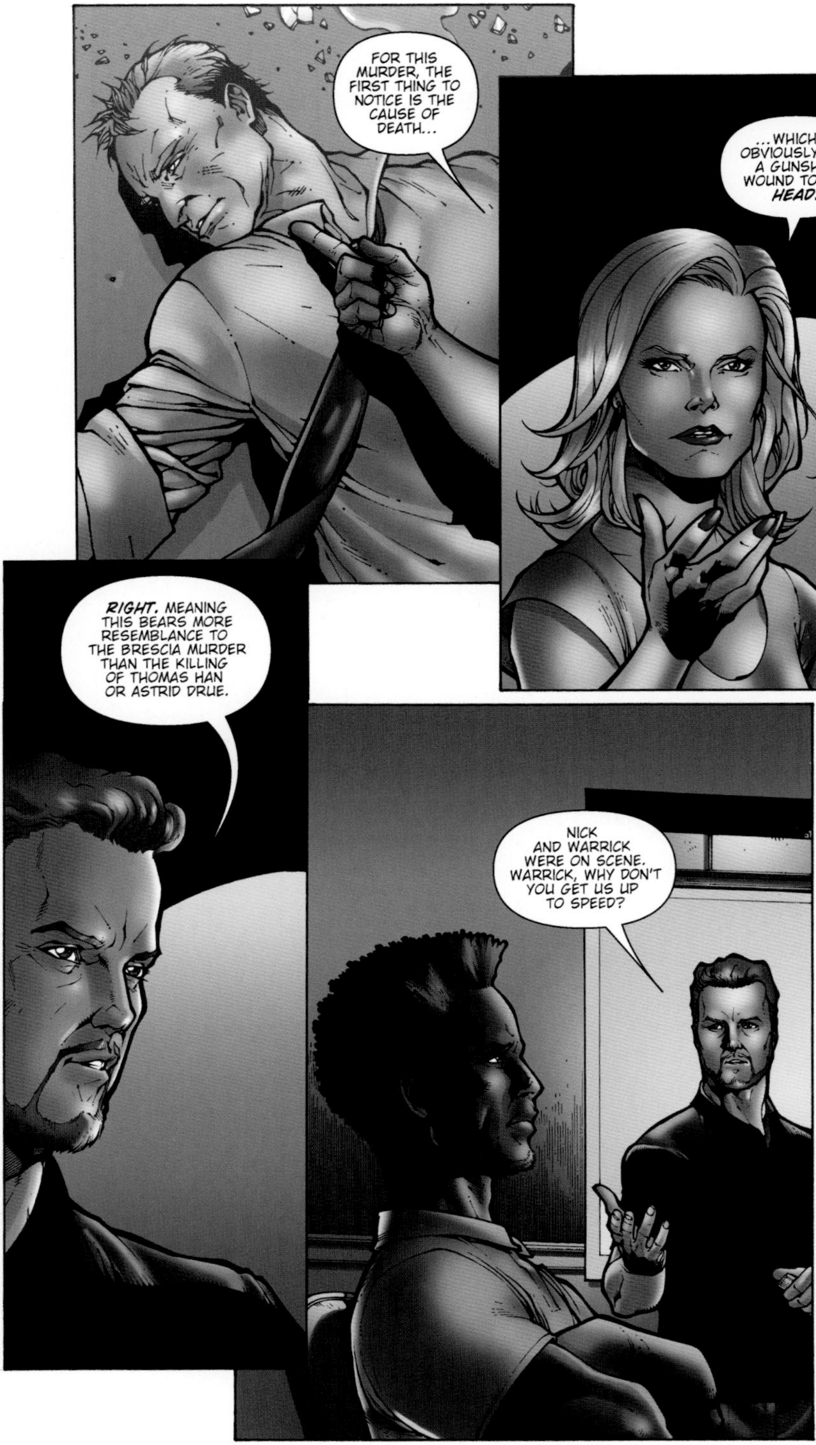
FOR THIS MURDER, THE FIRST THING TO NOTICE IS THE CAUSE OF DEATH...
...WHICH IS OBVIOUSLY NOT A GUNSHOT WOUND TO THE HEAD.
RIGHT. MEANING THIS BEARS MORE RESEMBLANCE TO THE BRESCIA MURDER THAN THE KILLING OF THOMAS HAN OR ASTRID DRUE.
NICK AND WARRICK WERE ON SCENE. WARRICK, WHY DON'T YOU GET US UP TO SPEED?

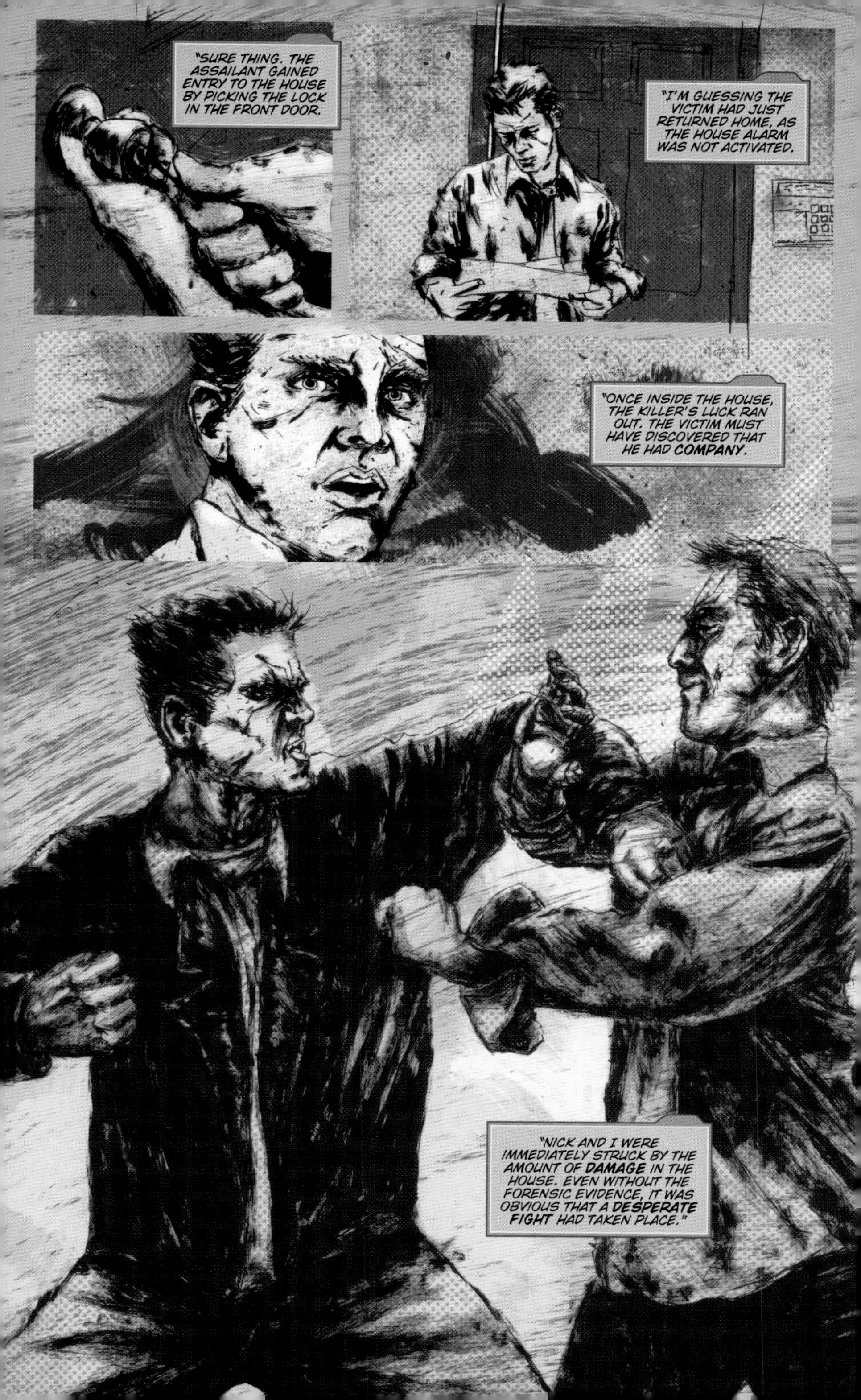
"SURE THING. THE ASSAILANT GAINED ENTRY TO THE HOUSE BY PICKING THE LOCK IN THE FRONT DOOR.
"I'M GUESSING THE VICTIM HAD JUST RETURNED HOME, AS THE HOUSE ALARM WAS NOT ACTIVATED.
"ONCE INSIDE THE HOUSE, THE KILLER'S LUCK RAN OUT. THE VICTIM MUST HAVE DISCOVERED THAT HE HAD COMPANY.
"NICK AND I WERE IMMEDIATELY STRUCK BY THE AMOUNT OF DAMAGE IN THE HOUSE. EVEN WITHOUT THE FORENSIC EVIDENCE, IT WAS OBVIOUS THAT A DESPERATE FIGHT HAD TAKEN PLACE."

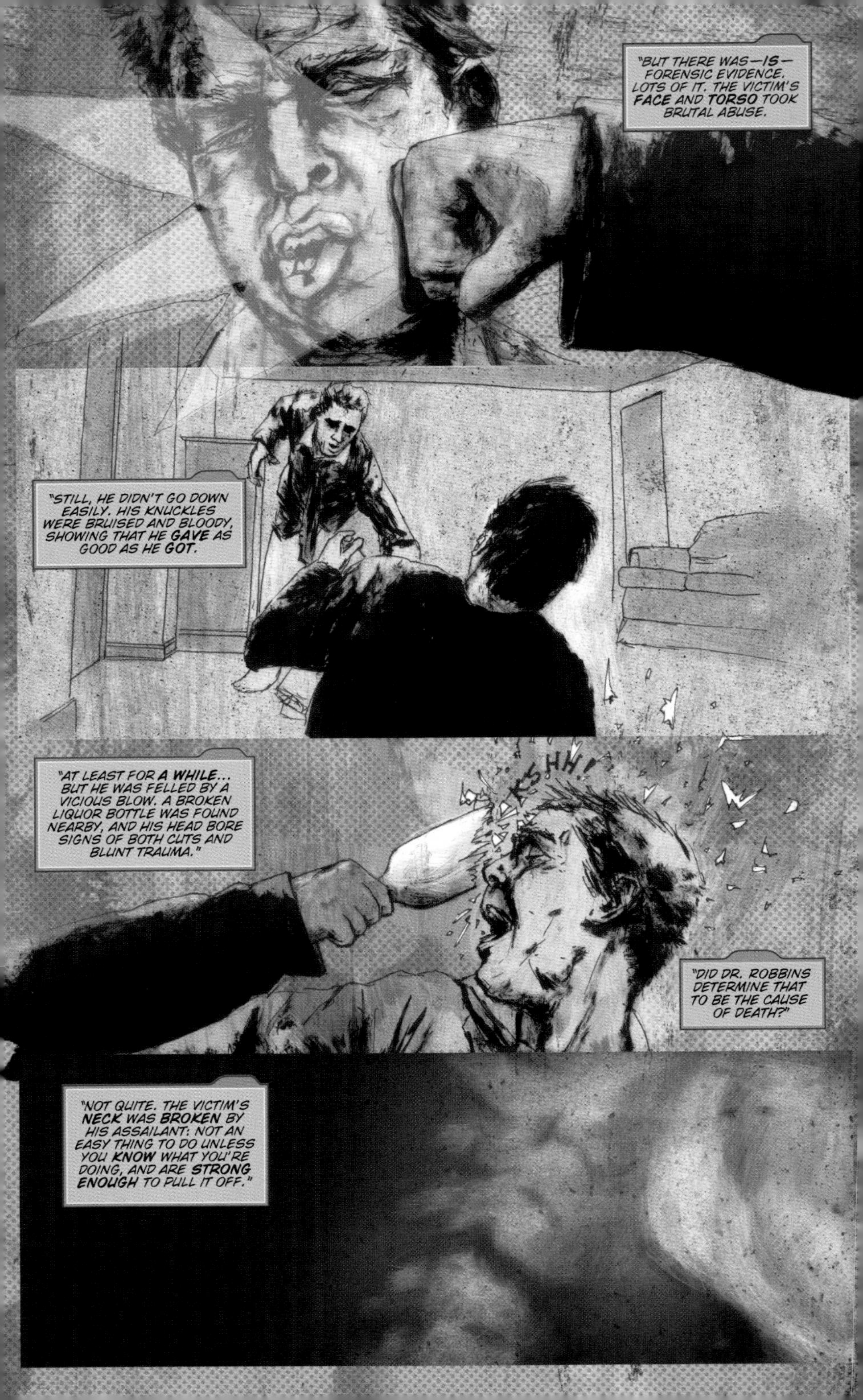
"BUT THERE WAS—IS—FORENSIC EVIDENCE. LOTS OF IT. THE VICTIM'S FACE AND TORSO TOOK BRUTAL ABUSE.
"STILL, HE DIDN'T GO DOWN EASILY. HIS KNUCKLES WERE BRUISED AND BLOODY, SHOWING THAT HE GAVE AS GOOD AS HE GOT.
"AT LEAST FOR A WHILE... BUT HE WAS FELLED BY A VICIOUS BLOW. A BROKEN LIQUOR BOTTLE WAS FOUND NEARBY, AND HIS HEAD BORE SIGNS OF BOTH CUTS AND BLUNT TRAUMA."
KSHH!
"DID DR. ROBBINS DETERMINE THAT TO BE THE CAUSE OF DEATH?"
"NOT QUITE. THE VICTIM'S NECK WAS BROKEN BY HIS ASSAILANT: NOT AN EASY THING TO DO UNLESS YOU KNOW WHAT YOU'RE DOING, AND ARE STRONG ENOUGH TO PULL IT OFF."

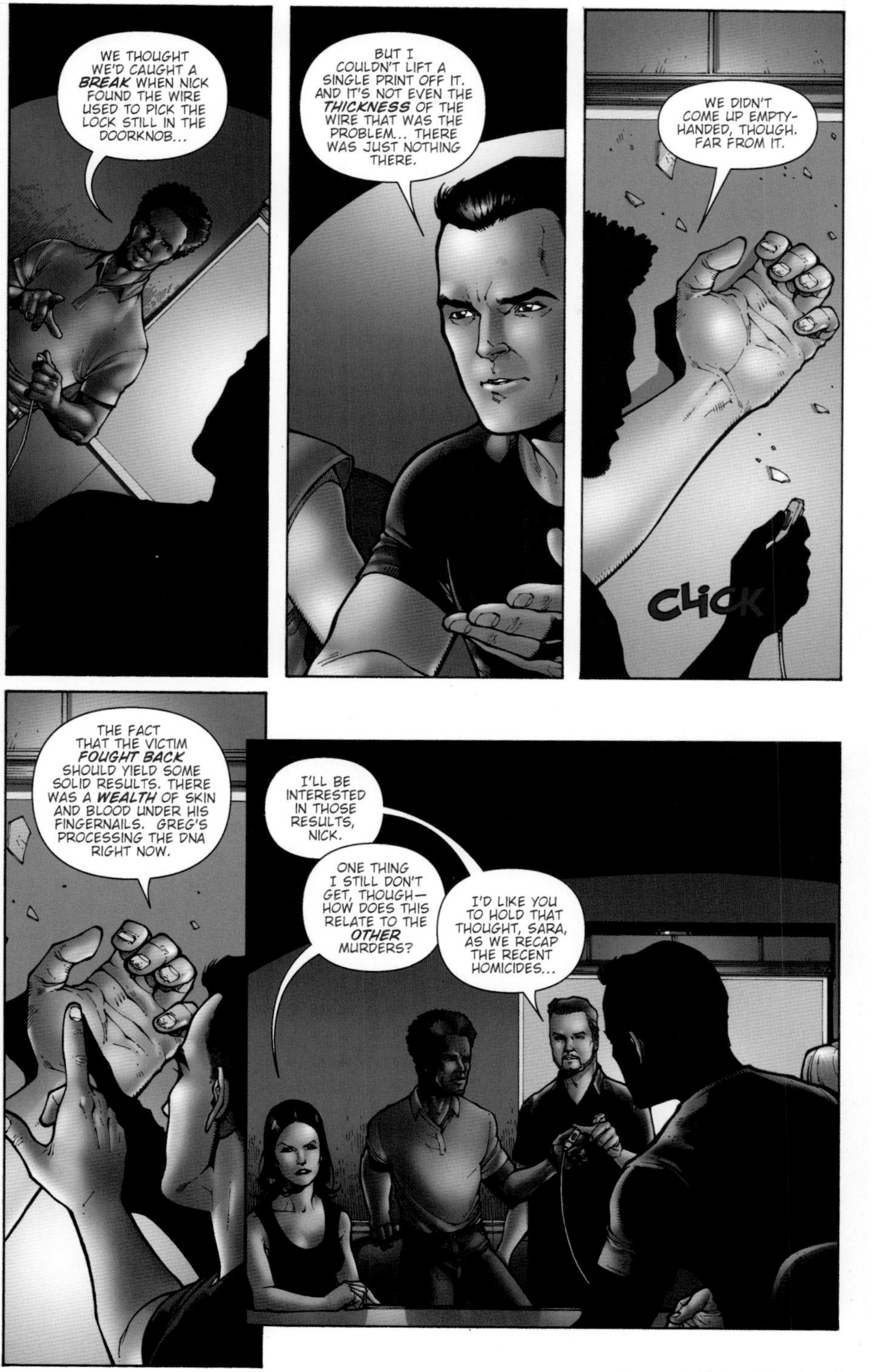
WE THOUGHT WE'D CAUGHT A BREAK WHEN NICK FOUND THE WIRE USED TO PICK THE LOCK STILL IN THE DOORKNOB...
BUT I COULDN'T LIFT A SINGLE PRINT OFF IT. AND IT'S NOT EVEN THE THICKNESS OF THE WIRE THAT WAS THE PROBLEM... THERE WAS JUST NOTHING THERE.
WE DIDN'T COME UP EMPTY-HANDED, THOUGH. FAR FROM IT.
CLICK
THE FACT THAT THE VICTIM FOUGHT BACK SHOULD YIELD SOME SOLID RESULTS. THERE WAS A WEALTH OF SKIN AND BLOOD UNDER HIS FINGERNAILS. GREG'S PROCESSING THE DNA RIGHT NOW.
I'LL BE INTERESTED IN THOSE RESULTS, NICK.
ONE THING I STILL DON'T GET, THOUGH—HOW DOES THIS RELATE TO THE OTHER MURDERS?
I'D LIKE YOU TO HOLD THAT THOUGHT, SARA, AS WE RECAP THE RECENT HOMICIDES...

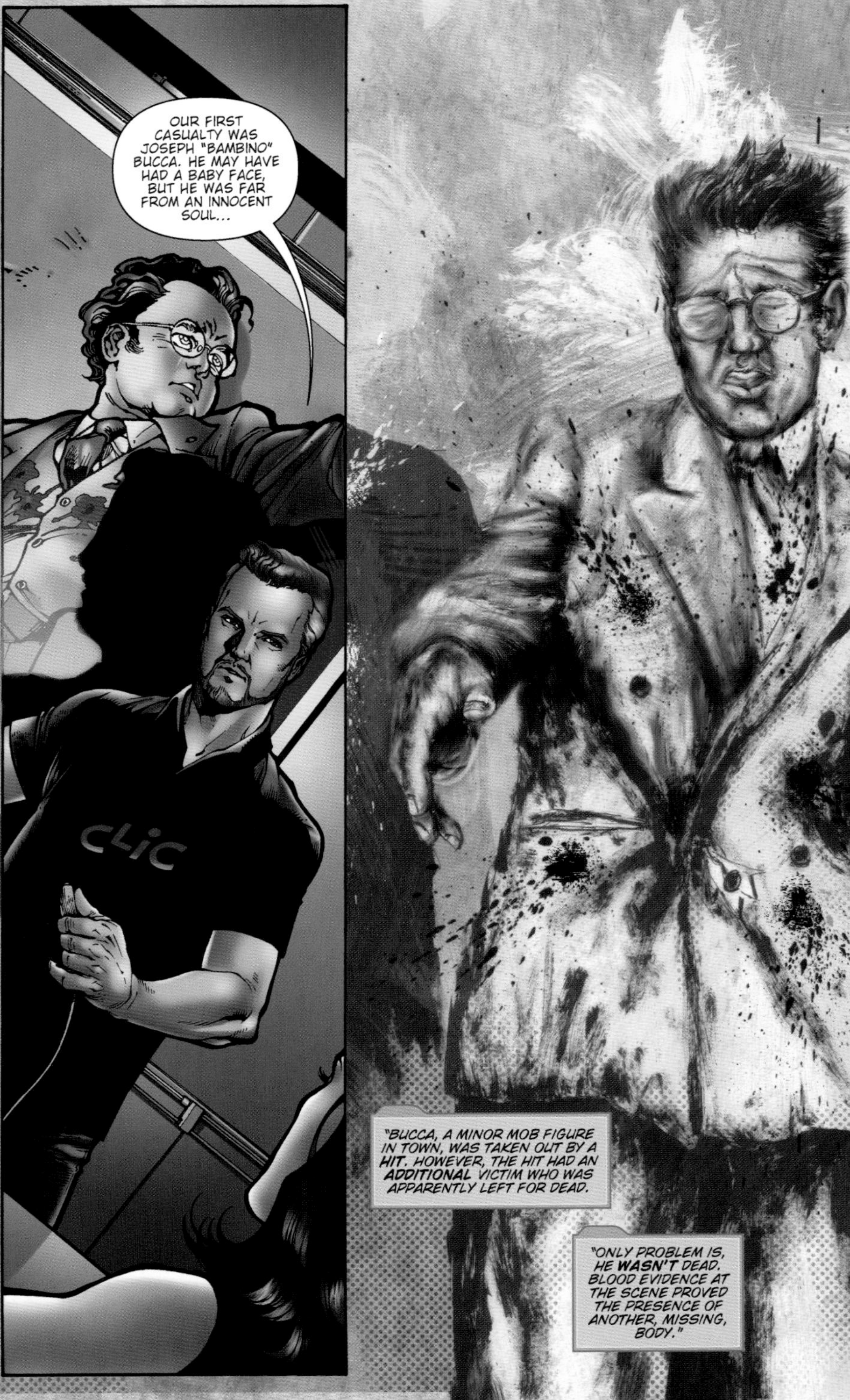
OUR FIRST CASUALTY WAS JOSEPH "BAMBINO" BUCCA. HE MAY HAVE HAD A BABY FACE, BUT HE WAS FAR FROM AN INNOCENT SOUL...
CLIC
"BUCCA, A MINOR MOB FIGURE IN TOWN, WAS TAKEN OUT BY A HIT. HOWEVER, THE HIT HAD AN ADDITIONAL VICTIM WHO WAS APPARENTLY LEFT FOR DEAD.
"ONLY PROBLEM IS, HE WASN'T DEAD. BLOOD EVIDENCE AT THE SCENE PROVED THE PRESENCE OF ANOTHER, MISSING, BODY."

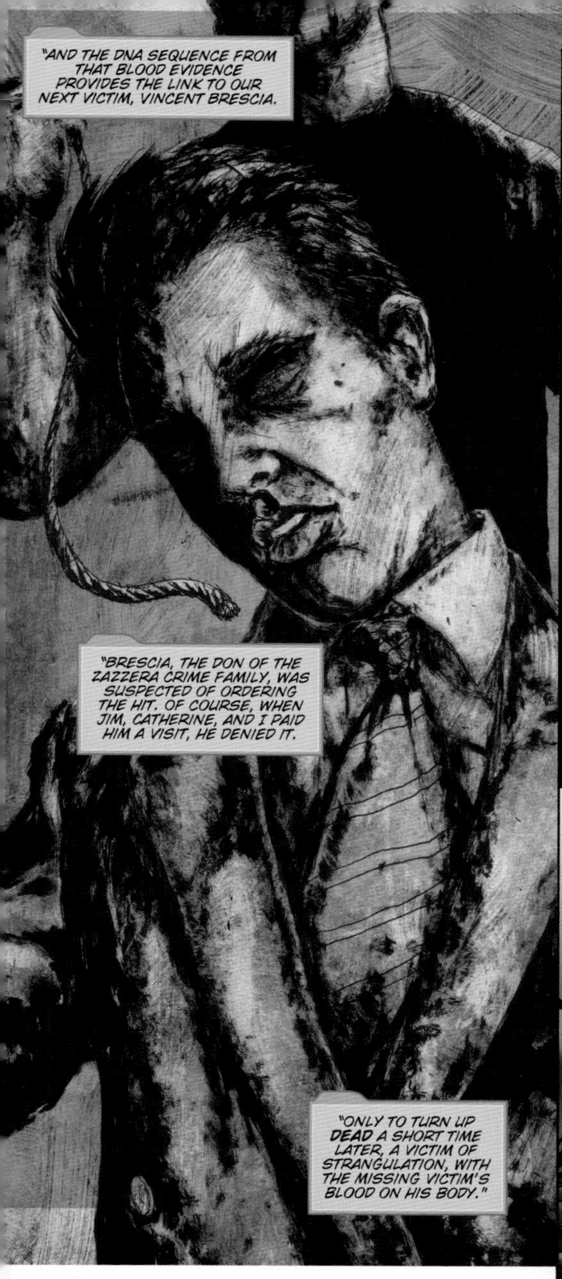
"AND THE DNA SEQUENCE FROM THAT BLOOD EVIDENCE PROVIDES THE LINK TO OUR NEXT VICTIM, VINCENT BRESCIA.
"BRESCIA, THE DON OF THE ZAZZERA CRIME FAMILY, WAS SUSPECTED OF ORDERING THE HIT. OF COURSE, WHEN JIM, CATHERINE, AND I PAID HIM A VISIT, HE DENIED IT.
"ONLY TO TURN UP DEAD A SHORT TIME LATER, A VICTIM OF STRANGULATION, WITH THE MISSING VICTIM'S BLOOD ON HIS BODY."

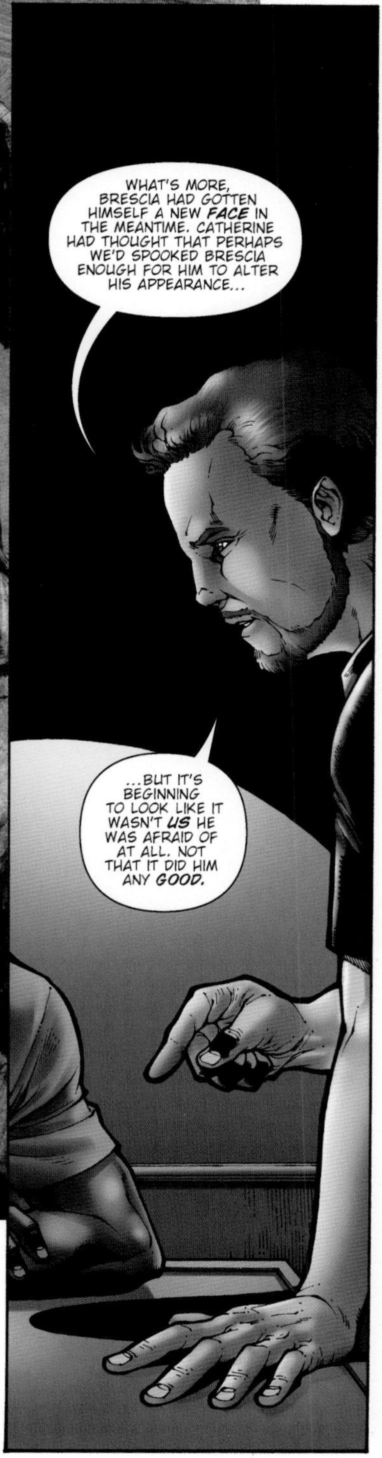
WHAT'S MORE, BRESCIA HAD GOTTEN HIMSELF A NEW FACE IN THE MEANTIME. CATHERINE HAD THOUGHT THAT PERHAPS WE'D SPOOKED BRESCIA ENOUGH FOR HIM TO ALTER HIS APPEARANCE...
...BUT IT'S BEGINNING TO LOOK LIKE IT WASN'T US HE WAS AFRAID OF AT ALL. NOT THAT IT DID HIM ANY GOOD.

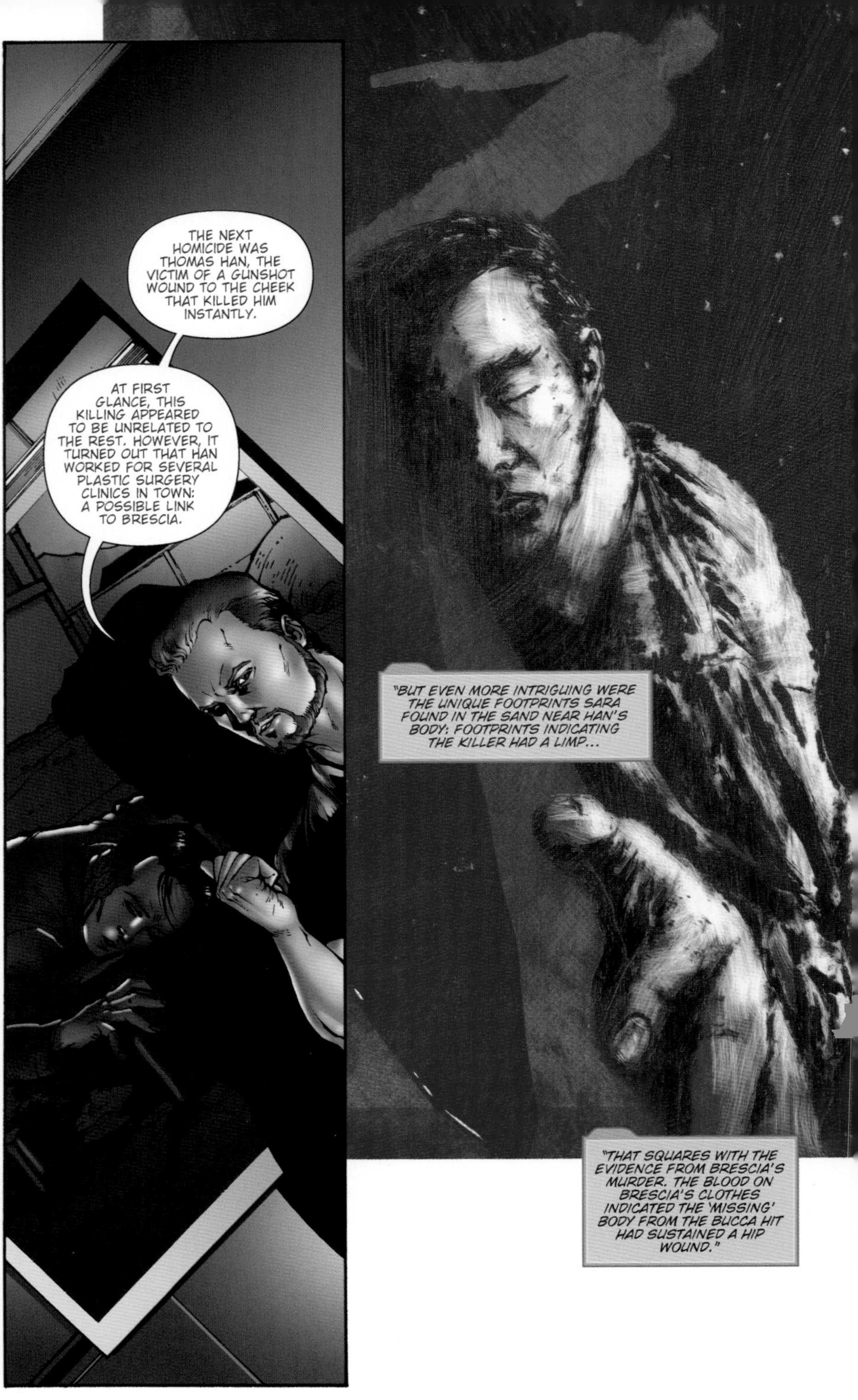
THE NEXT HOMICIDE WAS THOMAS HAN, THE VICTIM OF A GUNSHOT WOUND TO THE CHEEK THAT KILLED HIM INSTANTLY.
AT FIRST GLANCE, THIS KILLING APPEARED TO BE UNRELATED TO THE REST. HOWEVER, IT TURNED OUT THAT HAN WORKED FOR SEVERAL PLASTIC SURGERY CLINICS IN TOWN: A POSSIBLE LINK TO BRESCIA.
"BUT EVEN MORE INTRIGUING WERE THE UNIQUE FOOTPRINTS SARA FOUND IN THE SAND NEAR HAN'S BODY: FOOTPRINTS INDICATING THE KILLER HAD A LIMP...
"THAT SQUARES WITH THE EVIDENCE FROM BRESCIA'S MURDER. THE BLOOD ON BRESCIA'S CLOTHES INDICATED THE 'MISSING' BODY FROM THE BUCCA HIT HAD SUSTAINED A HIP WOUND."

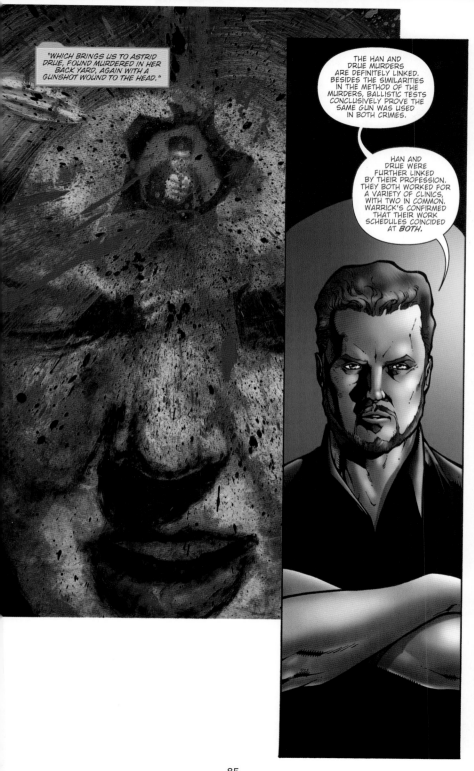

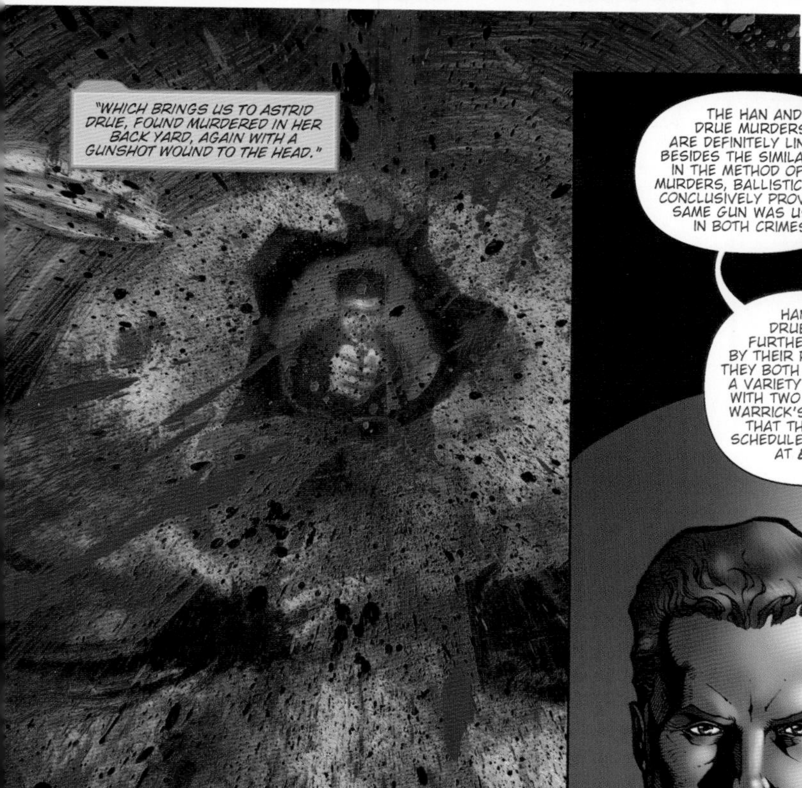
"WHICH BRINGS US TO ASTRID DRUE, FOUND MURDERED IN HER BACK YARD, AGAIN WITH A GUNSHOT WOUND TO THE HEAD."

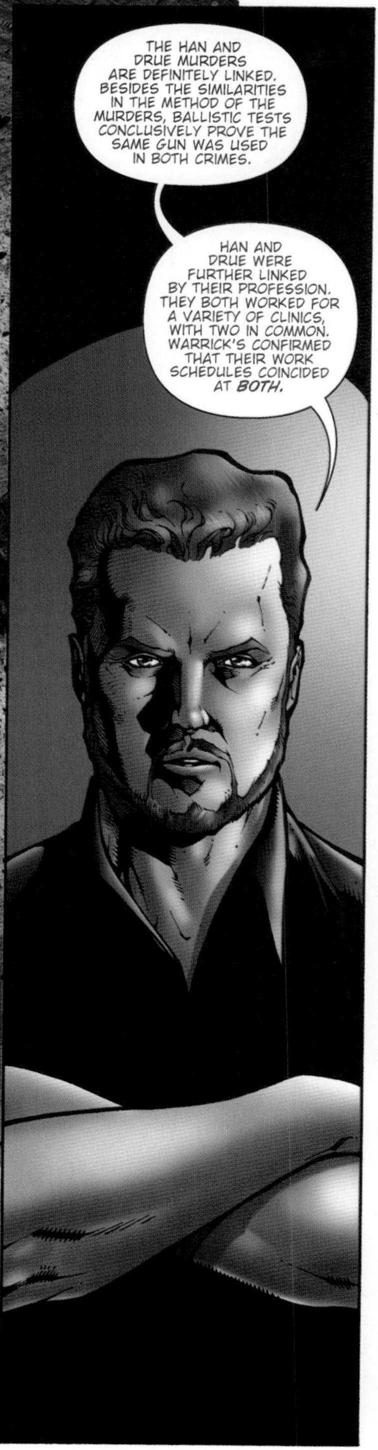
THE HAN AND DRUE MURDERS ARE DEFINITELY LINKED. BESIDES THE SIMILARITIES IN THE METHOD OF THE MURDERS, BALLISTIC TESTS CONCLUSIVELY PROVE THE SAME GUN WAS USED IN BOTH CRIMES.
HAN AND DRUE WERE FURTHER LINKED BY THEIR PROFESSION. THEY BOTH WORKED FOR A VARIETY OF CLINICS, WITH TWO IN COMMON. WARRICK'S CONFIRMED THAT THEIR WORK SCHEDULES COINCIDED AT *BOTH*.

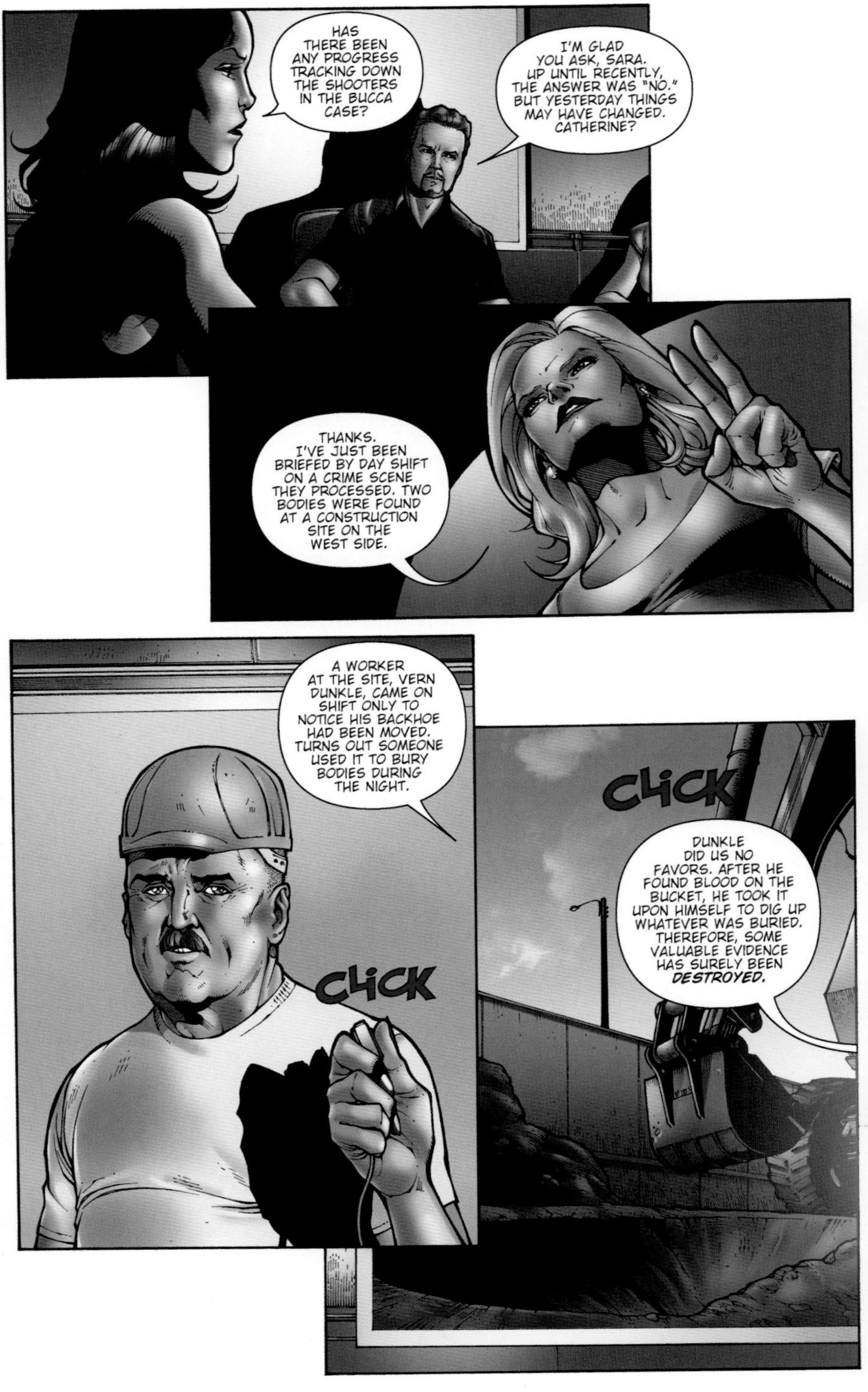
HAS THERE BEEN ANY PROGRESS TRACKING DOWN THE SHOOTERS IN THE BUCCA CASE?
I'M GLAD YOU ASK, SARA. UP UNTIL RECENTLY, THE ANSWER WAS "NO." BUT YESTERDAY THINGS MAY HAVE CHANGED. CATHERINE?
THANKS. I'VE JUST BEEN BRIEFED BY DAY SHIFT ON A CRIME SCENE THEY PROCESSED. TWO BODIES WERE FOUND AT A CONSTRUCTION SITE ON THE WEST SIDE.
A WORKER AT THE SITE, VERN DUNKLE, CAME ON SHIFT ONLY TO NOTICE HIS BACKHOE HAD BEEN MOVED. TURNS OUT SOMEONE USED IT TO BURY BODIES DURING THE NIGHT.
CLICK
CLICK
DUNKLE DID US NO FAVORS. AFTER HE FOUND BLOOD ON THE BUCKET, HE TOOK IT UPON HIMSELF TO DIG UP WHATEVER WAS BURIED. THEREFORE, SOME VALUABLE EVIDENCE HAS SURELY BEEN ***DESTROYED.***

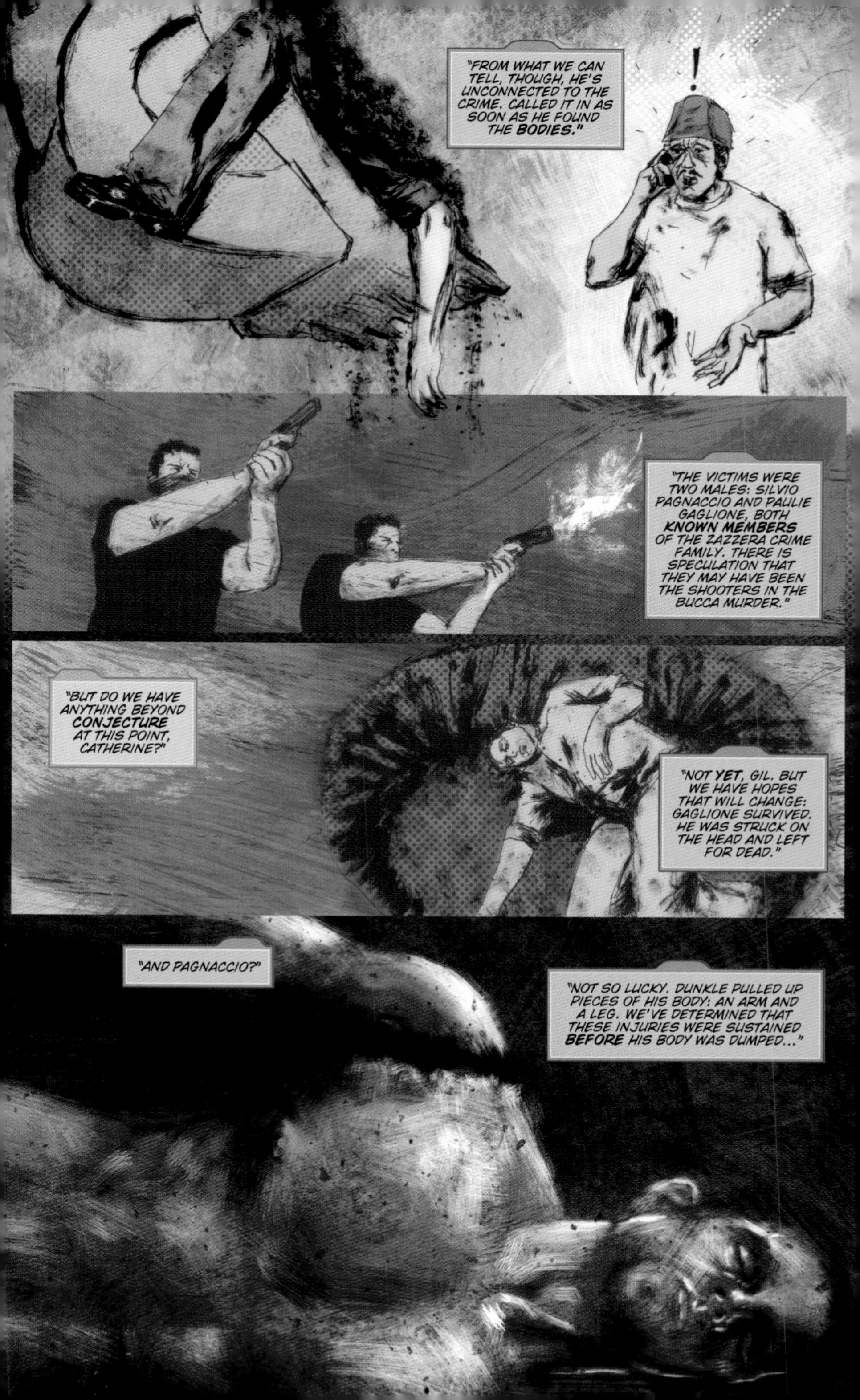
"FROM WHAT WE CAN TELL, THOUGH, HE'S UNCONNECTED TO THE CRIME. CALLED IT IN AS SOON AS HE FOUND THE BODIES."
!
"THE VICTIMS WERE TWO MALES: SILVIO PAGNACCIO AND PAULIE GAGLIONE, BOTH KNOWN MEMBERS OF THE ZAZZERA CRIME FAMILY. THERE IS SPECULATION THAT THEY MAY HAVE BEEN THE SHOOTERS IN THE BUCCA MURDER."
"BUT DO WE HAVE ANYTHING BEYOND CONJECTURE AT THIS POINT, CATHERINE?"
"NOT YET, GIL. BUT WE HAVE HOPES THAT WILL CHANGE: GAGLIONE SURVIVED. HE WAS STRUCK ON THE HEAD AND LEFT FOR DEAD."
"AND PAGNACCIO?"
"NOT SO LUCKY. DUNKLE PULLED UP PIECES OF HIS BODY: AN ARM AND A LEG. WE'VE DETERMINED THAT THESE INJURIES WERE SUSTAINED BEFORE HIS BODY WAS DUMPED..."

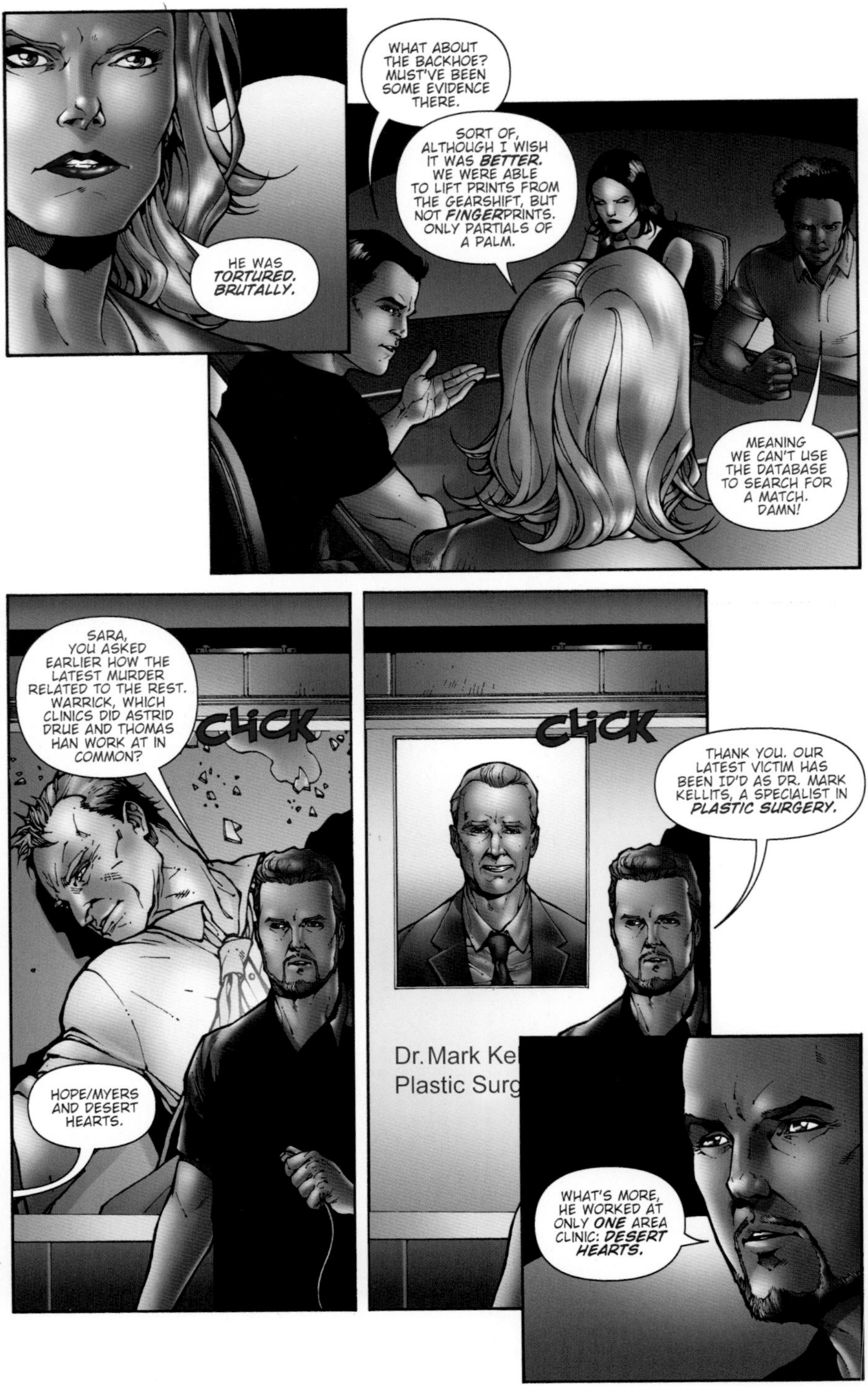
WHAT ABOUT THE BACKHOE? MUST'VE BEEN SOME EVIDENCE THERE.
HE WAS TORTURED. BRUTALLY.
SORT OF, ALTHOUGH I WISH IT WAS BETTER. WE WERE ABLE TO LIFT PRINTS FROM THE GEARSHIFT, BUT NOT FINGERPRINTS. ONLY PARTIALS OF A PALM.
MEANING WE CAN'T USE THE DATABASE TO SEARCH FOR A MATCH. DAMN!
SARA, YOU ASKED EARLIER HOW THE LATEST MURDER RELATED TO THE REST. WARRICK, WHICH CLINICS DID ASTRID DRUE AND THOMAS HAN WORK AT IN COMMON?
CLICK
HOPE/MYERS AND DESERT HEARTS.
CLICK
THANK YOU. OUR LATEST VICTIM HAS BEEN ID'D AS DR. MARK KELLITS, A SPECIALIST IN PLASTIC SURGERY.
Dr. Mark Kel
Plastic Surg
WHAT'S MORE, HE WORKED AT ONLY ONE AREA CLINIC: DESERT HEARTS.

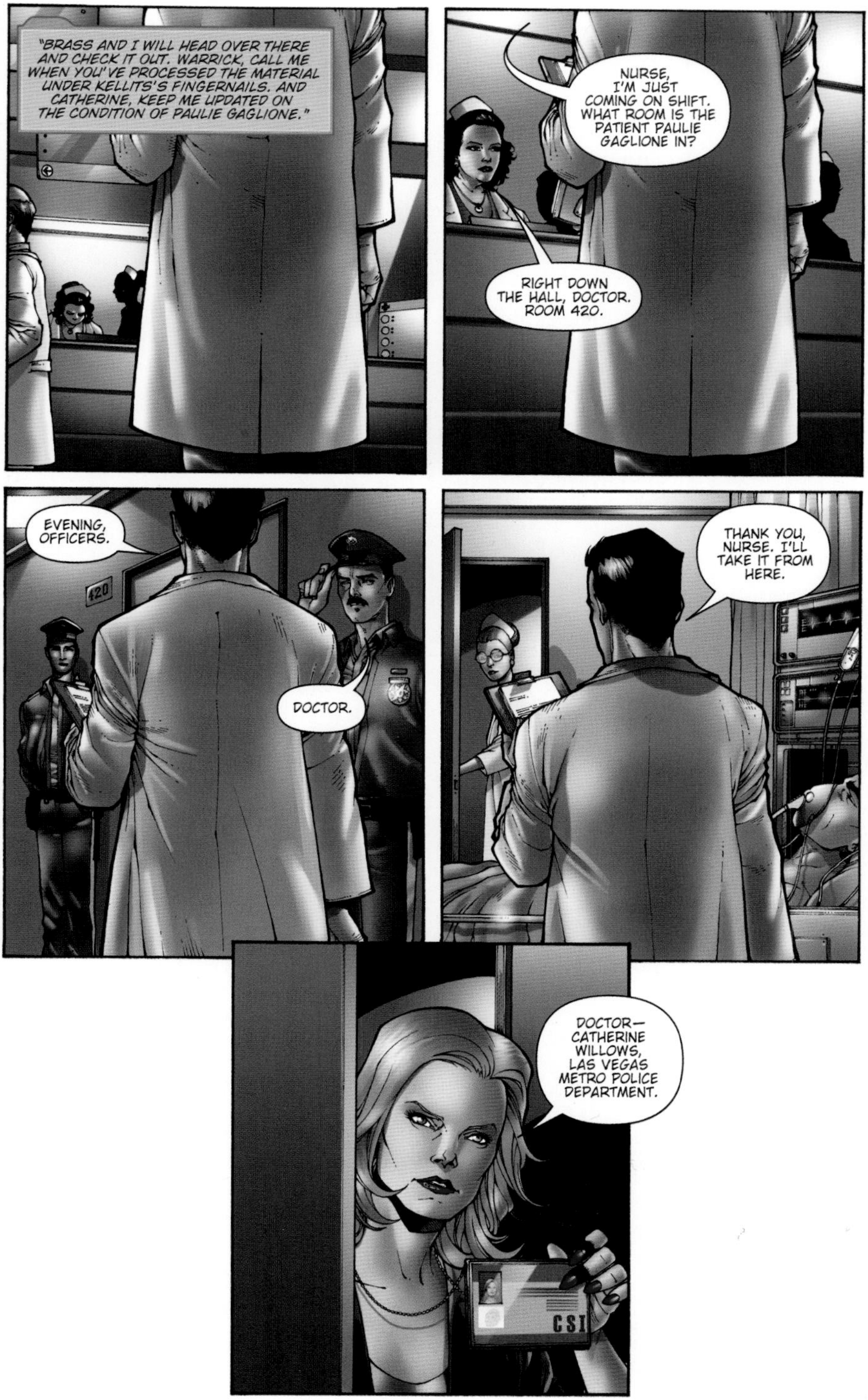
"BRASS AND I WILL HEAD OVER THERE AND CHECK IT OUT. WARRICK, CALL ME WHEN YOU'VE PROCESSED THE MATERIAL UNDER KELLITS'S FINGERNAILS. AND CATHERINE, KEEP ME UPDATED ON THE CONDITION OF PAULIE GAGLIONE."
NURSE, I'M JUST COMING ON SHIFT. WHAT ROOM IS THE PATIENT PAULIE GAGLIONE IN?
RIGHT DOWN THE HALL, DOCTOR. ROOM 420.
EVENING, OFFICERS.
420
DOCTOR.
THANK YOU, NURSE. I'LL TAKE IT FROM HERE.
DOCTOR— CATHERINE WILLOWS, LAS VEGAS METRO POLICE DEPARTMENT.
CSI

PLEASED TO MEET YOU. MR. GAGLIONE'S YOUR CASE?

THAT'S RIGHT. ANY CHANGE IN HIS CONDITION?

NOT YET. HIS VITAL SIGNS ARE *STEADY*, BUT THERE'S NO BRAIN ACTIVITY TO SPEAK OF. HE'S STILL IN A *DEEP COMA.*

WELL, I'VE GOT ROUNDS TO MAKE. BEST OF LUCK!

C'MON, PAULIE. YOU'VE GOT TO WAKE UP. WHAT DO YOU *KNOW?*

DAMN!

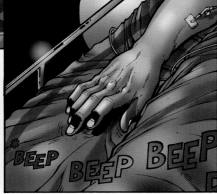

BEEP BEEP BEEP

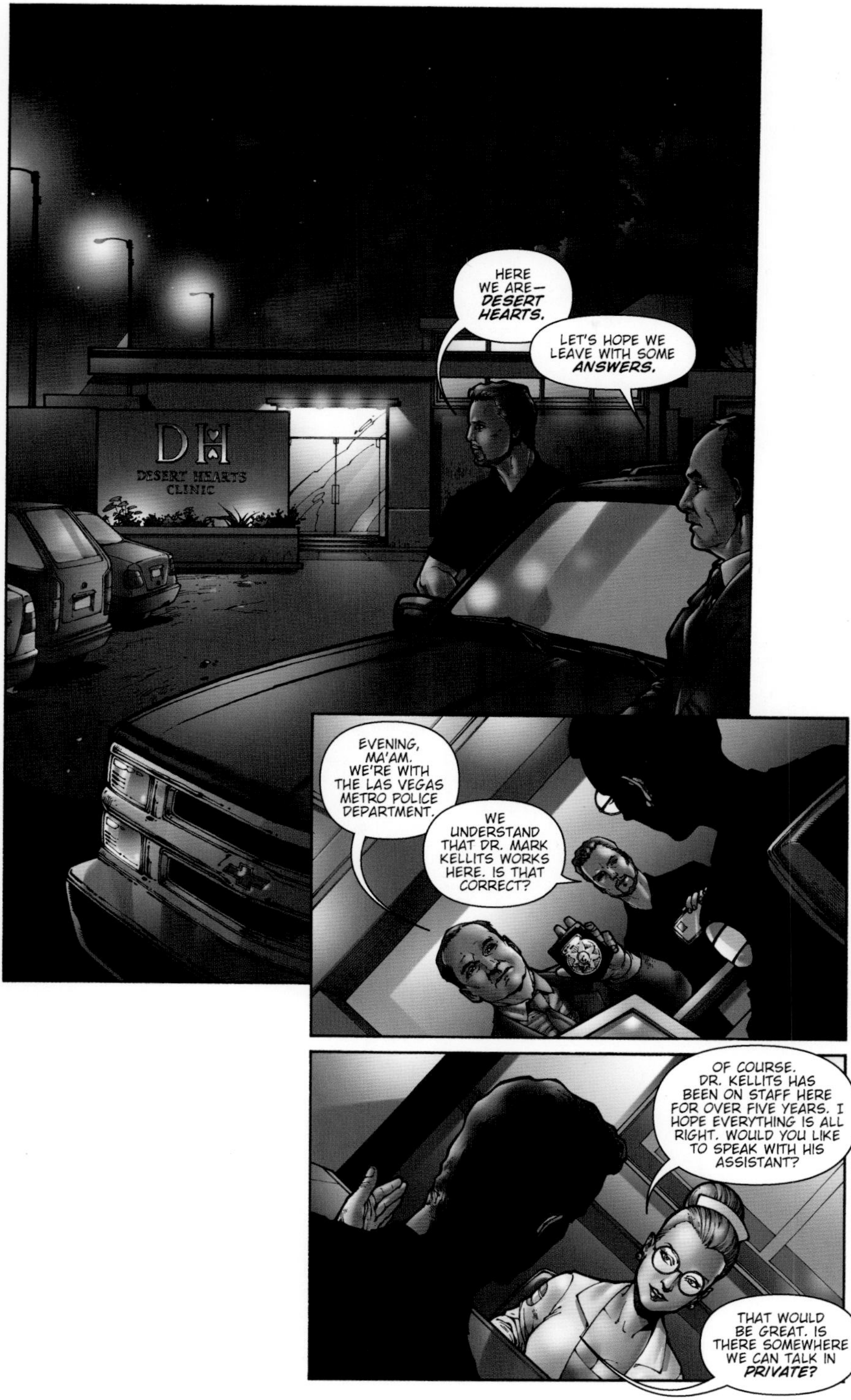
HERE WE ARE—*DESERT HEARTS.*
LET'S HOPE WE LEAVE WITH SOME *ANSWERS.*
DH
DESERT HEARTS CLINIC
EVENING, MA'AM. WE'RE WITH THE LAS VEGAS METRO POLICE DEPARTMENT.
WE UNDERSTAND THAT DR. MARK KELLITS WORKS HERE. IS THAT CORRECT?
OF COURSE. DR. KELLITS HAS BEEN ON STAFF HERE FOR OVER FIVE YEARS. I HOPE EVERYTHING IS ALL RIGHT. WOULD YOU LIKE TO SPEAK WITH HIS ASSISTANT?
THAT WOULD BE GREAT. IS THERE SOMEWHERE WE CAN TALK IN *PRIVATE?*

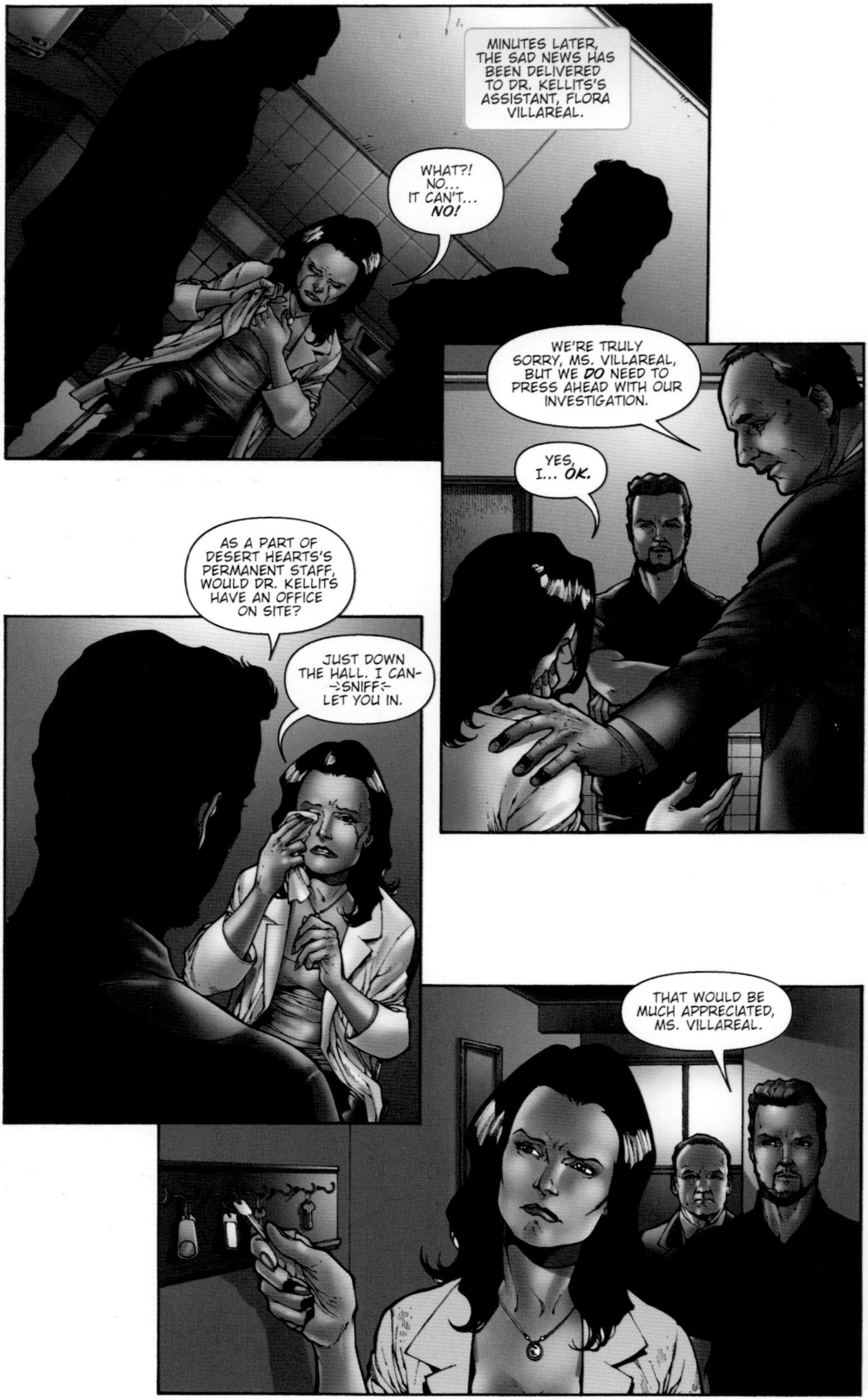
MINUTES LATER, THE SAD NEWS HAS BEEN DELIVERED TO DR. KELLITS'S ASSISTANT, FLORA VILLAREAL.
WHAT?! NO... IT CAN'T... NO!
WE'RE TRULY SORRY, MS. VILLAREAL, BUT WE DO NEED TO PRESS AHEAD WITH OUR INVESTIGATION.
YES, I... OK.
AS A PART OF DESERT HEARTS'S PERMANENT STAFF, WOULD DR. KELLITS HAVE AN OFFICE ON SITE?
JUST DOWN THE HALL. I CAN- -SNIFF- LET YOU IN.
THAT WOULD BE MUCH APPRECIATED, MS. VILLAREAL.

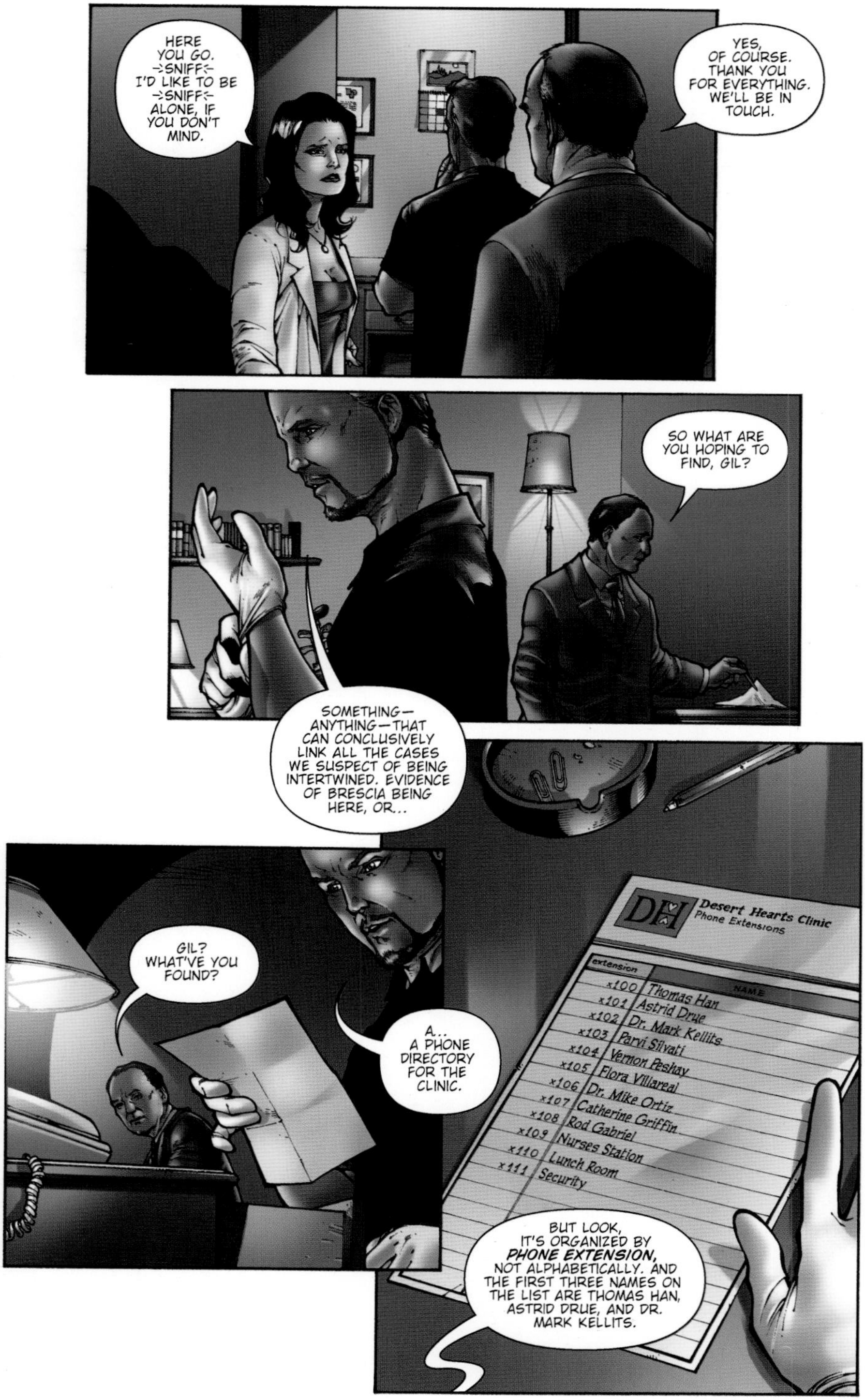
HERE YOU GO. SNIFF I'D LIKE TO BE SNIFF ALONE, IF YOU DON'T MIND.
YES, OF COURSE. THANK YOU FOR EVERYTHING. WE'LL BE IN TOUCH.
SO WHAT ARE YOU HOPING TO FIND, GIL?
SOMETHING—ANYTHING—THAT CAN CONCLUSIVELY LINK ALL THE CASES WE SUSPECT OF BEING INTERTWINED. EVIDENCE OF BRESCIA BEING HERE, OR...
GIL? WHAT'VE YOU FOUND?
A... A PHONE DIRECTORY FOR THE CLINIC.
DH
Desert Hearts Clinic
Phone Extensions
extension
NAME
x100 Thomas Han
x101 Astrid Drue
x102 Dr. Mark Kellits
x103 Parvi Silvati
x104 Vernon Peshay
x105 Flora Villareal
x106 Dr. Mike Ortiz
x107 Catherine Griffin
x108 Rod Gabriel
x109 Nurses Station
x110 Lunch Room
x111 Security
BUT LOOK, IT'S ORGANIZED BY ***PHONE EXTENSION,*** NOT ALPHABETICALLY. AND THE FIRST THREE NAMES ON THE LIST ARE THOMAS HAN, ASTRID DRUE, AND DR. MARK KELLITS.

"MY GOD... DO WE HAVE A **SERIAL KILLER** ON OUR HANDS HERE?"

Desert Hearts Clinic
Phone Extensions

extension	NAME
x100	Thomas Hun
x101	Astrid Dove
x102	Dr. Mark Keihs
x103	Parvi Silvati
x104	Vernon Peshay
x105	Flora Villarreal
x106	Dr. Mike Ortiz
x107	Catherine Griffin
x108	Rod Gabriel
x109	Nurses Station
x110	Lunch Room
x111	Security

BUT WE STILL CAN'T TIE THESE "DESERT HEARTS" MURDERS WITH VINCENT BRESCIA, GIL.

I KNOW, I KNOW. WE NEED **HARD** EVIDENCE THAT HE WAS HERE.

EXCUSE ME, MA'AM, BUT I NEED TO KNOW IF IT IS CLINIC POLICY TO RETAIN TISSUE SPECIMENS FROM CLIENTS YOU'VE TREATED HERE.

TISSUE SPECIMENS?

NO, OF COURSE NOT. ALL BIOLOGICAL MATERIAL IS DISPOSED OF AFTER EACH PROCEDURE.

I THOUGHT AS MUCH, BUT I HAD TO ASK. THANK YOU FOR ALL YOUR HELP.

NO LUCK THERE, GIL, BUT WE'RE REALLY ON TO SOMETHING NOW.

YES. I'LL SEE IF WARRICK AND NICK HAVE ANY NEWS.

YOU FOUND *WHAT?!* YEAH, I UNDERSTAND THE URGENCY! I'LL CALL YOU BACK THE SECOND I KNOW SOMETHING.

WARRICK FILLS NICK IN ON THE DESERT HEARTS PHONE LIST, ADDING TO THEIR HASTE IN PROCESSING THE MATERIAL FOUND UNDER DR. KELLITS'S FINGERNAILS.

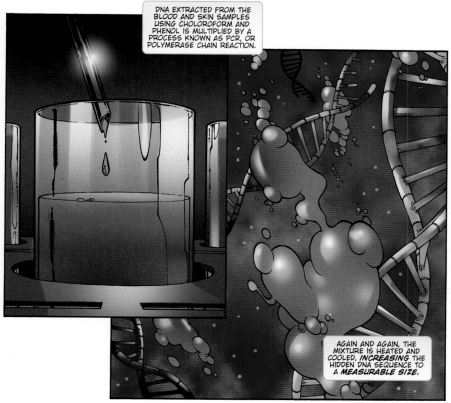

DNA EXTRACTED FROM THE BLOOD AND SKIN SAMPLES USING CHOLOROFORM AND PHENOL IS MULTIPLIED BY A PROCESS KNOWN AS PCR, OR POLYMERASE CHAIN REACTION.

AGAIN AND AGAIN, THE MIXTURE IS HEATED AND COOLED, *INCREASING* THE HIDDEN DNA SEQUENCE TO A *MEASURABLE SIZE.*

95

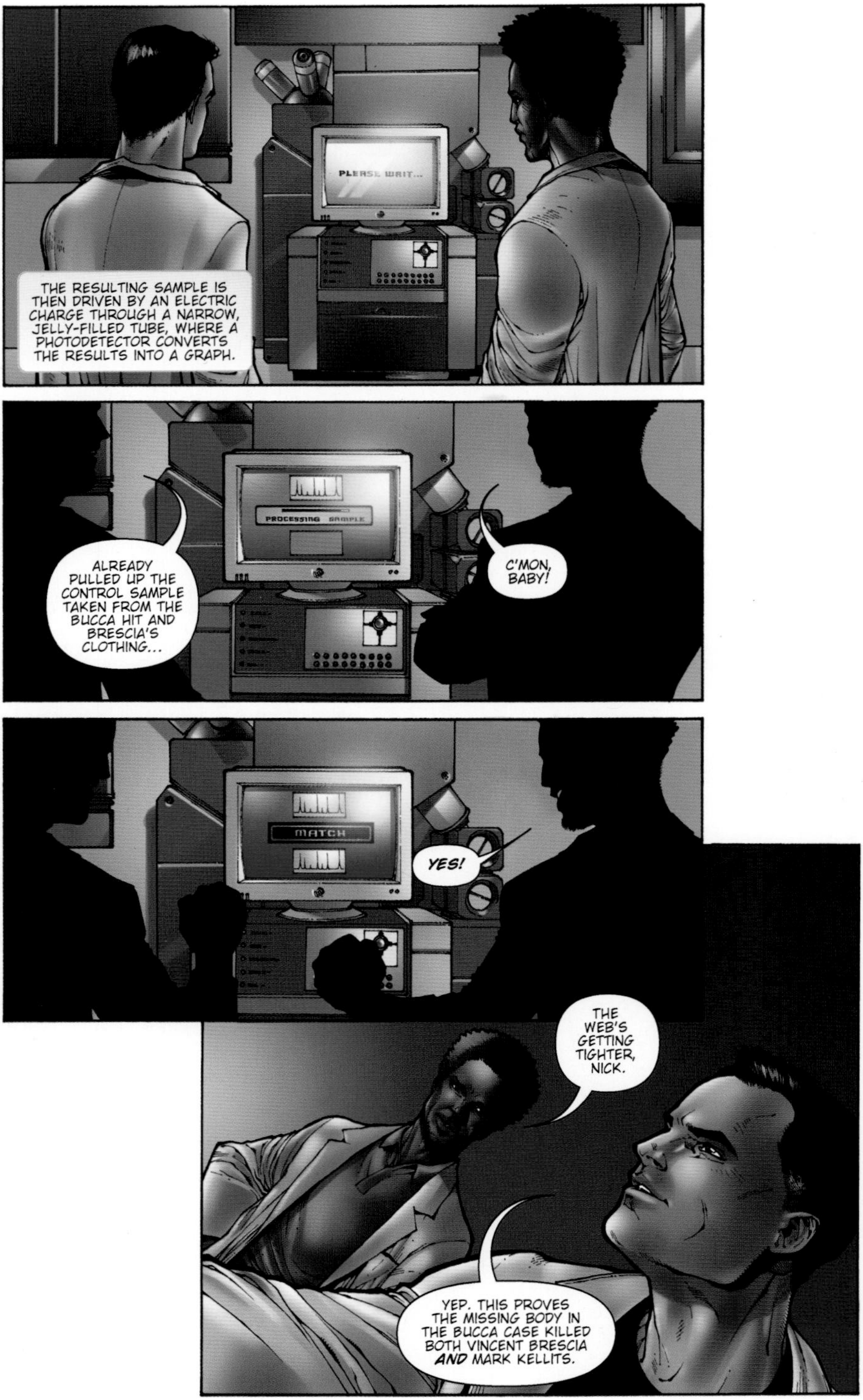

THE RESULTING SAMPLE IS THEN DRIVEN BY AN ELECTRIC CHARGE THROUGH A NARROW, JELLY-FILLED TUBE, WHERE A PHOTODETECTOR CONVERTS THE RESULTS INTO A GRAPH.
PLEASE WAIT...
PROCESSING SAMPLE
ALREADY PULLED UP THE CONTROL SAMPLE TAKEN FROM THE BUCCA HIT AND BRESCIA'S CLOTHING...
C'MON, BABY!
MATCH
YES!
THE WEB'S GETTING TIGHTER, NICK.
YEP. THIS PROVES THE MISSING BODY IN THE BUCCA CASE KILLED BOTH VINCENT BRESCIA ***AND*** MARK KELLITS.

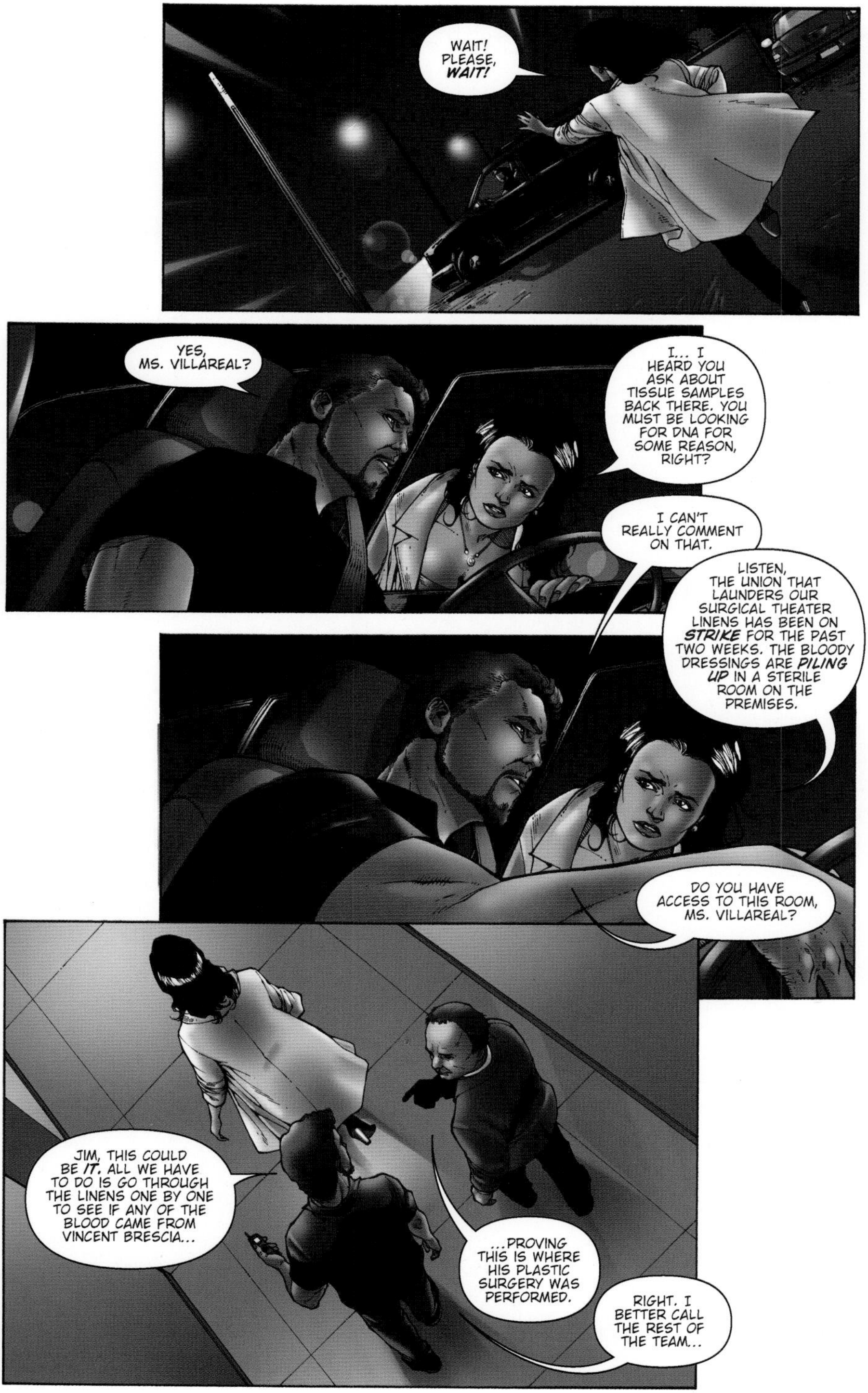
WAIT! PLEASE, WAIT!
YES, MS. VILLAREAL?
I... I HEARD YOU ASK ABOUT TISSUE SAMPLES BACK THERE. YOU MUST BE LOOKING FOR DNA FOR SOME REASON, RIGHT?
I CAN'T REALLY COMMENT ON THAT.
LISTEN, THE UNION THAT LAUNDERS OUR SURGICAL THEATER LINENS HAS BEEN ON STRIKE FOR THE PAST TWO WEEKS. THE BLOODY DRESSINGS ARE PILING UP IN A STERILE ROOM ON THE PREMISES.
DO YOU HAVE ACCESS TO THIS ROOM, MS. VILLAREAL?
JIM, THIS COULD BE IT. ALL WE HAVE TO DO IS GO THROUGH THE LINENS ONE BY ONE TO SEE IF ANY OF THE BLOOD CAME FROM VINCENT BRESCIA...
...PROVING THIS IS WHERE HIS PLASTIC SURGERY WAS PERFORMED.
RIGHT. I BETTER CALL THE REST OF THE TEAM...

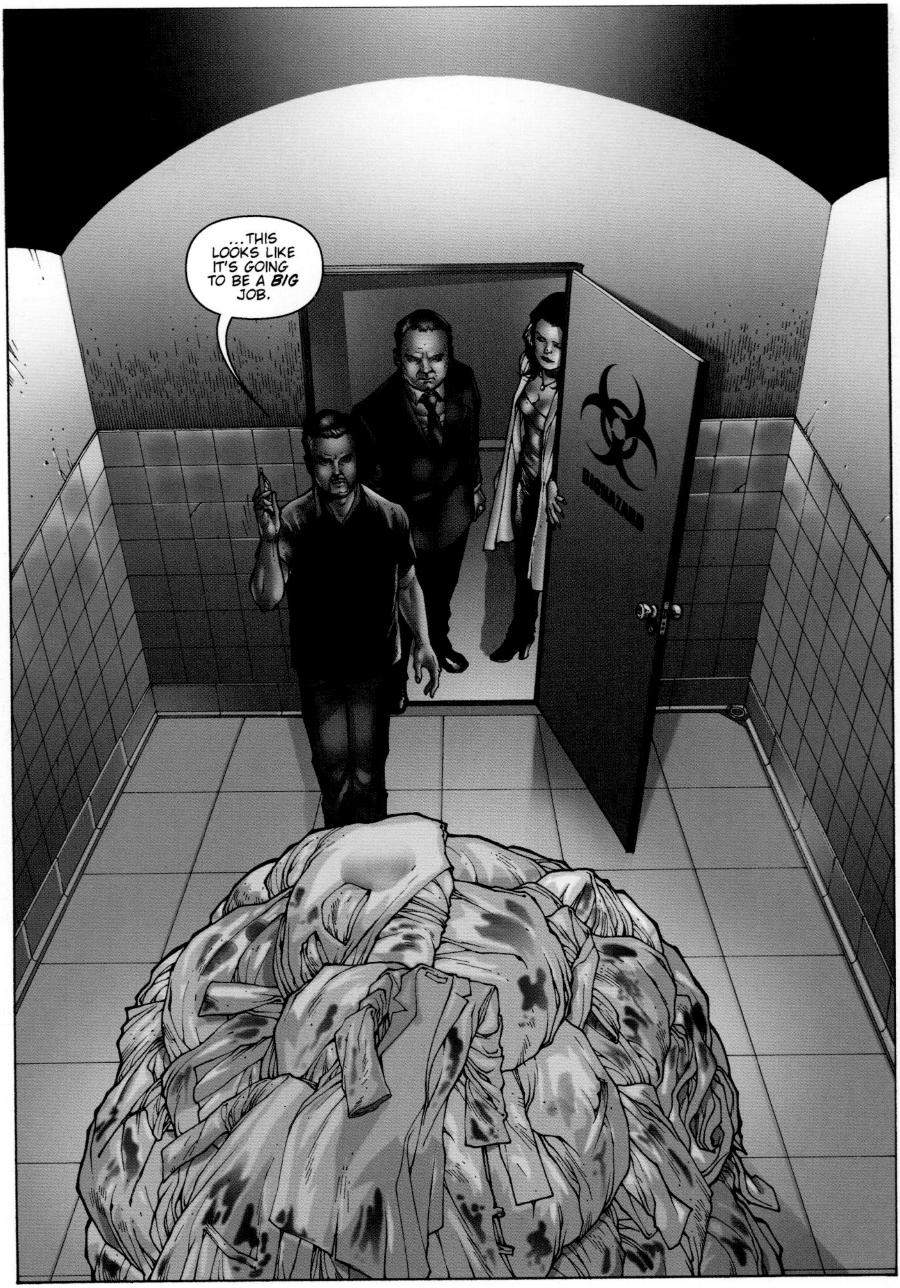
...THIS LOOKS LIKE IT'S GOING TO BE A *BIG* JOB.
BIOHAZARD

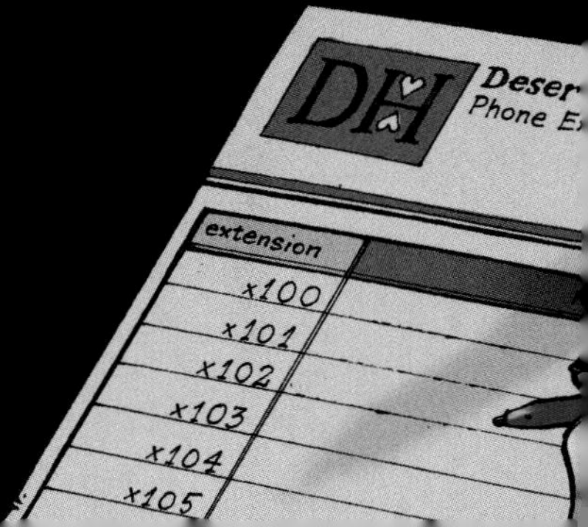
extension
x100
x101
x102
x103
x104
x105

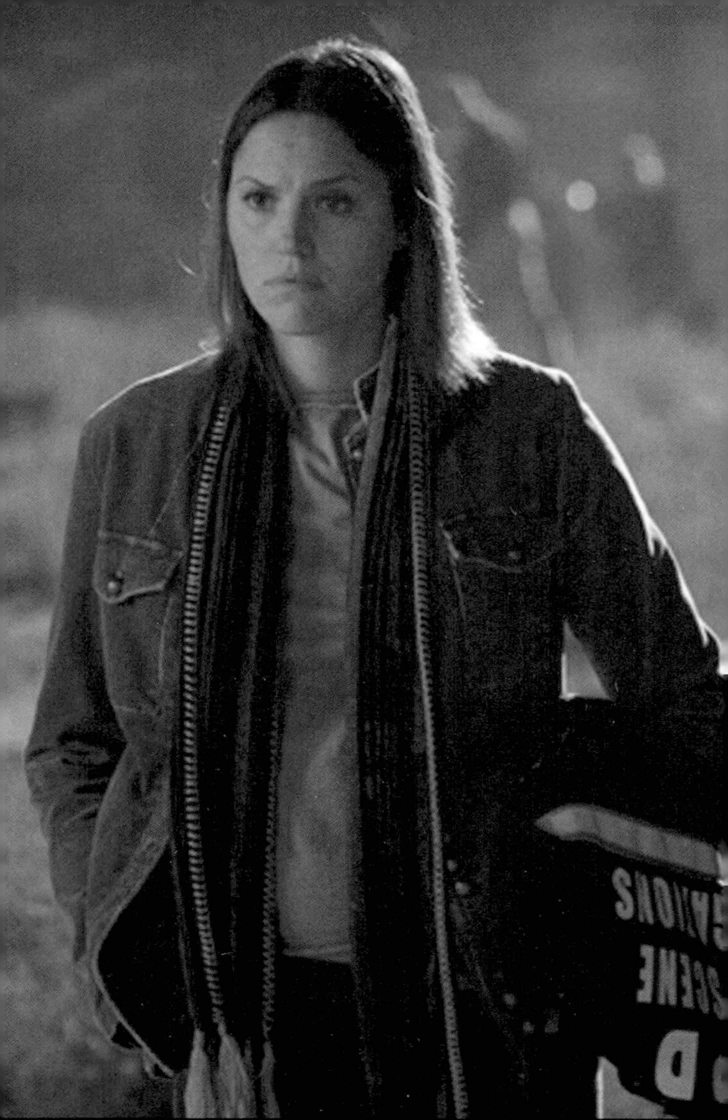

Chapter Five

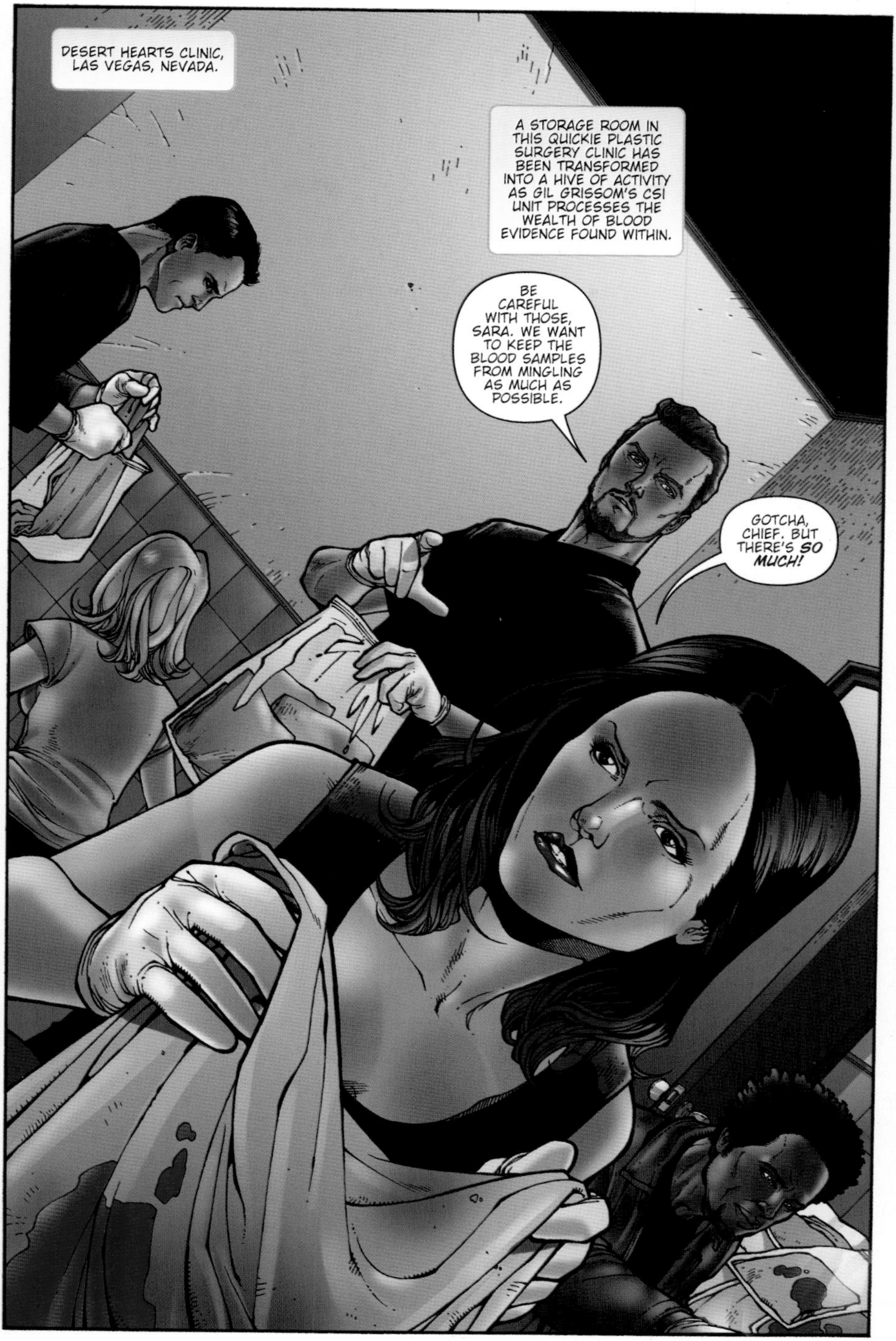
DESERT HEARTS CLINIC, LAS VEGAS, NEVADA.
A STORAGE ROOM IN THIS QUICKIE PLASTIC SURGERY CLINIC HAS BEEN TRANSFORMED INTO A HIVE OF ACTIVITY AS GIL GRISSOM'S CSI UNIT PROCESSES THE WEALTH OF BLOOD EVIDENCE FOUND WITHIN.
BE CAREFUL WITH THOSE, SARA. WE WANT TO KEEP THE BLOOD SAMPLES FROM MINGLING AS MUCH AS POSSIBLE.
GOTCHA, CHIEF. BUT THERE'S ***SO MUCH!***

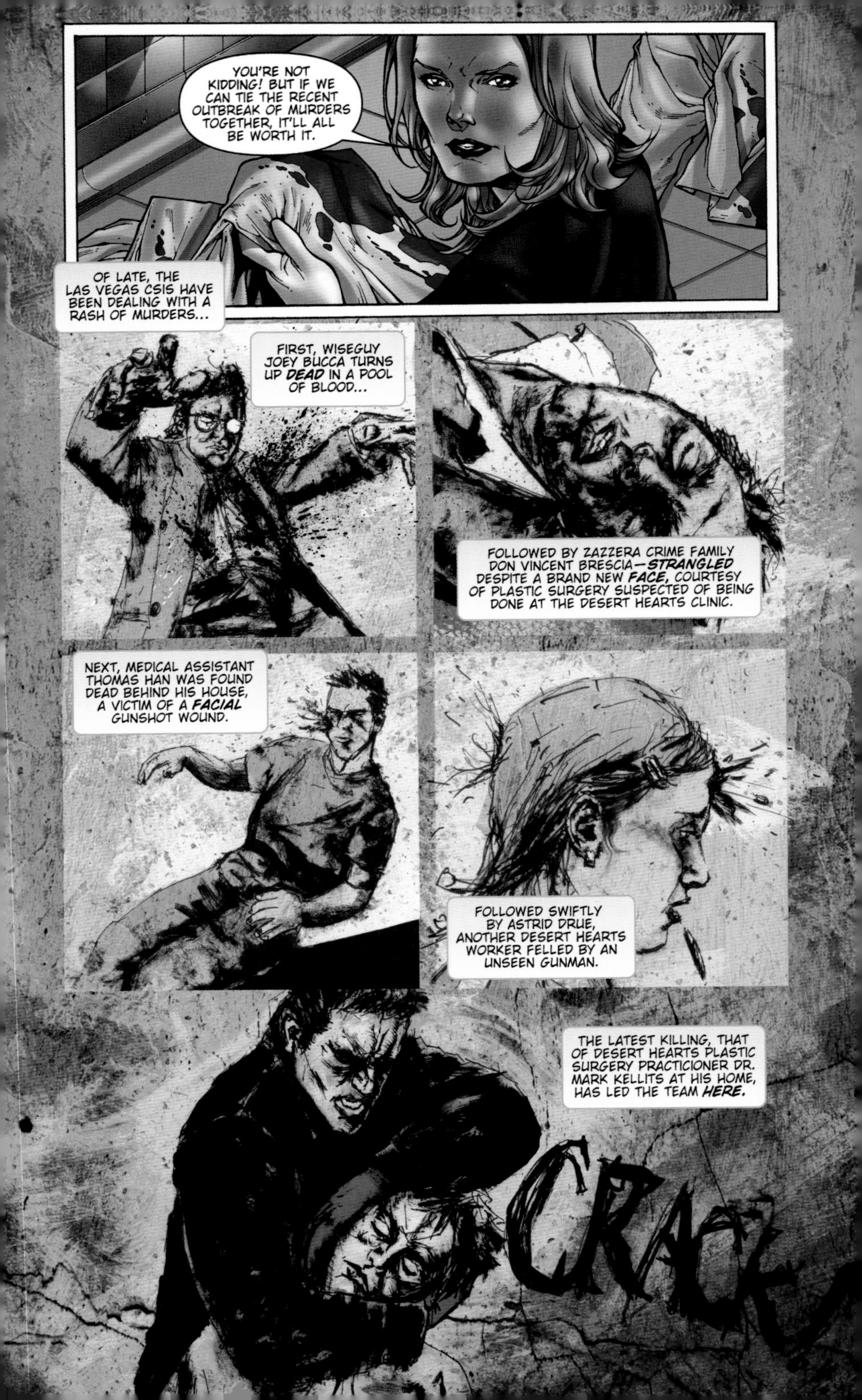
YOU'RE NOT KIDDING! BUT IF WE CAN TIE THE RECENT OUTBREAK OF MURDERS TOGETHER, IT'LL ALL BE WORTH IT.
OF LATE, THE LAS VEGAS CSIS HAVE BEEN DEALING WITH A RASH OF MURDERS...
FIRST, WISEGUY JOEY BUCCA TURNS UP DEAD IN A POOL OF BLOOD...
FOLLOWED BY ZAZZERA CRIME FAMILY DON VINCENT BRESCIA—STRANGLED DESPITE A BRAND NEW FACE, COURTESY OF PLASTIC SURGERY SUSPECTED OF BEING DONE AT THE DESERT HEARTS CLINIC.
NEXT, MEDICAL ASSISTANT THOMAS HAN WAS FOUND DEAD BEHIND HIS HOUSE, A VICTIM OF A FACIAL GUNSHOT WOUND.
FOLLOWED SWIFTLY BY ASTRID DRUE, ANOTHER DESERT HEARTS WORKER FELLED BY AN UNSEEN GUNMAN.
THE LATEST KILLING, THAT OF DESERT HEARTS PLASTIC SURGERY PRACTICIONER DR. MARK KELLITS AT HIS HOME, HAS LED THE TEAM HERE.
CRACK

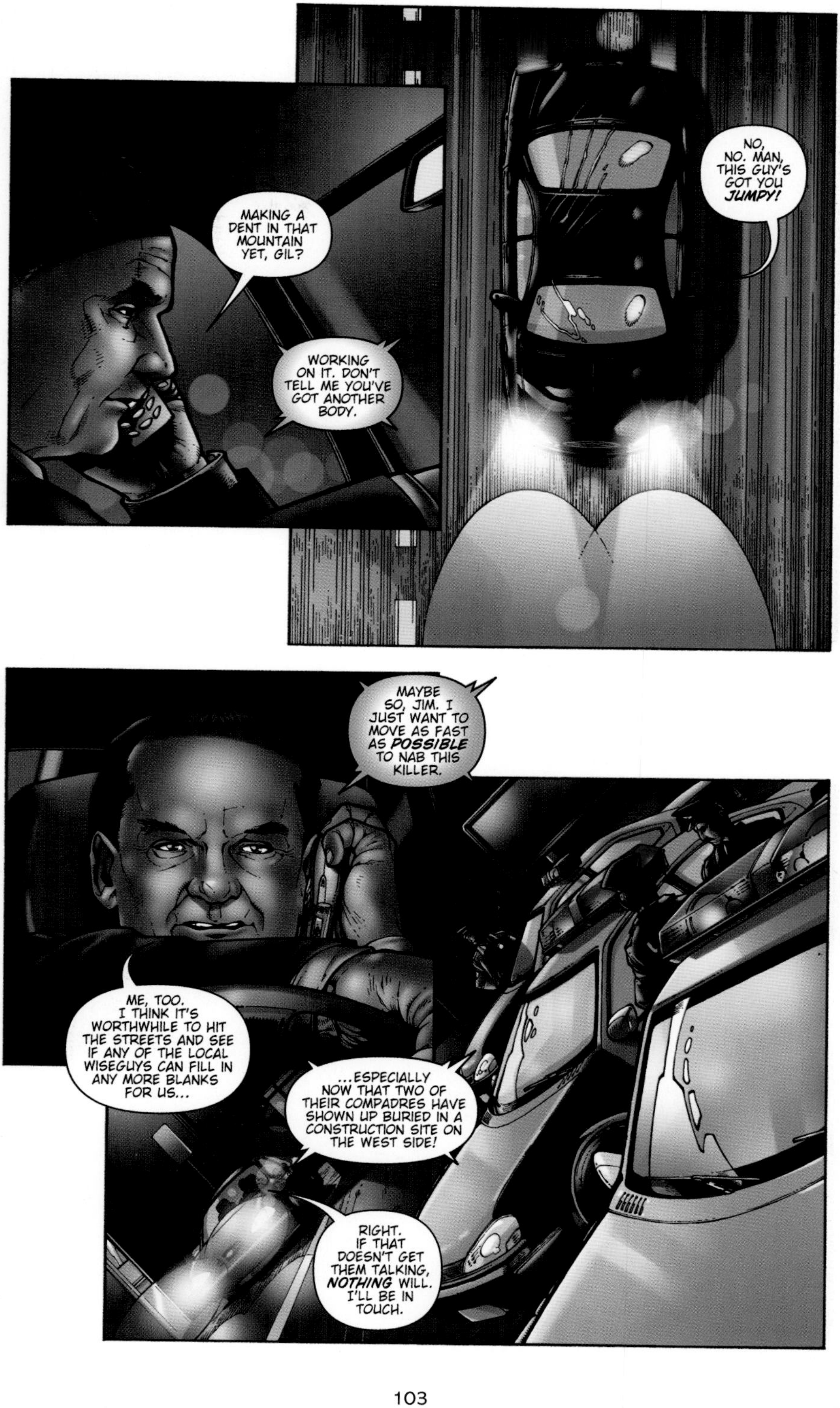
MAKING A DENT IN THAT MOUNTAIN YET, GIL?
WORKING ON IT. DON'T TELL ME YOU'VE GOT ANOTHER BODY.
NO, NO. MAN, THIS GUY'S GOT YOU **JUMPY!**
MAYBE SO, JIM. I JUST WANT TO MOVE AS FAST AS **POSSIBLE** TO NAB THIS KILLER.
ME, TOO. I THINK IT'S WORTHWHILE TO HIT THE STREETS AND SEE IF ANY OF THE LOCAL WISEGUYS CAN FILL IN ANY MORE BLANKS FOR US...
...ESPECIALLY NOW THAT TWO OF THEIR COMPADRES HAVE SHOWN UP BURIED IN A CONSTRUCTION SITE ON THE WEST SIDE!
RIGHT. IF THAT DOESN'T GET THEM TALKING, **NOTHING** WILL. I'LL BE IN TOUCH.

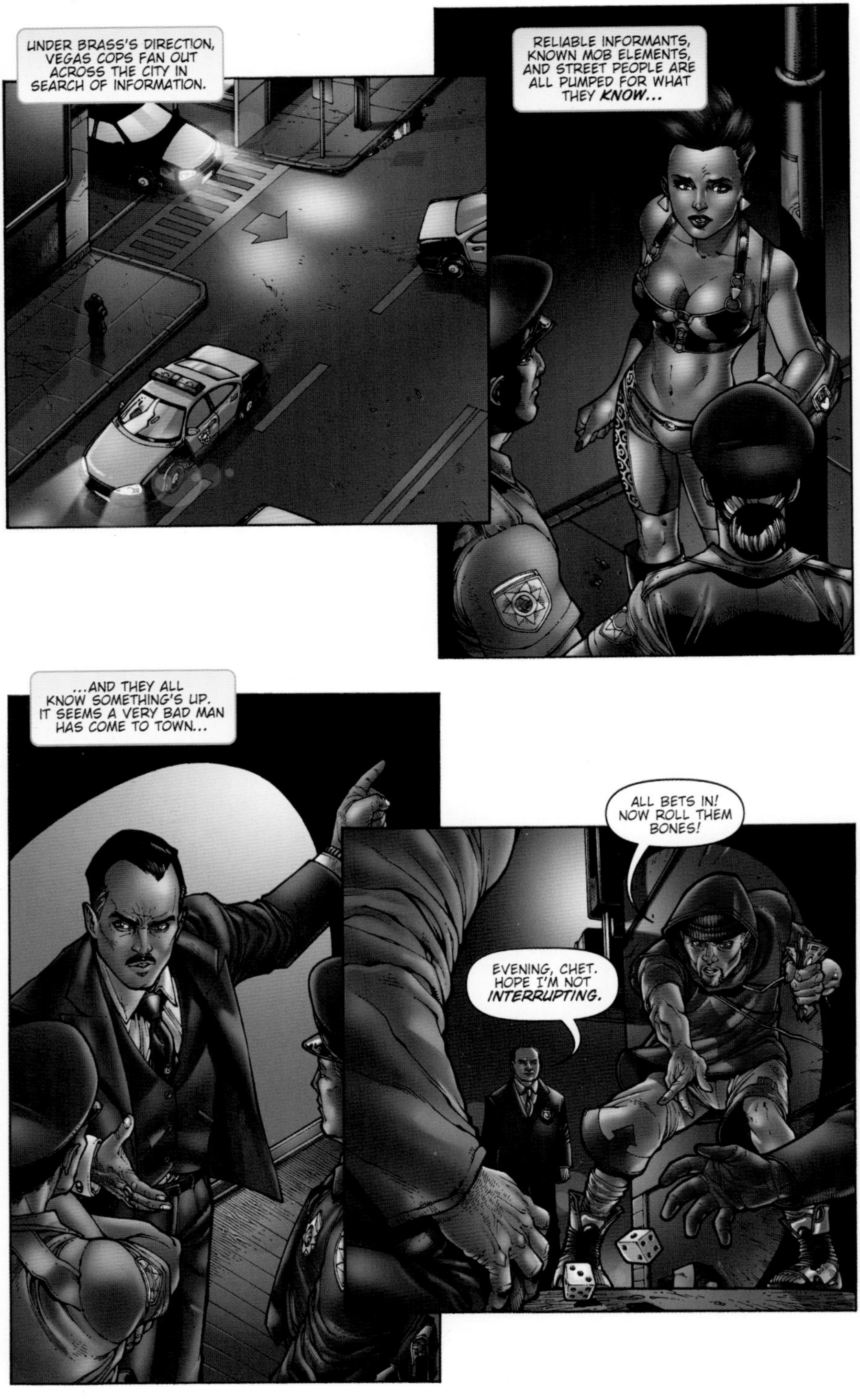
UNDER BRASS'S DIRECTION, VEGAS COPS FAN OUT ACROSS THE CITY IN SEARCH OF INFORMATION.
RELIABLE INFORMANTS, KNOWN MOB ELEMENTS, AND STREET PEOPLE ARE ALL PUMPED FOR WHAT THEY *KNOW*...
...AND THEY ALL KNOW SOMETHING'S UP. IT SEEMS A VERY BAD MAN HAS COME TO TOWN...
ALL BETS IN! NOW ROLL THEM BONES!
EVENING, CHET. HOPE I'M NOT *INTERRUPTING.*

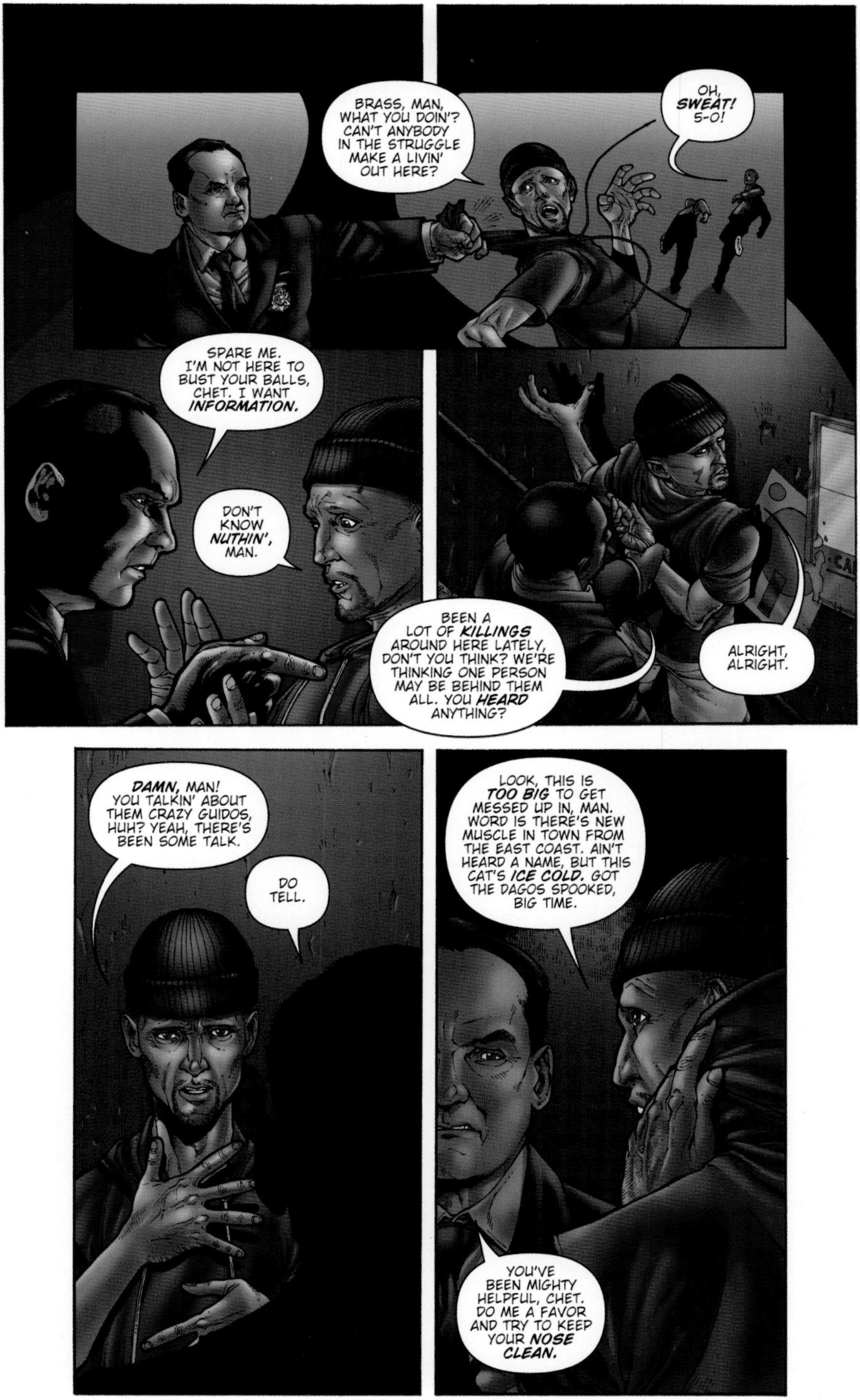
BRASS, MAN, WHAT YOU DOIN'? CAN'T ANYBODY IN THE STRUGGLE MAKE A LIVIN' OUT HERE?
OH, SWEAT! 5-0!
SPARE ME. I'M NOT HERE TO BUST YOUR BALLS, CHET. I WANT INFORMATION.
DON'T KNOW NUTHIN', MAN.
BEEN A LOT OF KILLINGS AROUND HERE LATELY, DON'T YOU THINK? WE'RE THINKING ONE PERSON MAY BE BEHIND THEM ALL. YOU HEARD ANYTHING?
ALRIGHT, ALRIGHT.
DAMN, MAN! YOU TALKIN' ABOUT THEM CRAZY GUIDOS, HUH? YEAH, THERE'S BEEN SOME TALK.
DO TELL.
LOOK, THIS IS TOO BIG TO GET MESSED UP IN, MAN. WORD IS THERE'S NEW MUSCLE IN TOWN FROM THE EAST COAST. AIN'T HEARD A NAME, BUT THIS CAT'S ICE COLD. GOT THE DAGOS SPOOKED, BIG TIME.
YOU'VE BEEN MIGHTY HELPFUL, CHET. DO ME A FAVOR AND TRY TO KEEP YOUR NOSE CLEAN.

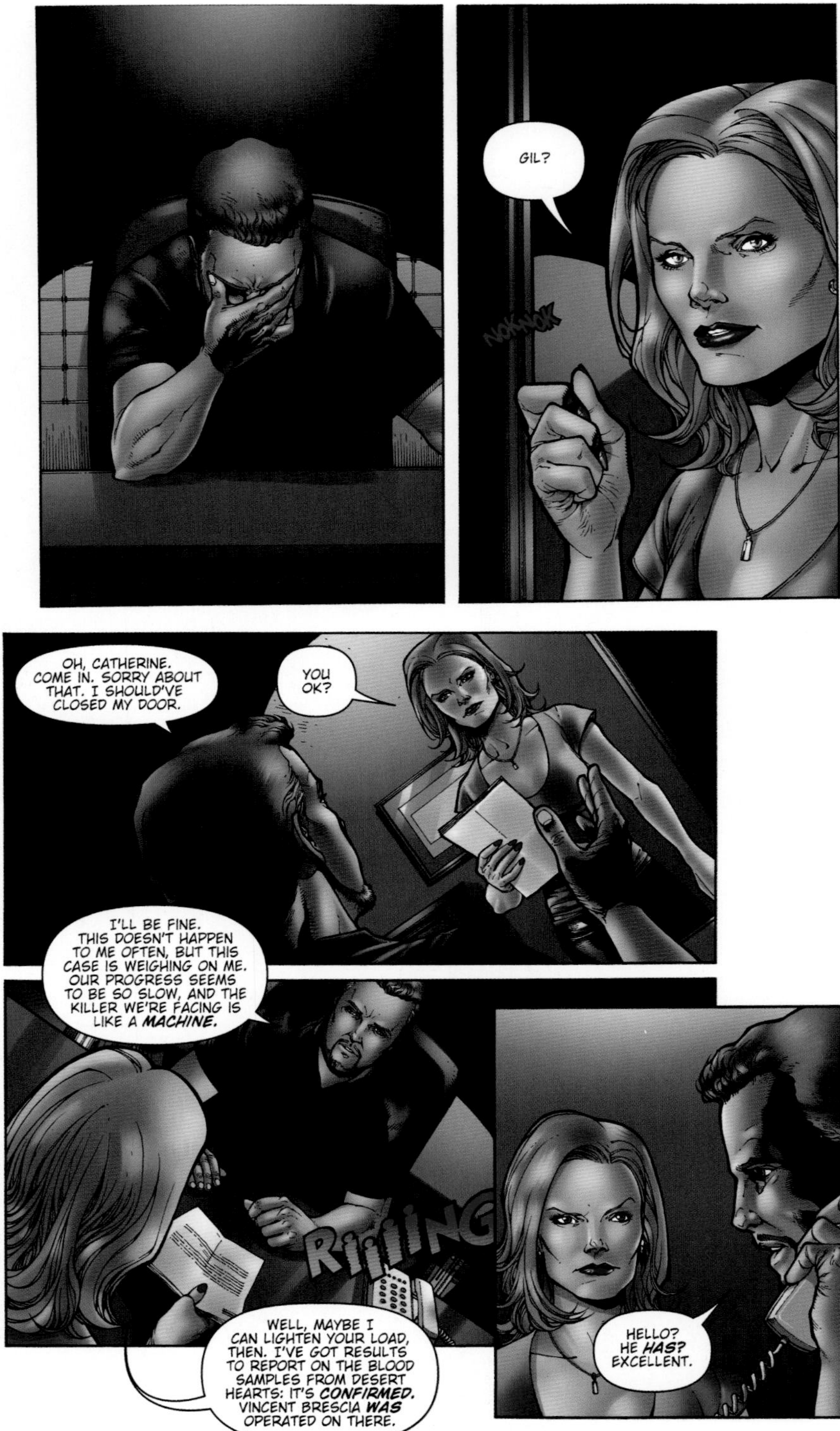
GIL?
NOKNOK
OH, CATHERINE. COME IN. SORRY ABOUT THAT. I SHOULD'VE CLOSED MY DOOR.
YOU OK?
I'LL BE FINE. THIS DOESN'T HAPPEN TO ME OFTEN, BUT THIS CASE IS WEIGHING ON ME. OUR PROGRESS SEEMS TO BE SO SLOW, AND THE KILLER WE'RE FACING IS LIKE A ***MACHINE.***
RiiiING
WELL, MAYBE I CAN LIGHTEN YOUR LOAD, THEN. I'VE GOT RESULTS TO REPORT ON THE BLOOD SAMPLES FROM DESERT HEARTS: IT'S ***CONFIRMED.*** VINCENT BRESCIA ***WAS*** OPERATED ON THERE.
HELLO? HE ***HAS?*** EXCELLENT.

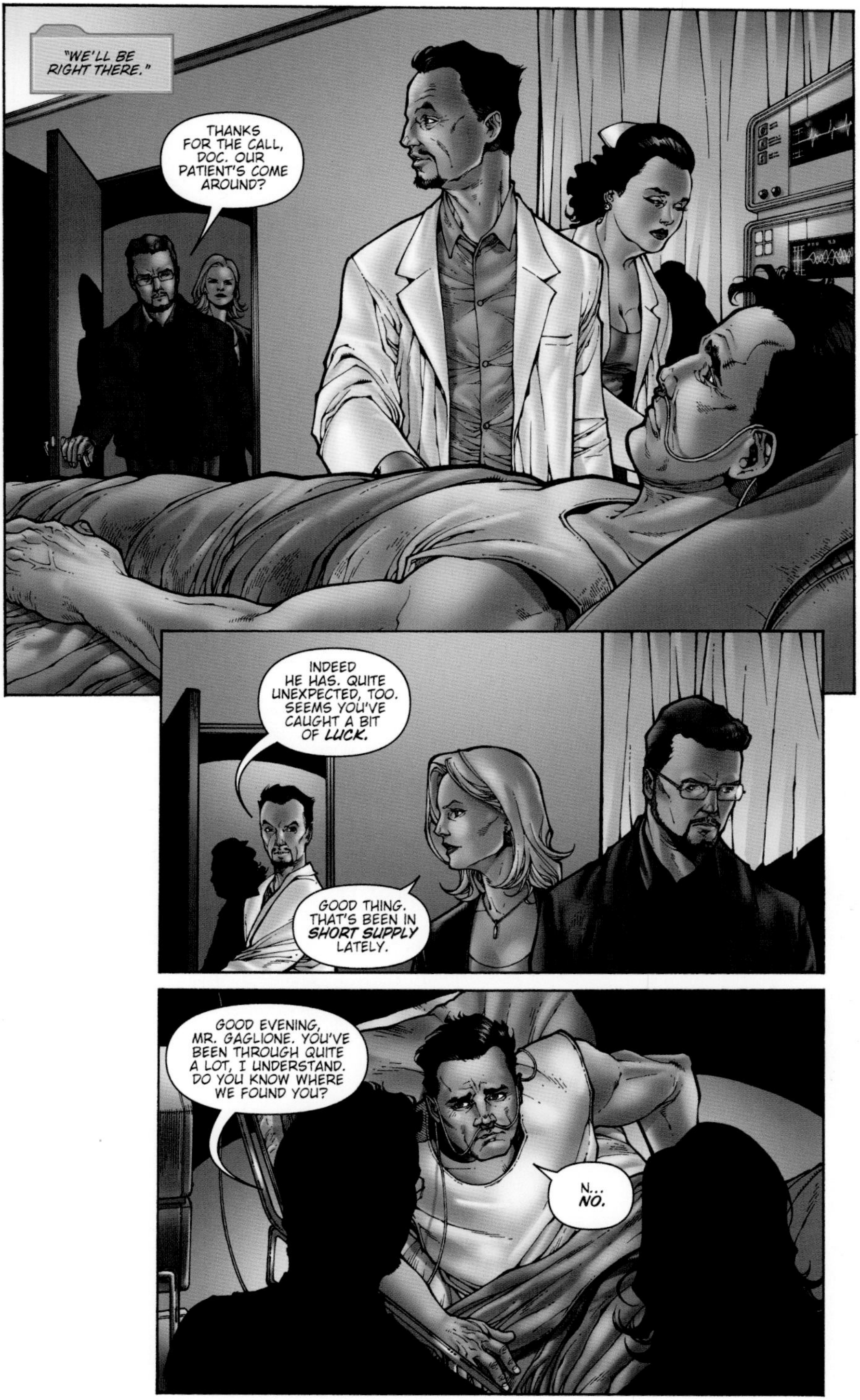
"WE'LL BE RIGHT THERE."
THANKS FOR THE CALL, DOC. OUR PATIENT'S COME AROUND?
INDEED HE HAS. QUITE UNEXPECTED, TOO. SEEMS YOU'VE CAUGHT A BIT OF LUCK.
GOOD THING. THAT'S BEEN IN SHORT SUPPLY LATELY.
GOOD EVENING, MR. GAGLIONE. YOU'VE BEEN THROUGH QUITE A LOT, I UNDERSTAND. DO YOU KNOW WHERE WE FOUND YOU?
N... NO.

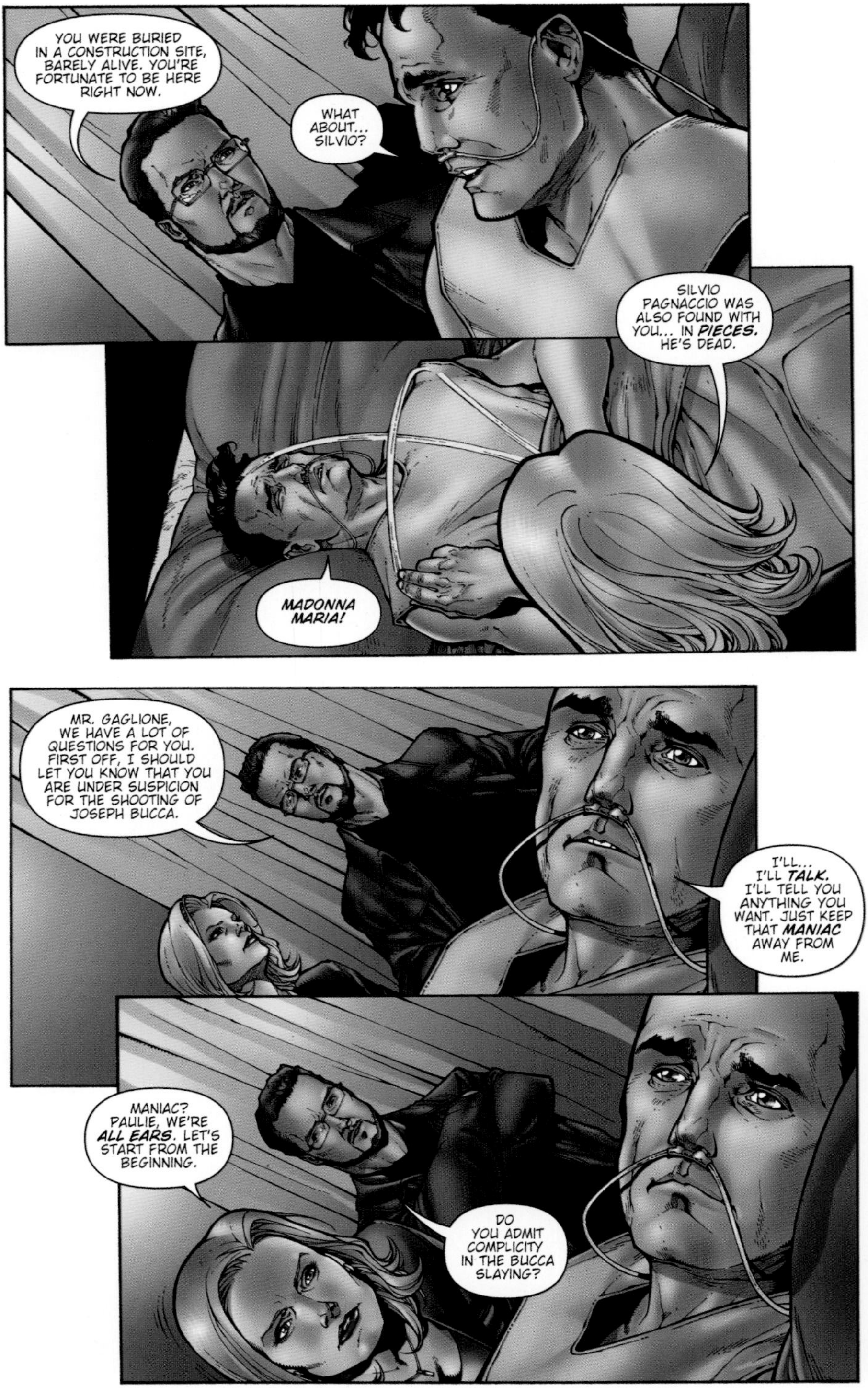
YOU WERE BURIED IN A CONSTRUCTION SITE, BARELY ALIVE. YOU'RE FORTUNATE TO BE HERE RIGHT NOW.
WHAT ABOUT... SILVIO?
SILVIO PAGNACCIO WAS ALSO FOUND WITH YOU... IN PIECES. HE'S DEAD.
MADONNA MARIA!
MR. GAGLIONE, WE HAVE A LOT OF QUESTIONS FOR YOU. FIRST OFF, I SHOULD LET YOU KNOW THAT YOU ARE UNDER SUSPICION FOR THE SHOOTING OF JOSEPH BUCCA.
I'LL... I'LL TALK. I'LL TELL YOU ANYTHING YOU WANT. JUST KEEP THAT MANIAC AWAY FROM ME.
MANIAC? PAULIE, WE'RE ALL EARS. LET'S START FROM THE BEGINNING.
DO YOU ADMIT COMPLICITY IN THE BUCCA SLAYING?

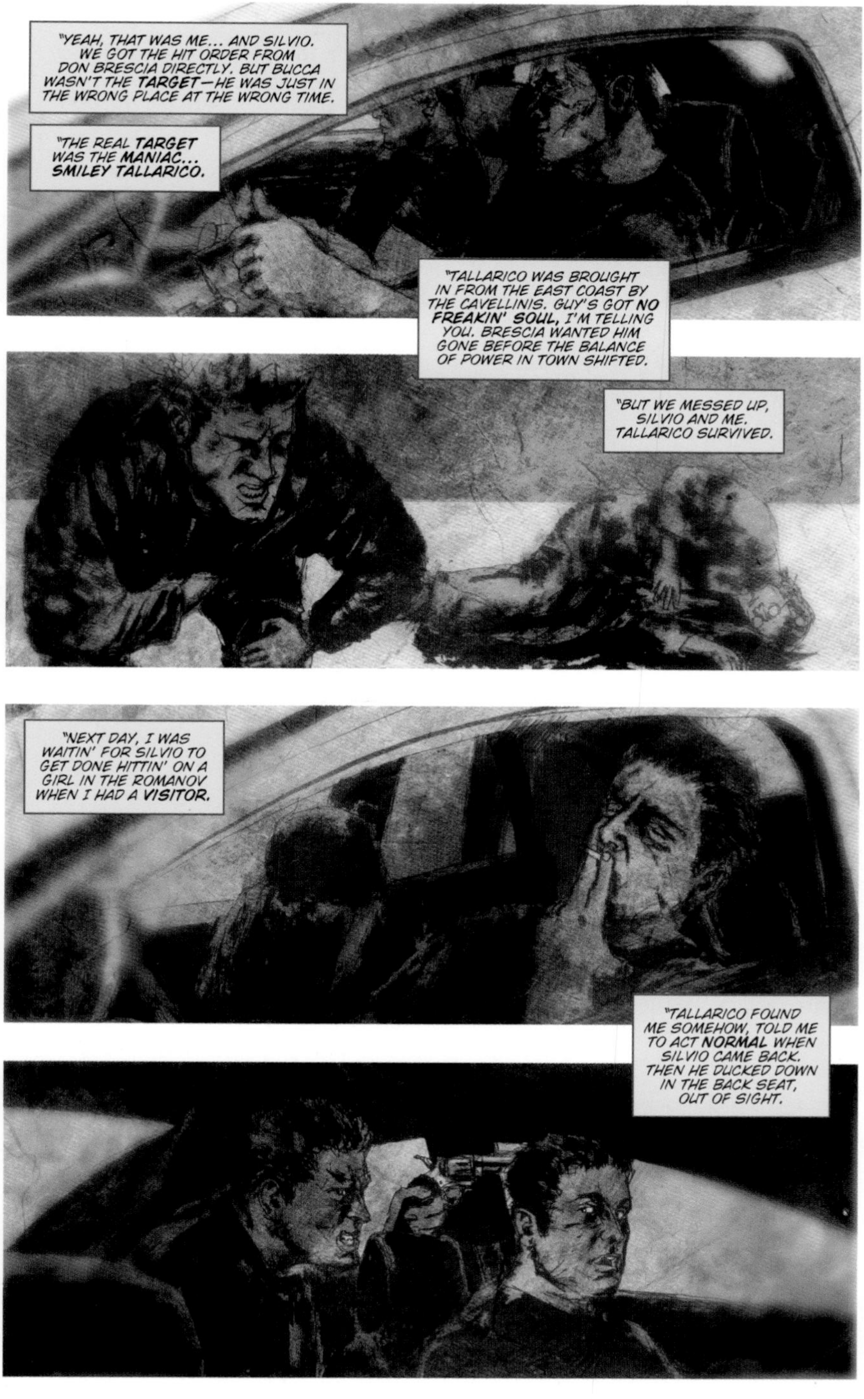
"YEAH, THAT WAS ME... AND SILVIO. WE GOT THE HIT ORDER FROM DON BRESCIA DIRECTLY. BUT BUCCA WASN'T THE TARGET—HE WAS JUST IN THE WRONG PLACE AT THE WRONG TIME.
"THE REAL TARGET WAS THE MANIAC... SMILEY TALLARICO.
"TALLARICO WAS BROUGHT IN FROM THE EAST COAST BY THE CAVELLINIS. GUY'S GOT NO FREAKIN' SOUL, I'M TELLING YOU. BRESCIA WANTED HIM GONE BEFORE THE BALANCE OF POWER IN TOWN SHIFTED.
"BUT WE MESSED UP, SILVIO AND ME. TALLARICO SURVIVED.
"NEXT DAY, I WAS WAITIN' FOR SILVIO TO GET DONE HITTIN' ON A GIRL IN THE ROMANOV WHEN I HAD A VISITOR.
"TALLARICO FOUND ME SOMEHOW, TOLD ME TO ACT NORMAL WHEN SILVIO CAME BACK. THEN HE DUCKED DOWN IN THE BACK SEAT, OUT OF SIGHT.

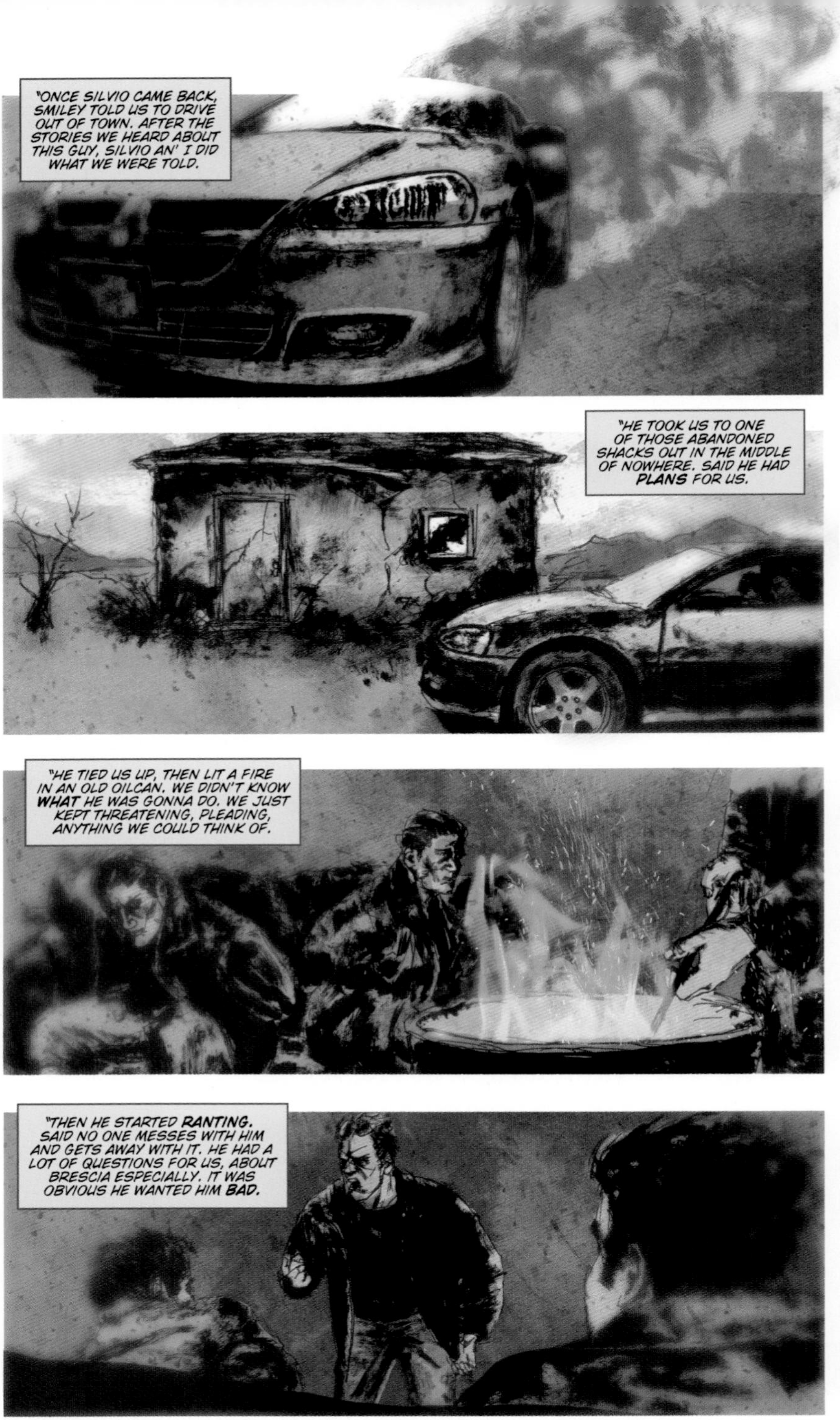
"ONCE SILVIO CAME BACK, SMILEY TOLD US TO DRIVE OUT OF TOWN. AFTER THE STORIES WE HEARD ABOUT THIS GUY, SILVIO AN' I DID WHAT WE WERE TOLD.
"HE TOOK US TO ONE OF THOSE ABANDONED SHACKS OUT IN THE MIDDLE OF NOWHERE. SAID HE HAD **PLANS** FOR US.
"HE TIED US UP, THEN LIT A FIRE IN AN OLD OILCAN. WE DIDN'T KNOW **WHAT** HE WAS GONNA DO. WE JUST KEPT THREATENING, PLEADING, ANYTHING WE COULD THINK OF.
"THEN HE STARTED **RANTING**. SAID NO ONE MESSES WITH HIM AND GETS AWAY WITH IT. HE HAD A LOT OF QUESTIONS FOR US, ABOUT BRESCIA ESPECIALLY. IT WAS OBVIOUS HE WANTED HIM **BAD**.

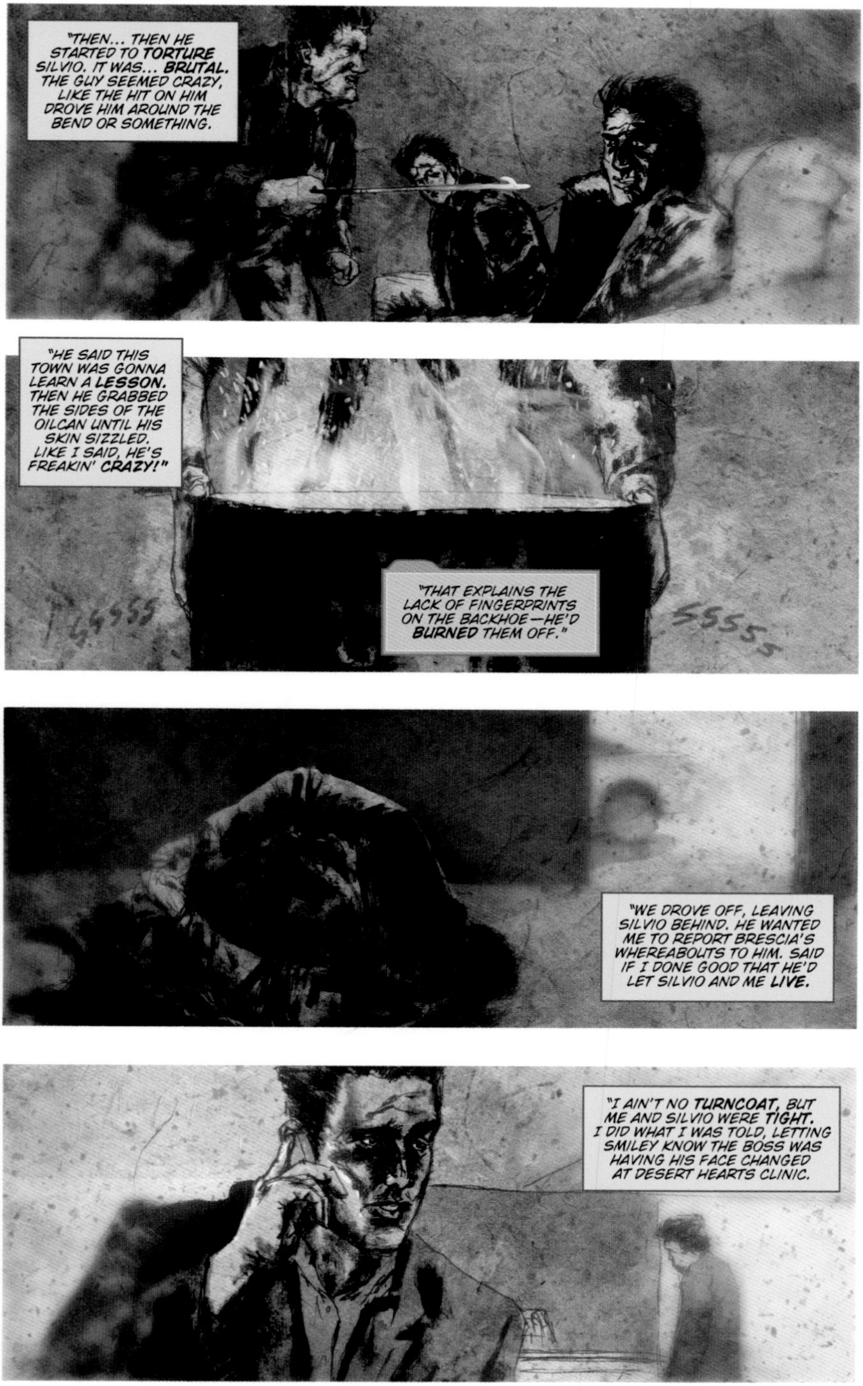
"THEN... THEN HE STARTED TO **TORTURE** SILVIO. IT WAS... **BRUTAL.** THE GUY SEEMED CRAZY, LIKE THE HIT ON HIM DROVE HIM AROUND THE BEND OR SOMETHING.
"HE SAID THIS TOWN WAS GONNA LEARN A **LESSON.** THEN HE GRABBED THE SIDES OF THE OILCAN UNTIL HIS SKIN SIZZLED. LIKE I SAID, HE'S FREAKIN' **CRAZY!"**
"THAT EXPLAINS THE LACK OF FINGERPRINTS ON THE BACKHOE—HE'D **BURNED** THEM OFF."
SSSSS
"WE DROVE OFF, LEAVING SILVIO BEHIND. HE WANTED ME TO REPORT BRESCIA'S WHEREABOUTS TO HIM. SAID IF I DONE GOOD THAT HE'D LET SILVIO AND ME **LIVE.**
"I AIN'T NO **TURNCOAT,** BUT ME AND SILVIO WERE **TIGHT.** I DID WHAT I WAS TOLD, LETTING SMILEY KNOW THE BOSS WAS HAVING HIS FACE CHANGED AT DESERT HEARTS CLINIC.

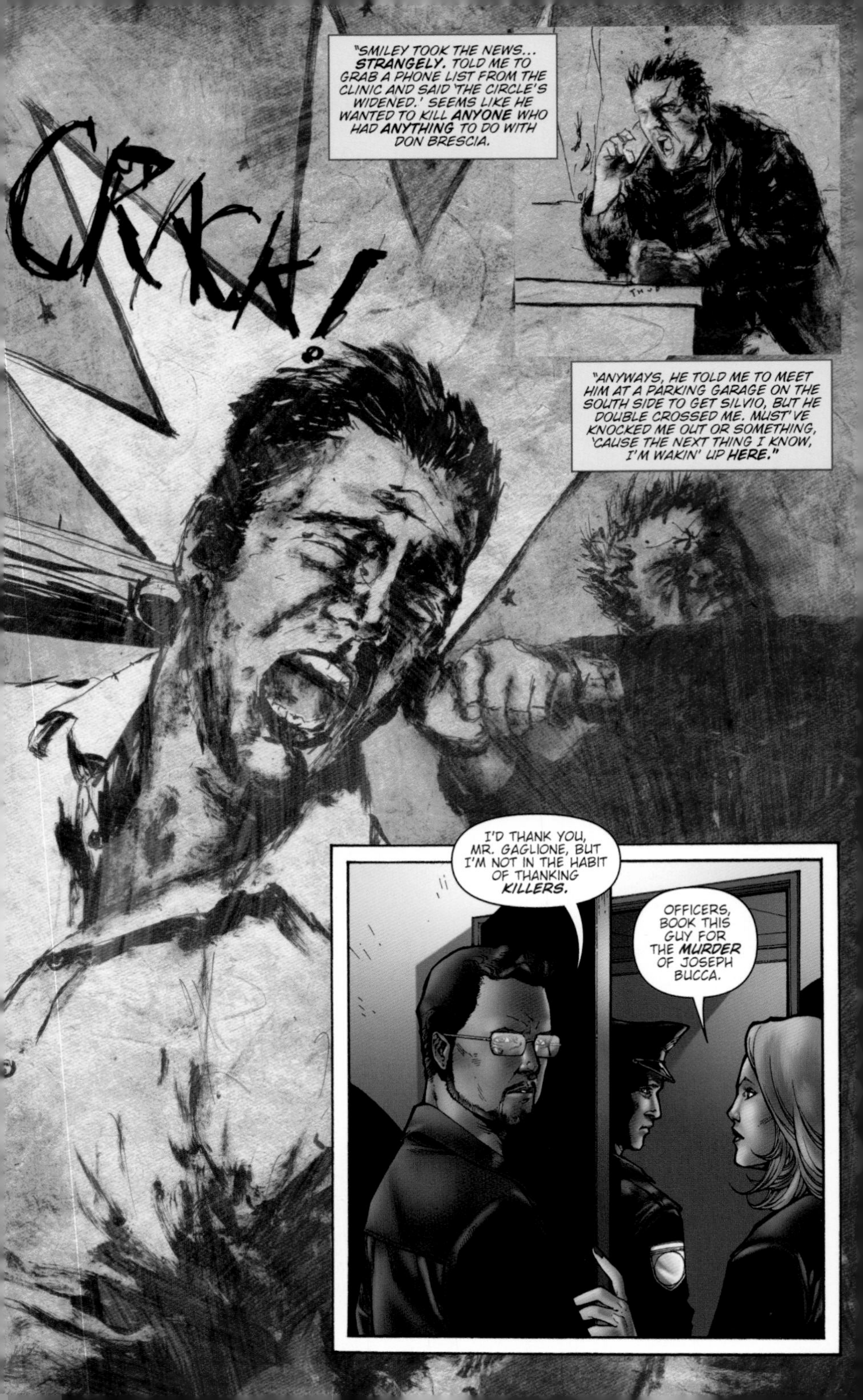
CRACK!
"SMILEY TOOK THE NEWS... STRANGELY. TOLD ME TO GRAB A PHONE LIST FROM THE CLINIC AND SAID 'THE CIRCLE'S WIDENED.' SEEMS LIKE HE WANTED TO KILL ANYONE WHO HAD ANYTHING TO DO WITH DON BRESCIA.
"ANYWAYS, HE TOLD ME TO MEET HIM AT A PARKING GARAGE ON THE SOUTH SIDE TO GET SILVIO, BUT HE DOUBLE CROSSED ME. MUST'VE KNOCKED ME OUT OR SOMETHING, 'CAUSE THE NEXT THING I KNOW, I'M WAKIN' UP HERE."
I'D THANK YOU, MR. GAGLIONE, BUT I'M NOT IN THE HABIT OF THANKING KILLERS.
OFFICERS, BOOK THIS GUY FOR THE MURDER OF JOSEPH BUCCA.

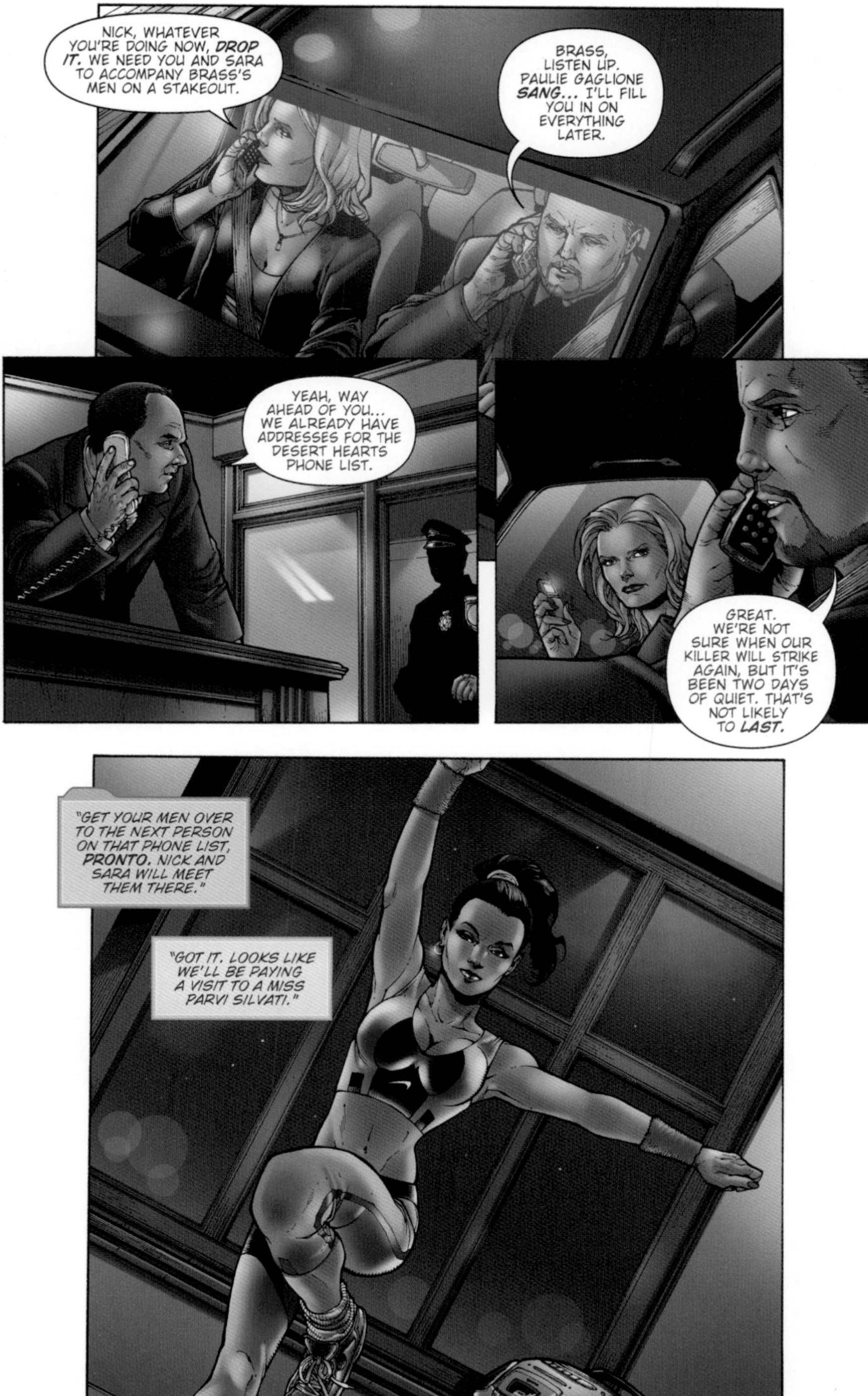
NICK, WHATEVER YOU'RE DOING NOW, **DROP IT.** WE NEED YOU AND SARA TO ACCOMPANY BRASS'S MEN ON A STAKEOUT.
BRASS, LISTEN UP. PAULIE GAGLIONE **SANG...** I'LL FILL YOU IN ON EVERYTHING LATER.
YEAH, WAY AHEAD OF YOU... WE ALREADY HAVE ADDRESSES FOR THE DESERT HEARTS PHONE LIST.
GREAT. WE'RE NOT SURE WHEN OUR KILLER WILL STRIKE AGAIN, BUT IT'S BEEN TWO DAYS OF QUIET. THAT'S NOT LIKELY TO **LAST.**
"GET YOUR MEN OVER TO THE NEXT PERSON ON THAT PHONE LIST, **PRONTO.** NICK AND SARA WILL MEET THEM THERE."
"GOT IT. LOOKS LIKE WE'LL BE PAYING A VISIT TO A MISS PARVI SILVATI."

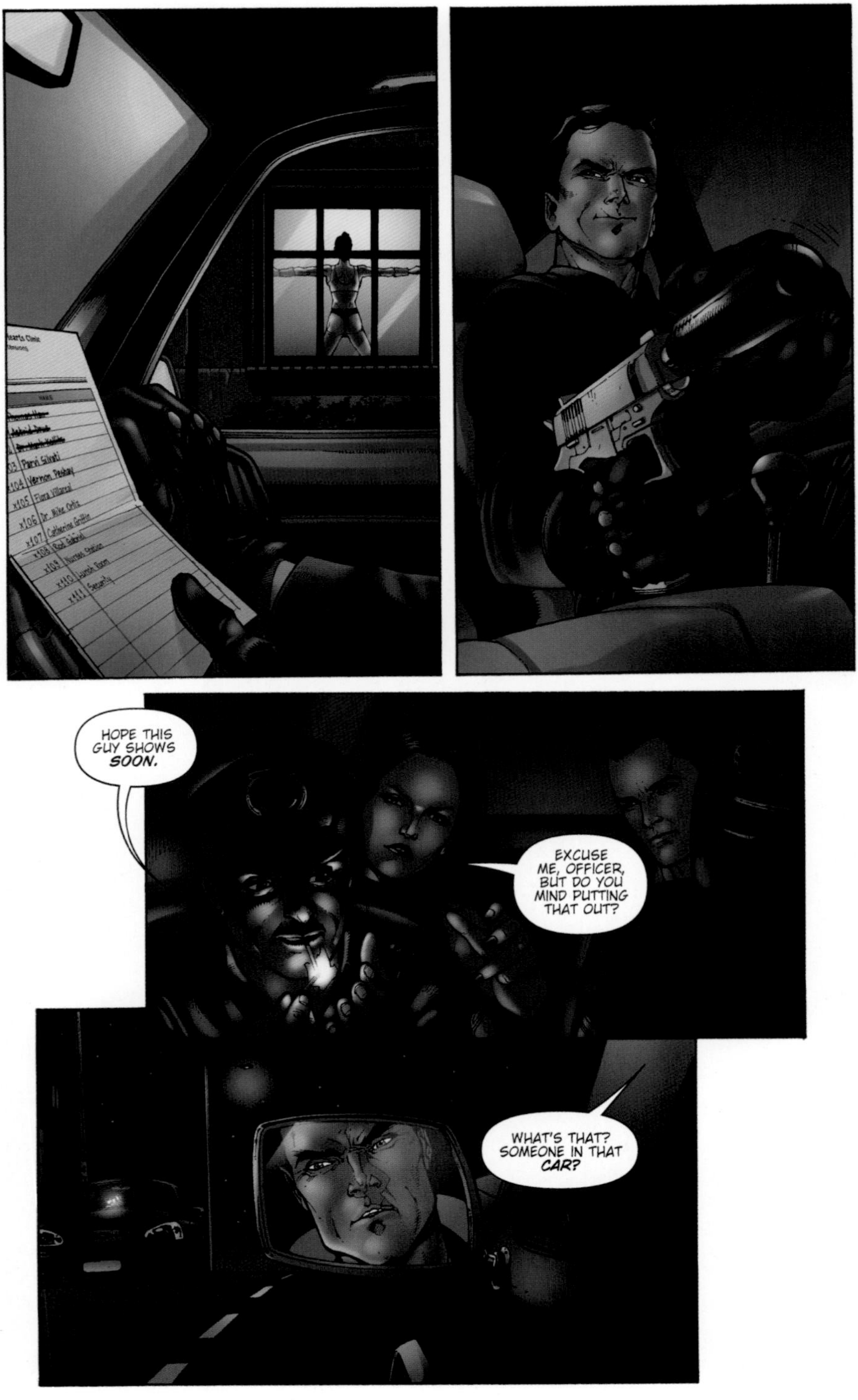
x104 Vernon Peshay
x105 Flora Villarreal
x106 Dr. Mike Ortiz
x107 Catherine Griffin
x108 Rod Gabriel
x109 Nurses Station
x110 Lunch Room
x111 Security
HOPE THIS GUY SHOWS **SOON.**
EXCUSE ME, OFFICER, BUT DO YOU MIND PUTTING THAT OUT?
WHAT'S THAT? SOMEONE IN THAT **CAR?**

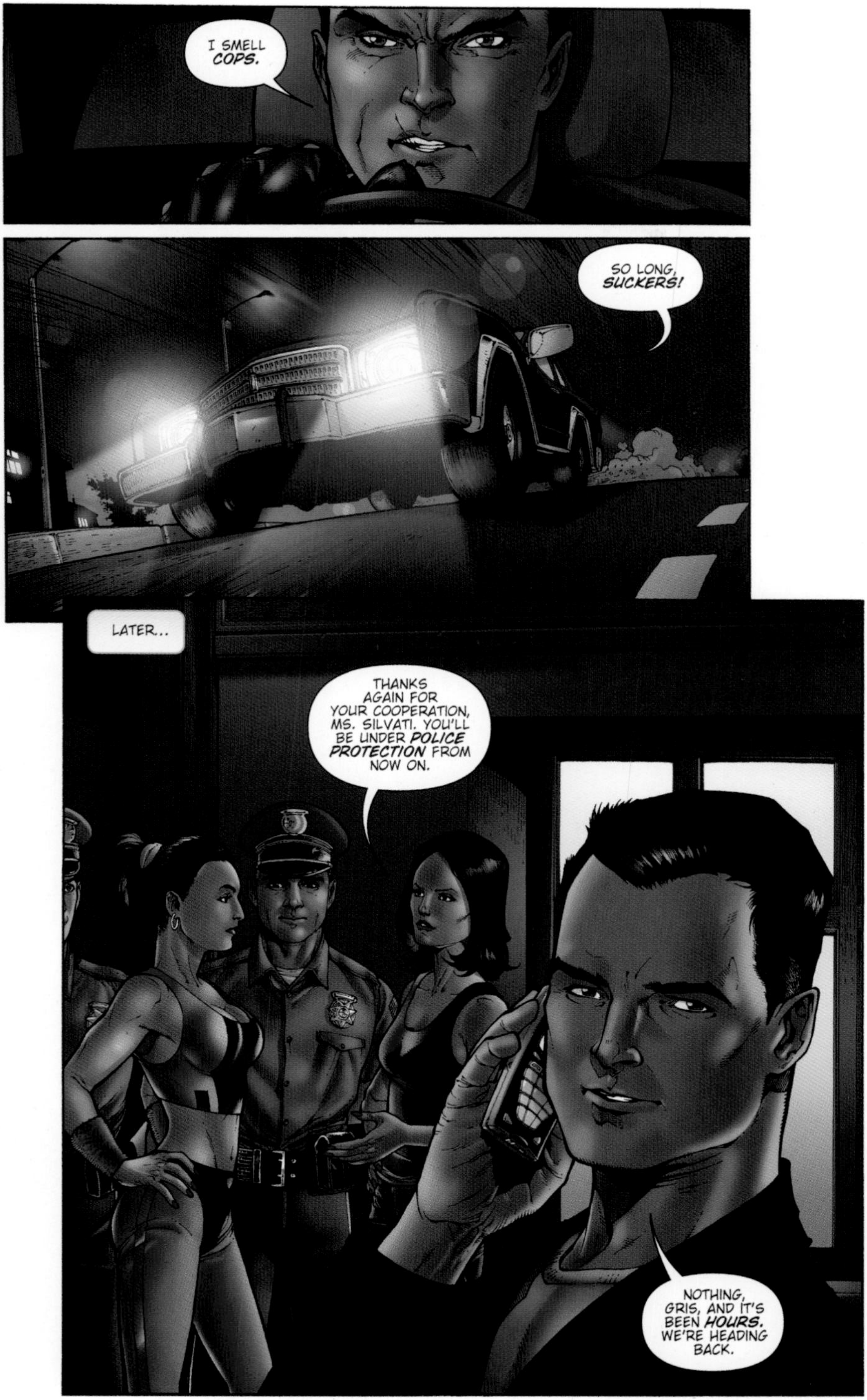
I SMELL COPS.
SO LONG, SUCKERS!
LATER...
THANKS AGAIN FOR YOUR COOPERATION, MS. SILVATI. YOU'LL BE UNDER POLICE PROTECTION FROM NOW ON.
NOTHING, GRIS, AND IT'S BEEN HOURS. WE'RE HEADING BACK.

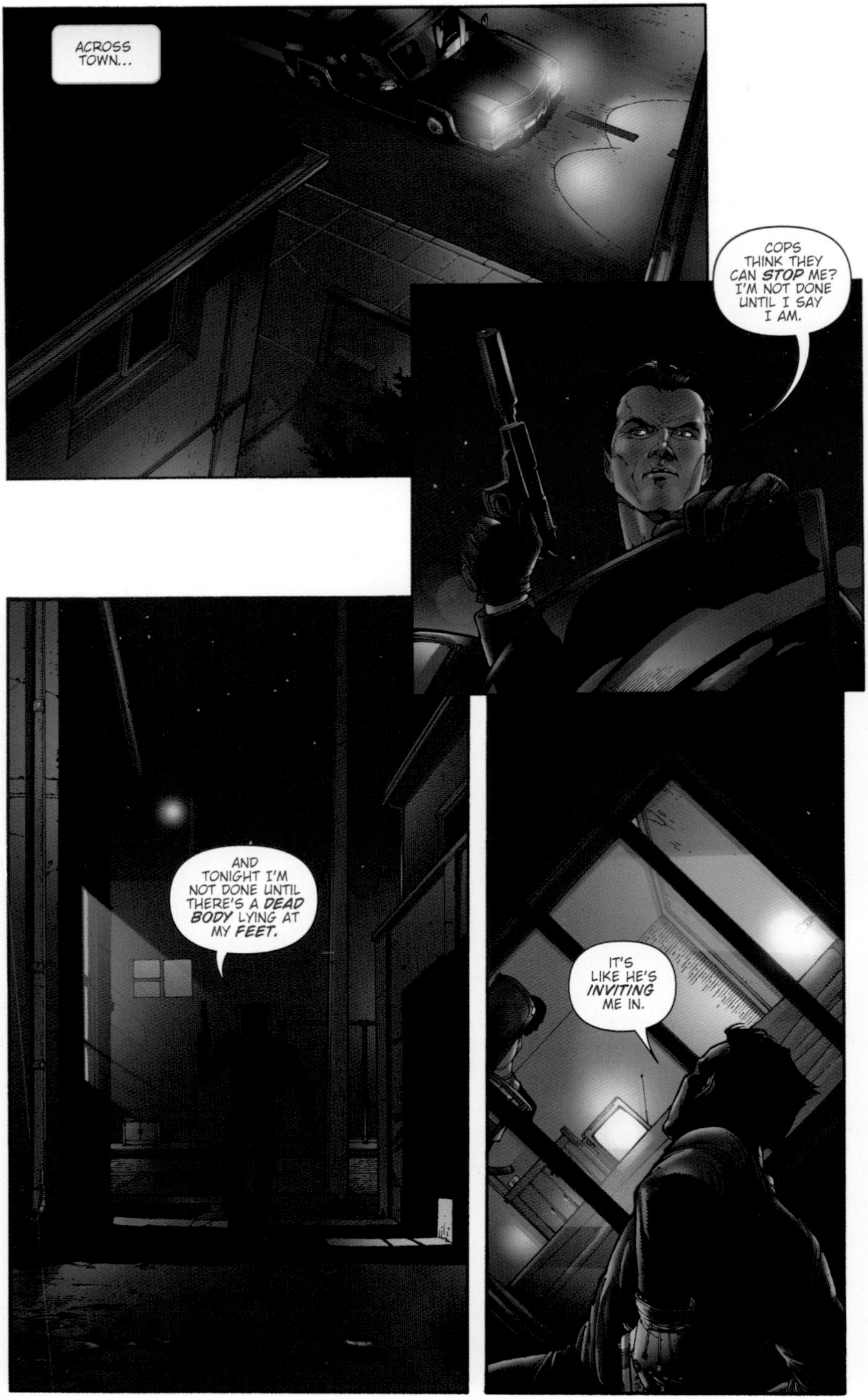
ACROSS TOWN...
COPS THINK THEY CAN STOP ME? I'M NOT DONE UNTIL I SAY I AM.
AND TONIGHT I'M NOT DONE UNTIL THERE'S A DEAD BODY LYING AT MY FEET.
IT'S LIKE HE'S INVITING ME IN.

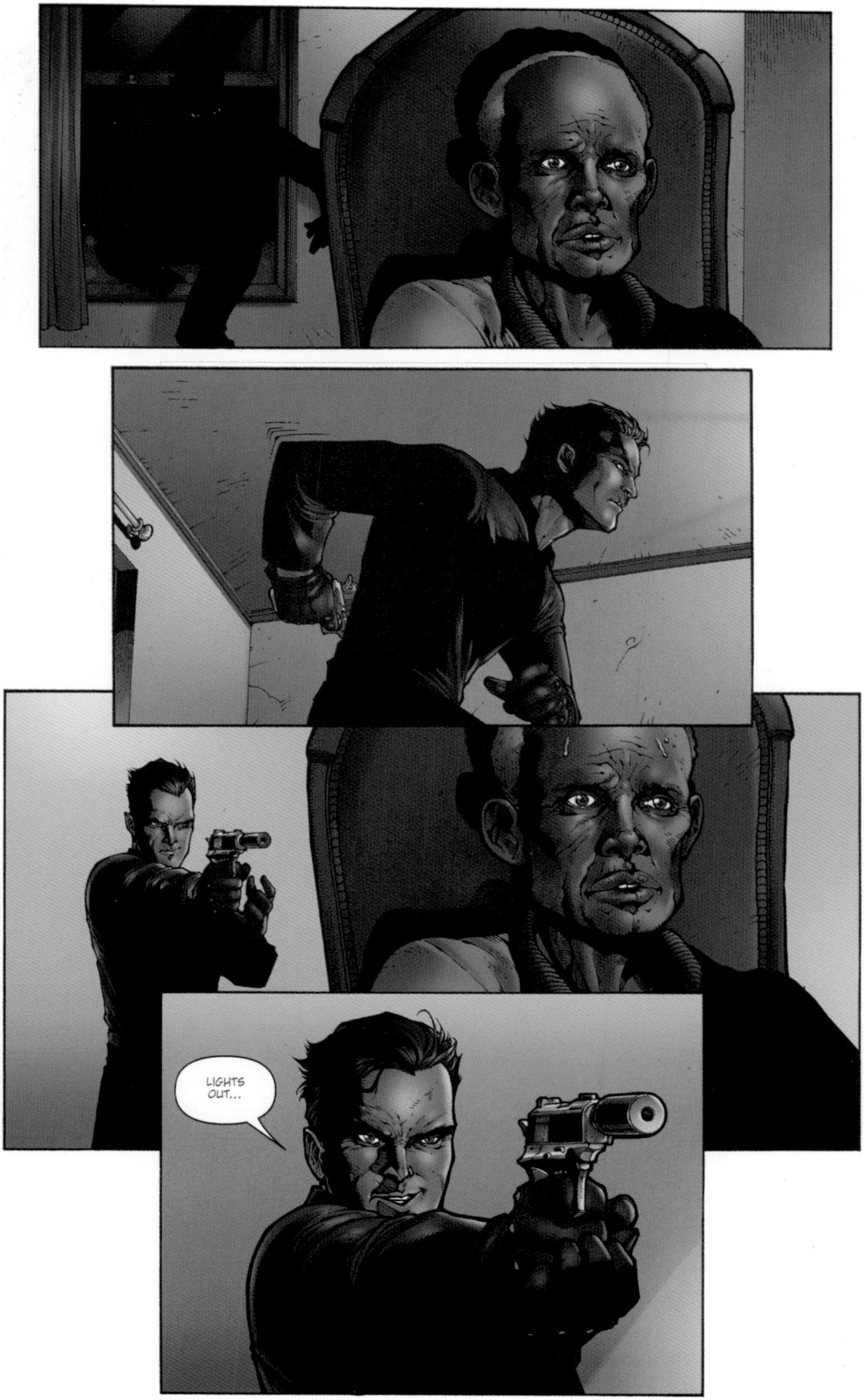
LIGHTS OUT...

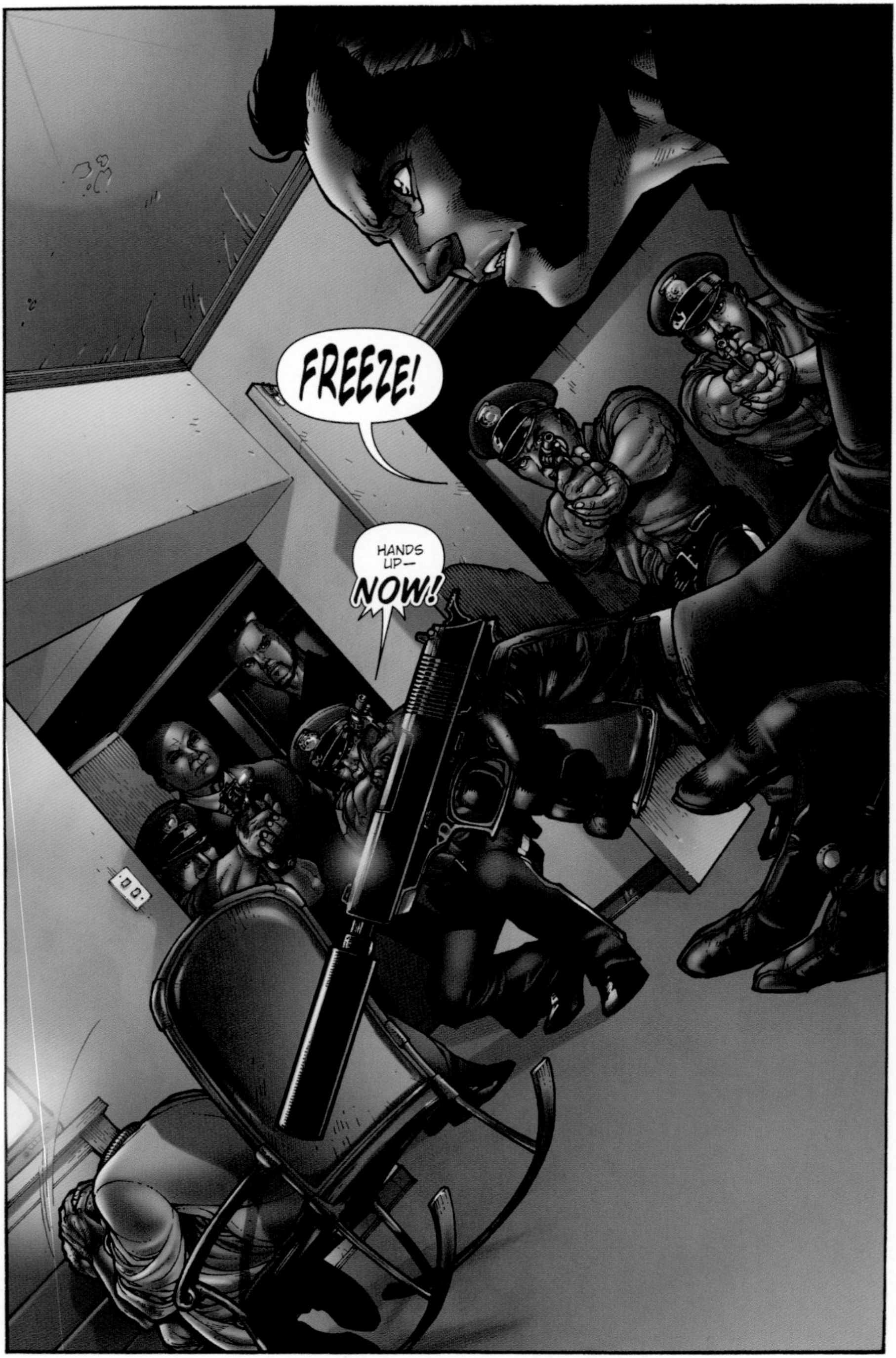
FREEZE!
HANDS UP—NOW!

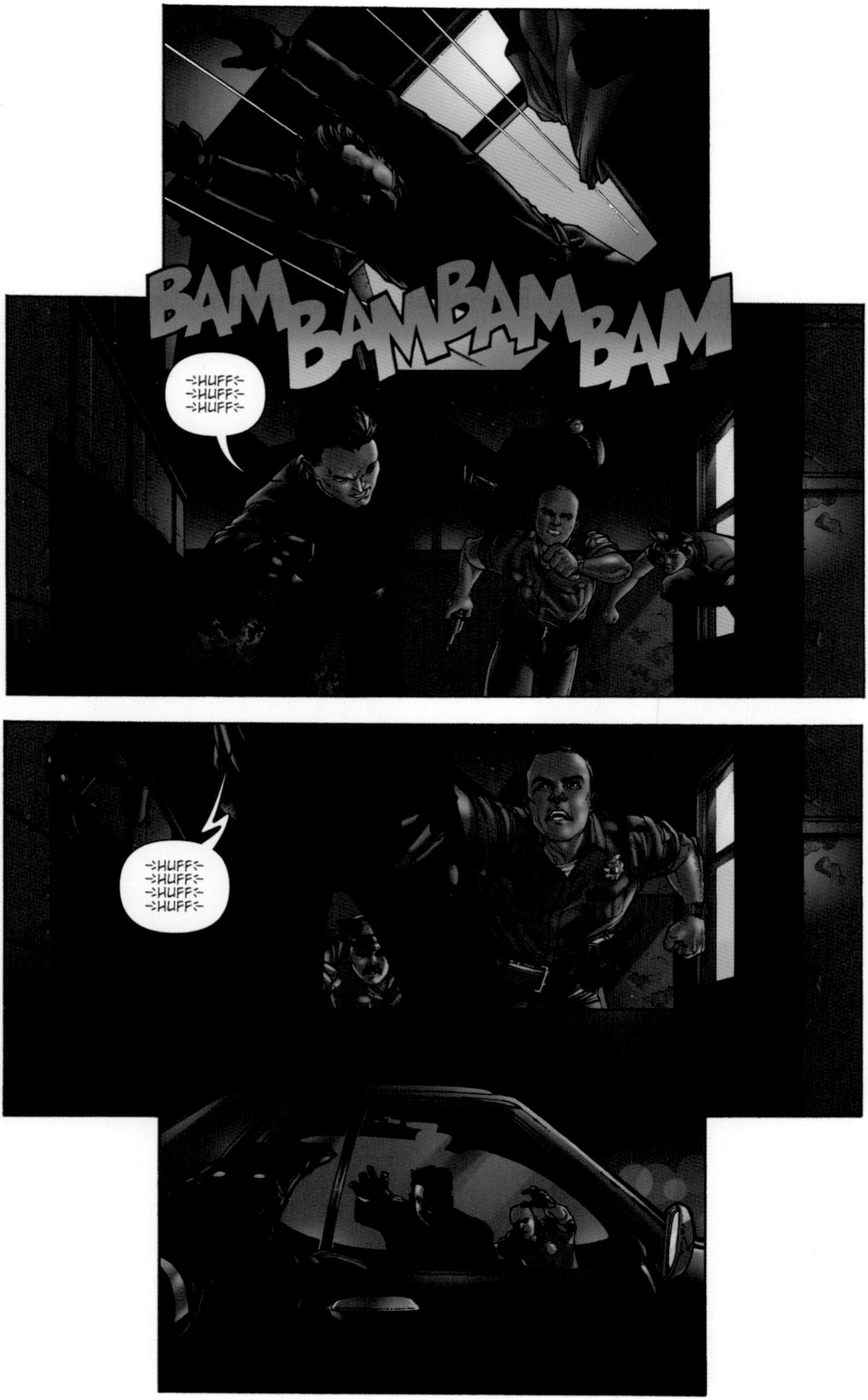
BAM BAM BAM BAM BAM
HUFF HUFF HUFF
HUFF HUFF HUFF HUFF

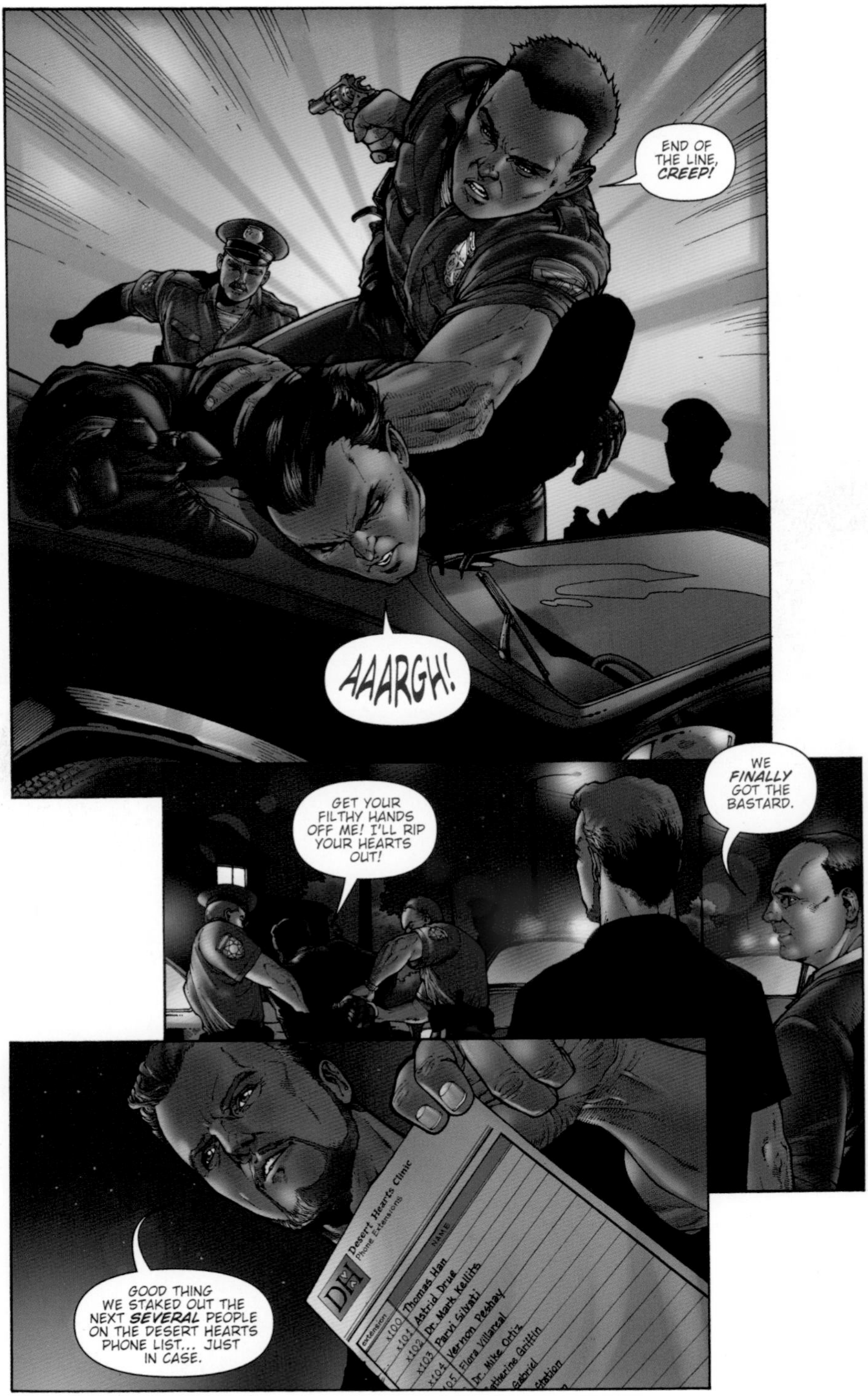

END OF THE LINE, CREEP!
AAARGH!
GET YOUR FILTHY HANDS OFF ME! I'LL RIP YOUR HEARTS OUT!
WE FINALLY GOT THE BASTARD.
GOOD THING WE STAKED OUT THE NEXT SEVERAL PEOPLE ON THE DESERT HEARTS PHONE LIST... JUST IN CASE.
Desert Hearts Clinic
Phone Extensions
extension
NAME
x100 Thomas Han
x101 Astrid Drue
x102 Dr. Mark Kallits
x103 Parvi Silvati
x104 Vernon Peshay
Flora Villarreal
Dr. Mike Ortiz

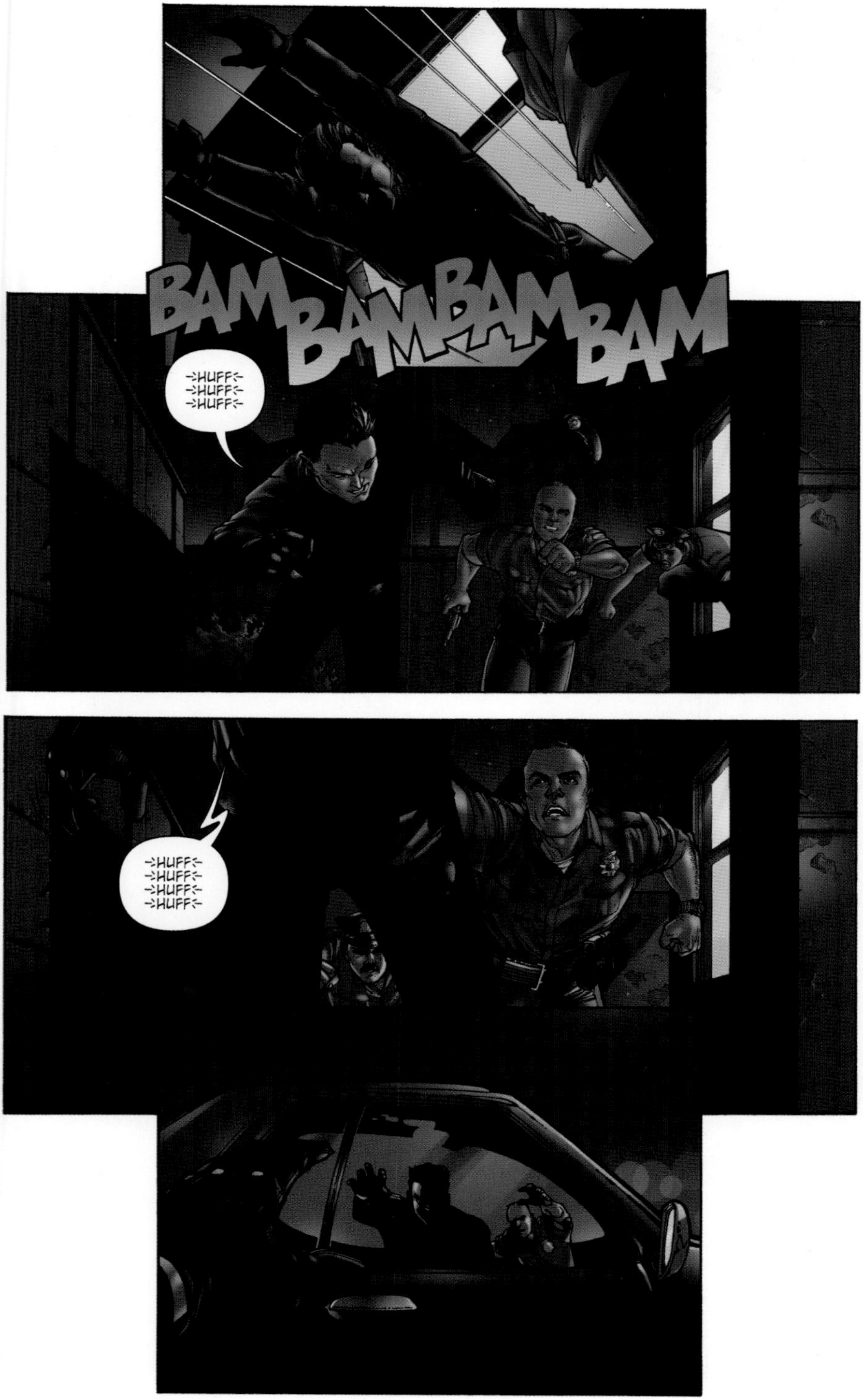
BAM BAM BAM BAM
-HUFF- -HUFF- -HUFF-
-HUFF- -HUFF- -HUFF- -HUFF-

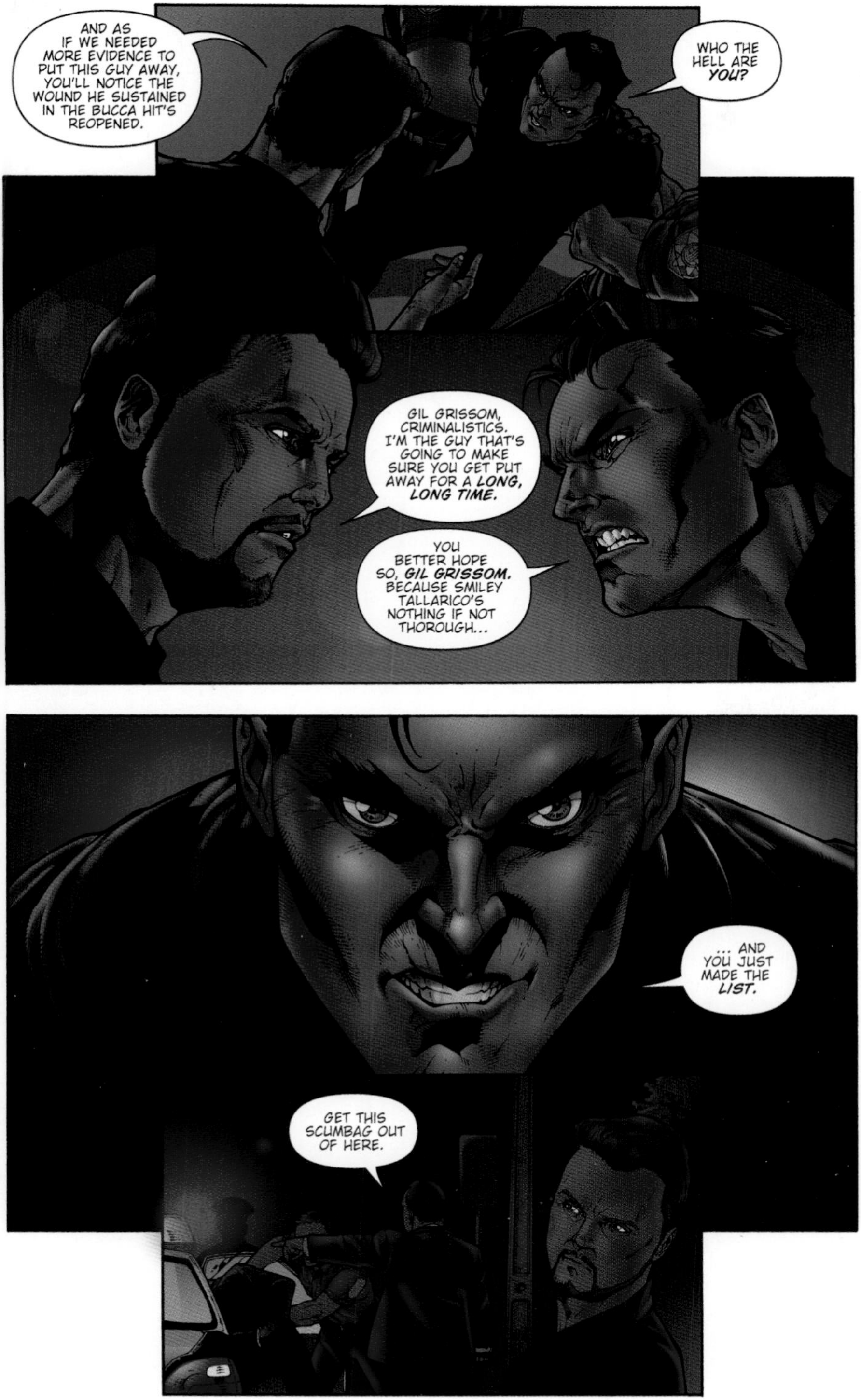
AND AS IF WE NEEDED MORE EVIDENCE TO PUT THIS GUY AWAY, YOU'LL NOTICE THE WOUND HE SUSTAINED IN THE BUCCA HIT'S REOPENED.
WHO THE HELL ARE *YOU?*
GIL GRISSOM, CRIMINALISTICS. I'M THE GUY THAT'S GOING TO MAKE SURE YOU GET PUT AWAY FOR A *LONG, LONG TIME.*
YOU BETTER HOPE SO, *GIL GRISSOM.* BECAUSE SMILEY TALLARICO'S NOTHING IF NOT THOROUGH...
... AND YOU JUST MADE THE *LIST.*
GET THIS SCUMBAG OUT OF HERE.

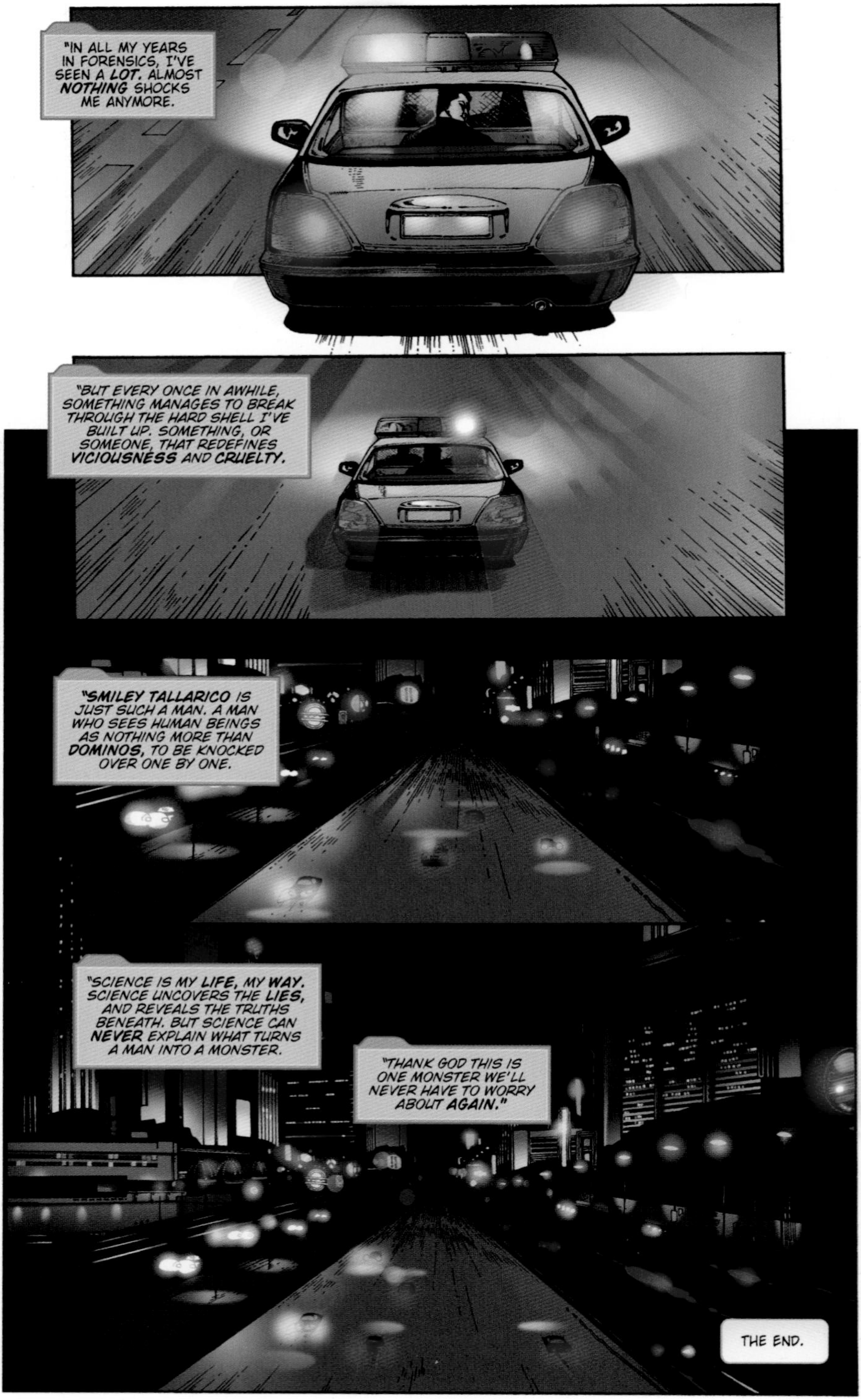
"IN ALL MY YEARS IN FORENSICS, I'VE SEEN A LOT. ALMOST NOTHING SHOCKS ME ANYMORE.
"BUT EVERY ONCE IN AWHILE, SOMETHING MANAGES TO BREAK THROUGH THE HARD SHELL I'VE BUILT UP. SOMETHING, OR SOMEONE, THAT REDEFINES VICIOUSNESS AND CRUELTY.
"SMILEY TALLARICO IS JUST SUCH A MAN. A MAN WHO SEES HUMAN BEINGS AS NOTHING MORE THAN DOMINOS, TO BE KNOCKED OVER ONE BY ONE.
"SCIENCE IS MY LIFE, MY WAY. SCIENCE UNCOVERS THE LIES, AND REVEALS THE TRUTHS BENEATH. BUT SCIENCE CAN NEVER EXPLAIN WHAT TURNS A MAN INTO A MONSTER.
"THANK GOD THIS IS ONE MONSTER WE'LL NEVER HAVE TO WORRY ABOUT AGAIN."
THE END.

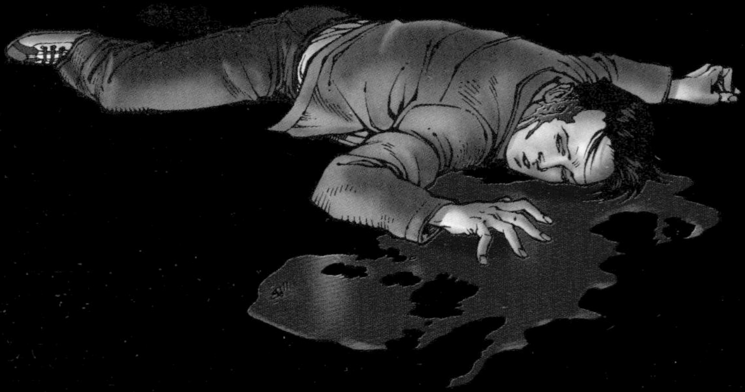

IDW